Computational Models of Language Evolution

Editors: Luc Steels, Remi van Trijp

In this series:

ISSN: 2364-7809

The evolution of grounded spatial language

Michael Spranger

Michael Spranger. 2016. *The evolution of grounded spatial language*
(Computational Models of Language Evolution 5). Berlin: Language Science
Press.

This title can be downloaded at:
http://langsci-press.org/catalog/book/53
© 2016, Michael Spranger
Published under the Creative Commons Attribution 4.0 Licence (CC BY 4.0):
http://creativecommons.org/licenses/by/4.0/
ISBN: 978-3-946234-14-2 (Digital)
      978-3-946234-15-9 (Hardcover)
      978-3-944675-46-6 (Softcover)
      978-1-523743-49-0 (Softcover US)
ISSN: 2364-7809
DOI:10.17169/langsci.b53.183

Cover and concept of design: Ulrike Harbort
Fonts: Linux Libertine, Arimo, DejaVu Sans Mono
Typesetting software: X∃LATEX

Language Science Press
Habelschwerdter Allee 45
14195 Berlin, Germany
langsci-press.org

Storage and cataloguing done by FU Berlin

Contents

Contents

Preface

This book contributes to our understanding of the origins of spatial language by carrying out language game experiments with artificial agents instantiated as humanoid robots. It tests the theory of language evolution by linguistic selection, which states that language emerges through a cultural process based on the recruitment of various cognitive capacities in the service of language. Agents generate possible paradigmatic choices in their language systems and explore different language strategies. Which ones survive and dominate depends on linguistic selection criteria, such as expressive adequacy with respect to the ecological challenges and conditions in the environment, minimization of cognitive effort, and communicative success.

To anchor this case study in empirical phenomena, the book reconstructs the syntax and semantics of German spatial language, in particular German locative phrases. Syntactic processing is organized using Fluid Construction Grammar (FCG), a computational formalism for representing linguistic knowledge. For the semantics the book focusses in particular on proximal, projective and absolute spatial categories as well as perspective, perspective reversal and frame of reference. The semantic investigations use the perspective of Embodied Cognitive Semantics. The spatial semantics is grounded in the sensory-motor experiences of the robot and made compositional by using the Incremental Recruitment Language (IRL) developed for this purpose. The complete reconstructed system allows humanoid robots to communicate successfully and efficiently using the German locative system and provides a performance base line. The reconstruction shows that the computational formalisms, i.e. FCG and IRL, are sufficient for tackling complex natural language phenomena. Moreover, the reconstruction efforts reveal the tight interaction of syntax and semantics in German locative phrases.

The second part of the book concentrates on the evolution of spatial language. First the focus is on the formation and acquisition of spatial language by proposing strategies in the form of invention, adoption, and alignment operators. The book shows the adequacy of these strategies in acquisition experiments in which some agents act as learners and others as tutors. It shows next in language formation experiments that these strategies are sufficient to allow a population to self-organize a spatial language system from scratch. The book continues by studying the origins and competition of language strategies. Different conceptual strategies are considered and studied systematically, particularly in relation to the properties of the environment, for example, whether a global landmark is available. Different linguistic strategies are studied as well, for instance, the problem of choosing a particular reference object on the scene can be solved by the invention of markers, which allows many different reference objects, or by converging to a standard single reference object, such as a global landmark.

The book demonstrates that the theory of language evolution by linguistic selection leads to operational experiments in which artificial agents self-organize semantically rich and syntactically complex language. Moreover, many issues in cognitive science, ranging from perception and conceptualization to language processing, had to be dealt with to instantiate this theory, so that this book contributes not only to the study of language evolution but to the investigation of the cognitive bases of spatial language as well.

This book would not have been possible without the hard work of the people at Sony Computer Science Laboratory Paris and the A.I. Lab at the Vrije Universiteit Brussels. Many of them have left traces in software and ideas that provide the background against which a book like this one becomes possible. Most notably I would like to thank the current and past members of the AI lab in Brussels and Sony CSL Paris who I have met and who have made contributions to the various software systems that underly the experiments described in this book: Katrien Beuls, Joris Bleys, Joachim De Beule, Wouter van den Broeck, Remi van Trijp and Pieter Wellens.

Martin Loetzsch and Simon Pauw had big impact on many issues discussed in this book. I am indebted to all of them for long discussions that have tremendously shaped my way of thinking and for their collaboration on different aspects of spatial language, conceptualization and embodiment.

Last but not least, I would like to thank Luc Steels who has had tremendous impact on the intellectual ideas put forth in this book, provided the necessary environment to conduct this research, and who continues to be an inspirational and visionary figure for future work.

1 Introduction

Spatial language is a vast topic. This book focusses on locative phrases, which are phrases that single out objects in the physical environment with the COMMUNICATIVE INTENTION to draw attention to these objects. The following shows an example of a locative phrase from German.

(1) der   Block   rechts   der   Kiste   von   dir
     the.NOM block.NOM right.PREP the.GEN box.GEN from.PREP your.DAT
     aus
     perspective
     'The block to the right of the box from your perspective'

Phrases like this can be seen as highly complex tools that help dialog partners to establish spatial reference. The utterance conveys to the hearer a number of instructions such as (1) apply the spatial relation right, (2) use a particular landmark and (3) take the perspective of the interlocutor. These instructions, when applied properly, allow an interlocutor to identify the object in question. The syntactic structure, i.e. the words and the grammatical relations of the utterance, encode which concepts and categories should be used and how the instructions work together. For instance, the fact that the hearer's perspective on the scene should be taken is conveyed by the phrase *von ... aus* ('from ... your perspective').

Languages vary widely in how they solve the problem of spatial reference – including both how they conceptualize space and how they talk about it (Levinson & Wilkins 2006; Levinson 2003). Spatial position of objects can be expressed using a variety of syntactic means including case, adpositions, particles, and verbs. But, maybe more importantly, there is a breathtaking variety in how people conceptualize space, which spatial relations they know, what counts as a landmark, how perspective is used, etc. Just to give a few simple examples, Spanish has three basic proximal distinctions, while German has two. In Barcelona people make active use of the topology of the surrounding landscape, referring regularly to the seaside and mountainside when giving navigation instructions. In other languages 'uphill' and 'downhill' are used to refer to proximal objects (Levinson 2003).

These examples show that spatial language is a highly developed tool for establishing reference in a spatial environment. How did spatial language become this way? There is an emerging view now that the most plausible answer to this question is that spatial language is a COMPLEX ADAPTIVE SYSTEM (see Steels 2000a for the general idea of language as a complex adaptive system), that is constructed and changed by its users for the same purpose it is used for today, namely to describe spatial scenes, establish reference to objects in the environment, give instructions for navigation, etc. This process is, of course, not the same process of construction that a group of engineers use when they are building a bridge. In such classic engineering problems, a team of people with a more or less complete view of the problem designs a top-down solution. By contrast, nobody has a global view on the state of a language. Rather, language lives in the individuals of the language community. Every individual has its own views on the state of the language, i.e. what words and grammatical relations are available.

When we combine the evidence from the complexity of particular spatial languages, such as German locative phrases, and the variation that can be seen across languages, it seems reasonable to consider results from a science that routinely deals with complexity and variation – biology. Biological species are highly complex solutions to particular environmental and social challenges. The solutions found by each species exhibit a high degree of variation. This simple observation has forced biology to come up with precise models and predictions to explain the origins of species. It comes as no surprise, then, that theories of language, particularly language evolution and language change, have adopted concepts from biology related to variation, complexity and the emergence of order in biological systems.

This book defends the SELECTIONIST THEORY OF LANGUAGE EVOLUTION, which exploits biological concepts to explain how language is shaped by the communicative needs and environmental conditions that a community or population faces. The theory hypothesizes that agents create variation within their language and select working solutions based on how successful they are in communication (COMMUNICATIVE SUCCESS), how complex they are in processing (COGNITIVE EFFORT) and other factors.

Studying language change from the perspective of communicative intentions requires a great deal of insight into how humans or artificial systems can realize their specific communicative intentions in social interactions in the physical world. Such holistic explanations necessitate a WHOLE SYSTEMS APPROACH (Steels 2001), in which great care is taken to ensure that perception, conceptualization and linguistic processing systems are integrated to an extent that interaction between agents is possible. Only when all of this machinery is in place can one attempt to examine questions of language change.

In particular, a whole systems approach requires an operational theory of language. How are utterances processed? How is space conceptualized? How is linguistic knowledge represented? How does language interact with the perception of the physical reality? A whole systems approach requires concrete answers to each of these important questions. The resulting burden placed on operational models is of course far greater than for high-level explanations or logical reasoning about these processes. But concrete, mechanistic accounts allow much greater insights into the phenomena studied. In the best case, a successful model of language evolution in a whole systems approach validates many aspects of the theory of language and language change at the same time.

This book contributes to the understanding of spatial language in two ways. First, it provides a detailed operational reconstruction of German locative phrases using a whole systems approach. Second, it explores the evolution of spatial language within the same computational framework. The two parts together argue for (1) the validity of the approach to language, and (2) the validity and explanatory power of the selectionist theory of language evolution.

1.1 Locative spatial language

If one wants to make an interesting claim about how language evolves, one needs a solid idea what language actually is, how linguistic knowledge is represented, and how to organize linguistic processing. These questions are best answered by reconstructing a complex natural language phenomenon such as German locative phrases. Such phrases are used for establishing reference to static objects and identifying them by denoting their spatial position (Miller & Johnson-Laird 1976). They can be distinguished from other parts of spatial language that are dealing with motion or navigation (Eschenbach 2004).

German locative phrases can be analyzed in terms of components or systems which together form a locative phrase. (1) consists of three parts: a SPATIAL RELATION, which is combined with a LANDMARK and a PERSPECTIVE.

Spatial Relations The defining quality of locative spatial phrases are that they contain locative spatial relations such as *rechts* ('right'), *vorne* ('front'), *nah* ('near'), *nördlich* ('north on' and so forth). These relations are called locative because they encode static spatial relationships and do not refer to change of position in time. In (1), *rechts* ('right') is the locative spatial relation. In this book we study three classes of spatial relations. *Proximal* relations are based on distance estimations. Examples of proximal relations in German are *nah* ('near') and *fern* ('far'). The second class is called *projective* relations and includes direction-based spatial relations such as *links* ('left') and *vor* ('front'). The last class considered are *absolute* relations such as *nördlich* ('north') and *östlich* ('east'). These are also direction-based, but the direction is related to a geocentric reference system such as the magnetic poles of the earth.

Landmarks A spatial relation is at least a binary and always relates to something. This something is typically called LANDMARK. In (1), the landmark is expressed in the determined noun phrase *der Kiste* ('the box') immediately following the spatial relation.

Perspective For certain spatial relations perspective is important. (1) features a perspective that is marked via the phrase *von ... aus* ('from ... viewpoint'). The marker expresses that the viewpoint on the scene is the hearer.

1.2 A theory of language evolution

Theories of language evolution have to explain the evolution of language by defining the role and contribution of four different factors on language: biology, cognition, social cognition, and culture (Steels 2009; 2011c).

Biology To study language evolution from the biological perspective is to ask questions about the relationship of biology, in particular genetics and ecology, with linguistic behavior. The question can be roughly split into two parts. First, what is the biological influence on the general capacity for language in the human population? Second, one can ask for the influence of biology on the particular language spoken by individuals. The first is a general question for the processing capabilities that need to be present for language. This includes that humans require sufficient memory and powerful neural circuitry for processing language, but also production organs for speech and auditory capacities. The second question is how much the biological basis determines the particular language individuals speak. In other words, how much the lexicon and/or the grammar of a language are influenced by genetic conditions.

Cognition Biology has provided us with neural circuitry that enables distinct cognitive capabilities. The cognitive perspective on language asks: what are the basic cognitive processing mechanisms underlying production and parsing of language, interpretation, conceptualization, but also categorization, perception etc.? Language depends on a number of capabilities that may or may not be prior to language, such as temporal clustering of events, spatial navigation, perception-action systems (Rizzolatti & Arbib 1998; Arbib 2002; Steels & Spranger 2012; 2008), memory and so on and so forth. For instance, some have linked the evolution of language to an increase in capacity for storing cognitive categories and their interrelations (Schoenemann 1999). Another strand of cognitive influences on language evolution are general cognitive operators such as analogy and learning operators, for instance sequential learning (Christiansen et al. 2001).

Social Cognition Inevitably, language is a social phenomenon that occurs when humans interact. Social cognition researchers, for instance, are interested in the social mechanisms that are needed for children to acquire language, but also in the social mechanisms that are prerequisite for the emergence of language. Proposals include things such as "theory of mind" (Dunbar 1998) which is the capacity to understand another individual's state of mind, "joint attention" (Carpenter et al. 1998) which is the ability to track interlocutor gaze and mutual attentiveness to the same object, "social learning skills" such as imitation learning (Tomasello 1992) and the ability and the urge to "share intentions" (Tomasello et al. 2005). Many of these mechanisms are deeply rooted in biology. For instance, Dunbar (2003) and Worden (1998) argue that theory of mind is a necessary preadaptation for language and that it has evolved via natural selection.

Culture Language is a cultural phenomenon that is undergoing steady change on the cultural level. New words, speech sounds, morphemes, semantic and syntactic structures arise all the time in language (Steels 2011c). This manifests in the incredible amount of cross-cultural variation on all levels of linguistic processing (Evans & Levinson 2009), for example, phonemes (Maddieson 1984; Oudeyer 2005), spatial semantics (Levinson 2003), and syntax (Levinson & Wilkins 2006). This evidence points to strong cultural negotiation processes in which continuous invention is channeled to produce complex useful communication systems. Many of such processes orchestrating change and diversification have been identified. Grammaticalization, for instance, tries to explain the shift from lexical items to grammatical items (Hopper & Traugott 2003). Others have pointed to generational change as the trigger for development in language (Smith, Kirby &

Brighton 2003). The question from the perspective of cultural evolution is what are the mechanisms that bring about change in language and what are the principles with which agents conventionalize language up to the point that interlocutors have a chance of understanding each other.

I emphasize the cultural point of view in this book. That is, my primary concern is with change in language on the cultural level independent of changes in the human biology. Language change occurs on a smaller time scale than, for instance, the adaptation of a new biological organ, let alone a new species. There is absolutely no doubt that languages evolve fast. One just has to look through a text by Shakespeare or Goethe to see that a few hundred years can have impact on vocabulary and grammatical structure. It took Vulgar Latin a mere 1500 years to evolve into about a dozen different languages such as French, Italian, Portuguese or Catalan (e.g., see Pope 1952 for French). If we observe languages today, we can easily see that new words are invented all the time. In academic and technological contexts, for instance, new concepts arise all the time. Roughly 30 years ago vocabulary such as *email* or *website* did not even exist. What drives change in language, in what circumstances does it take place and what are necessary requirements for language change to occur? These are questions that cultural evolution theories of language have to address.

1.2.1 Language systems and language strategies

Cultural theories of language evolution have to take a close look at individual trajectories of language change (Steels 2011c). For instance, how did the Russian aspectual system emerge or why does English have a system of determiners and Russian not? How do spatial language systems develop over time? In other words, cultural theories of language evolution must provide models for the emergence and evolution of concrete LANGUAGE SYSTEMS (Steels 2011c). Language systems package a particular SEMANTIC SYSTEM (e.g. a set of spatial categories) and a particular way of expressing these distinctions (e.g. a corresponding set of lexical items). The absolute German system, for instance, consists of four absolute spatial categories and the corresponding strings, e.g. *nördlich* ('north'), *südlich* ('south'). These spatial categories are the basic building blocks of absolute spatial conceptualization in German. They can be compositionally combined with landmarks to build complex spatial phrases. Interestingly, the German locative systems effectively consist of different conceptualization strategies that have distinct but converging evolutionary trajectories. For instance, the absolute system is connected to the invention of the compass, whereas projective systems often at least in part can be traced back to body parts (Traugott & Heine 1991). Nevertheless, many locative spatial relations are used in the same syntactic context.

Spatial language systems such as the proximal or projective system are characterized by a degree of cohesion and systematicity that points to an underlying principle that organizes acquisition, emergence and coordination. We call the mechanisms organizing a particular language system the LANGUAGE STRATEGY (Steels 2011c). Language strategies have a *linguistic* and a *conceptual* part. For example, on the conceptual side absolute spatial categories share that they are part of the same conceptualization strategy which uses absolute directions to the magnetic poles of the earth. Syntactically all spatial relations share that they are expressed in a similar way namely lexically and that they can be expressed as adjective, adverb and preposition.

1.2.2 Selectionist theory of language evolution

In this book I follow the *selectionist* theory of language evolution (Steels 2011c), which applies the dominant theoretical construct in biology NATURAL SELECTION and uses it to explain language change on the level of language systems and language strategies. Additionally, the concepts of SELF-ORGANIZATION, RECRUITMENT and CO-EVOLUTION of syntax and semantics are used as theoretical pillars.

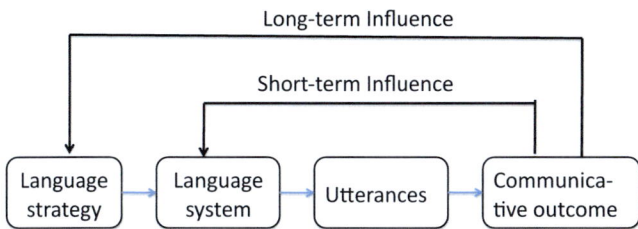

Figure 1.1: The fitness of utterances for communication affects both the language system and the language strategy. The effect of the success of a single utterance on the language strategy is smaller which leads to slower change on the level of the strategy. (Figure adapted from Steels 2011c)

Selection Selectionism rests on two principles: *generation* of possible variants and *selection* of variation based on fitness. The most important factor in determining the fitness of a particular language strategy, but also of a particular language system, is communicative success. A communicative interaction between two interlocutors is successful if the communicative intention of the speaker is reached. For instance, if the speaker wanted to draw attention to some object, the communication is successful if the hearer pays attention to that object. Communicative success drives selection on the levels of the language system, but also on the level of language strategies (see Figure 1.1).

Variation occurs in the systems for two reasons. First, agents are actively trying to solve problems in communication (Steels 2000a). Agents introduce new categories, new words and grammar when they detect problems that they cannot solve using the current language they know. Second, language is an inferential communication system (Sperber & Wilson 1986) which means that the information provided in an utterance is often incomplete and ambiguous. Interpreting phrases is an active process in which the hearer is fusing information from the context, from the dialogue and his knowledge about the language to arrive at the best possible interpretation. In this process of course hearers might interpret the utterance differently then intended. This is the second source of variation.

Self-organization Steels (2011c) assumes that selection is not enough to explain language change and proposes another driving force in the evolution of language: self-organization – a concept used to account for complex phenomena in physical and biological systems. In short, self-organization is a way to explain how global structure arises out of local interaction of subunits (Camazine et al. 2003). An example from biology for self-organization is swarm behavior in a school of fish. Each individual fish locally controls its behavior based on the estimation of the position and direction of its immediate neighbors. On the global level this leads to consistent swarm behavior. Self-organization is typically seen as a complementary mechanism to selection, although there is some discussion on how to reconcile the two mechanisms. Kauffman (1993), for instance, proposes the following idea. Local components and the interaction rules are determined by selection, whereas the global emergent behavior is explained using self-organization. Applied to the swarm behavior this means that the anatomy of fish as well as the perceptual feedback loop are a product of natural selection. The global emergent swarm behavior is the product of self-organization.

Similar to swarm behavior, agents in a population evolving a language have to achieve global coherence in the language they use. Each agent has its own private representations of the language that they speak and they can adjust their own representations based on local interactions with peers. How, from local interactions, agents can agree on a globally shared communication system is the problem of alignment. Psychologists have found that interlocutors align on all levels of linguistic processing even over the course of a few interactions, i.e., dialogue (Garrod & Doherty 1994; Pickering & Garrod 2004). Similar mechanisms applied over a long time span are required for driving populations to self-organize a sufficiently shared communication system (Steels & Kaplan 2002).

Recruitment The last problem for an account of how languages change in the selectionist theory of language evolution is the problem of language strategy generation. The hypothesis is that language strategies are recruited by assembling basic cognitive operations (Steels 2007). For instance, an absolute spatial conceptualization strategy involving distinctions such as "north" and "south" consists of basic categorization mechanisms and the ability to track ones own direction. The two abilities are assembled into the strategy which encompasses the different absolute spatial distinctions. The process is called RECRUITMENT because the cognitive mechanisms which are assembled could, in principle, have evolved or could be learned independently from language.

Co-evolution One of the tenants of the theory of linguistic selection is that syntax and semantics co-evolve. The idea is that recruitment of conceptualization strategies and the invention of new semantic distinctions and spatial relations trigger evolution of the syntax of a language (Steels 1997; 1998). For instance, presumably when the absolute system in German emerged based on a new way of construing reality, this at the same time triggered the invention of new words.

1.2.3 Evolutionary explanations

In every science one has to define what counts as an explanation. This book is guided by what counts as an evolutionary explanation in biology, ethology and psychology (Tinbergen 1963; Dunbar 1998). In order to explain a complex trait from the evolutionary perspective one has to provide explanations on four different levels: FUNCTION, MECHANISM, ONTOGENY and PHYLOGENY.

Function An explanation for a particular behavior has to show what the behavior is good for, i.e. what is its purpose. For Darwinian biology, the function of a behavior has to be explained in terms of its impact on survival or, more precisely, on the production of offspring. For evolutionary linguistics this turns into the question of how a particular language system or a particular strategy helps an agent to be more successful in communication. For example, one can explain particular spatial language systems with respect to their ability to help agents solve communicative problems in spatial navigation and spatial reference.

Mechanism Besides function, one has to identify the mechanisms that give rise to the behavior. This is actually called "causation" by Tinbergen (1963) and it refers to the cause and effect relations that generate a particular behavior. For instance, one can explain how aggressive behavior is generated by looking at changes in hormone levels in an organism, e.g., testosteron causes aggressive behavior. For spatial language this entails a detailed operational model of the production and parsing of spatial language.

Ontogeny The next question is how a particular behavior is acquired. To answer this question one has to identify the developmental steps that the behavior undergoes, but also what is the ontogenetic basis of the behavior. What is learned and what is instinct? For spatial language this requires insights into how spatial language is learned.

Phylogeny A fourth part of every evolutionary explanation has to identify the evolutionary history of a behavior. What are the sequential stages of evolution of a behavior? What are the prerequisites of a behavior? How do evolutionary older behaviors influence the behavior under question? These questions have to be answered with respect to the function of the behavior. In other words, one needs explanations of how the behavior evolved to fulfill its current function. For language evolution scholars have to identify how a particular strategy evolved over time. Was it adapted from an older strategy? How did syntax and semantics of the language system under consideration co-evolve over time?

1.3 Main hypothesis

This book provides experimental evidence for the theory of linguistic evolution. The hypothesis is that *spatial language syntax and spatial semantics co-evolve through a cultural process based on selection, self-organization and recruitment.*

This book explores the hypothesis for the different components of spatial language: spatial relations, landmarks and perspective. Computational experiments show the emergence of spatial relations, the negotiation of the use of landmarks and perspective. I also explore different strategies for expressing spatial conceptualizations: lexical and grammatical strategies.

1.4 Contributions

This book provides detailed accounts of the function, mechanisms, ontogeny and phylogeny of spatial language.

1. The first contribution is an explanation of the mechanisms behind spatial language for German locative phrases in a complete reconstruction including perception, semantic and syntactic processing. Once the mechanisms are in place, we test the function and impact of components of spatial language in experiments by removing the component in question and examining the effect the removal has on communication.

2. The second contribution is to explain steps in the co-evolution of spatial syntax and spatial semantics through computational models.

This book follows a whole systems approach which allows us to define external criteria for the progress in each of the objectives. The defining moment for the underlying conception of language is communication. A communication system is SUCCESSFUL if it allows robotic agents to achieve their communicative goals such as drawing the attention to an object in the environment.

1.4.1 Evolutionary stages

One way of understanding evolutionary processes is to try to identify evolutionary stages. Over the years, different steps in the evolution of language have been identified involving varying degrees of specificity (Bickerton 1999; Jackendoff 1999; Steels 2005). All of these proposals, while differing in detail and the exact number of stages, agree that language evolution starts at some pre-grammatical stage and increases in complexity to the form of language, in particular, grammar that we see today. Obviously any evolutionary account of language has to show how the current state of complexity of language can be traced back to earlier simple stages.

This book orients itself alongside Steels (2005), who proposes a number of stages of complexity which are relevant for this book: SINGLE-WORD UTTERANCES, MULTI-WORD UTTERANCES, and GRAMMATICAL UTTERANCES (see Figure 1.2).

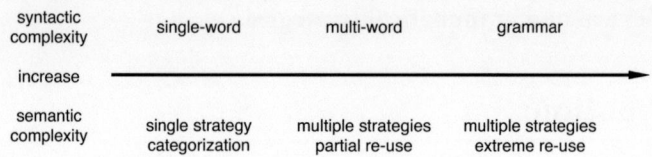

Figure 1.2: Co-evolution of syntactic and semantic complexity.

Single-word utterances In this stage agents utter single words that pertain to a particular concept or category used for discriminating objects. Examples for spatial language include utterances that directly refer to spatial regions such as *links* ('left') or *nördlich* ('north'). When agents can only express themselves using a single word, this single word necessarily encodes the complete conceptualization strategy. For instance, which landmark or perspective is used for conceptualization is holistically coded in the single word. Since there is no additional information about which conceptualization strategy the term is referring to, agents have to implicitly agree on the precise spatial construal the term is referring to. This limits the re-use of spatial categories in different spatial conceptualization strategies because agents have no way of disambiguating the use of the same spatial relation in different strategies.

Multi-word utterances Single-word communication systems are not very flexible. There is no compositionality and particularly there is no re-use. In German, for instance, projective relations can be used with different landmarks. In the multi-word utterance stage agents can express different constituents by using a number of lexical items. Besides expressing the spatial category used, agents can also mark landmarks. An example utterance is *links Kiste* ('left box') which is used to signal that the region left of the box is meant.

Grammatical utterances When we look at natural language, we can see that the *same* constituents can be part of different conceptualization strategies. Imagine an utterance like *Kiste link* ('box left') without the grammatical information, in particular, without word order and lexical class information. In that case a hearer does not know whether *link* is an adjective or an adverb.

This syntactic underdetermination has consequences for the semantic interpretation. If the phrase is interpreted as an adjective noun phrase as in *linke Kiste* ('left box'), the spatial category acts as a modifier on the set of boxes. If the spatial relation is interpreted as an adverb, then box might be a landmark and the whole phrase denotes a region next to the landmark as in *links der Kiste* ('to the left of the box'). Grammar signals the difference in these two semantic interpretations and disambiguates the conceptualization strategies. Consequently, agents equipped with grammatical strategies can disambiguate even more strategies and consequently, they can be more expressive.

The goal of this book is to identify, implement and test the mechanisms that drive the evolution of language on *each* of these stages. The mechanisms we are interested in are not descriptions of the phenomena but mechanistic explanations which identify the computational and cognitive components that enable robotic agents to self-organize communication systems. The procedure to find and validate mechanistic explanations is to

1. hypothesize INVENTION, ADOPTION and ALIGNMENT OPERATORS for the syntax and semantics according to each stage of complexity,

2. equip agents with these operators,

3. test the evolutionary dynamics in populations of equipped agents,

4. measure the communicative success, adaptivity and expressivity.

Invention, adoption and alignment operators are the backbone of the evolutionary models of this book. For instantiating the theory of linguistic selection one has to identify agent-level mechanisms that orchestrate the global behavior of the population. The mechanisms can be classified into the following three classes.

Invention operators Invention is the process of introducing variation into the system by inventing a new spatial relation or a word or even grammar in order to solve a problem in communication. A speaker, for instance, who is unable to discriminate an object might introduce a new spatial category to be able to identify the object. Subsequently, he might invent a new word to be able to express the new spatial category. Invention operators introduce variation and novelty into the system.

Adoption operators Adoption is the process by which an agent acquires a new word, a new spatial relation or a new piece of grammar. Acquisition is carried out by hearers in interactions when they observe new items that they are unable to process. Adoption is another source of novelty and variation. An agent that picks up a new word might have a different idea of what that word means than the speaker actually intended.

Alignment operators Invention is local to an interaction. When two agents communicate and one of them invents a new word, this word might be acquired by the interlocutor, but the knowledge about this word is still local. Alignment operators orchestrate the self-organization of the system and the global alignment of language.

1.4.2 Co-evolution of syntactic and semantic complexity

In each stage, syntactic complexity co-evolves with semantic complexity (see Figure 1.2). Syntactic complexity rises because the number of words per utterance increases (from the single-word stage to the multi-word stage) and because syntactic categorizations such as word order, morphology, agreement become important (from multi-word to grammar).

The notion of semantic complexity is harder to define. Obviously German spatial language is complex. But why does this seem obvious? What are the properties that make it a complex semantic system? For this book, complex semantics is defined with respect to spatial language as: the language supports a large number of conceptualizations of a spatial scene. There are two factors influencing the complexity of the space of possible conceptualizations of a spatial scene.

Number of relations A first level of semantic complexity is related to the number of spatial categories. For the part of German locative phrases considered in this book, we already have 12 spatial relations. But there are, of course, many more relations not considered in this book such as dynamic relations. For some scholars this is the only definition of semantic complexity (compare Schoenemann 1999).

Number of conceptualization strategies A second notion of semantic complexity is the number of conceptualization strategies a language supports. German, for instance, supports many different categorization systems: projective, e.g. *links* ('left') or *rechts* ('right'), proximal, e.g. *nah* ('near') and *fern* ('far'), and absolute, e.g. *nördlich* ('north') and *südlich* ('south'). This is one aspect. The other aspect is that these systems are part of different conceptualization strategies. Examples of this re-use were already given earlier with respect to adjectives and adverbs.

1.5 Structure of the book

This book is structured into three main parts besides this introduction and the conclusion. Part I explains the interaction model and the technical systems needed for studying spatial language. Part II deals with objective number one and details the reconstruction efforts for the German locative system. In Part III, I detail how spatial language evolves based on the model of evolutionary stages.

1.5.1 Part I: Spatial language games and technical background

1.5.1.1 Spatial language games

Spatial language occurs mainly in interactions of individuals in spatial scenes. To research spatial language in such a communication-based approach to language a number of things need to be in place. We need a model of interactions in spatial scenes. This is the topic of Chapter 2 which introduces spatial language games which are routinized interactions consisting of defined roles for interlocutors – speaker and hearer. The chapter explains the basic interaction scheme and the linguistic and non-linguistic behaviors that define a spatial language game.

1.5.1.2 Embodied cognitive semantics with IRL

In order to achieve the objectives of this book, we need computational formalisms that support the reconstruction and evolution investigations. One of such formalisms in part developed for this book is the Incremental Recruitment Language (IRL). IRL is (a) a formalism for representing semantics, (b) a set of planning algorithms for automatic conceptualization and interpretation, and (c) a set of tools that make semantics an open-ended adaptive system. Chapter 3 introduces the formalism and the technology behind it.

1.5.1.3 Construction grammar with FCG

Another important backbone of the investigations is Fluid Construction Grammar (FCG). FCG is a formalism for representing and processing linguistic knowledge. Chapter 4 details how mappings from semantics to syntax are implemented using FCG and gives an example of processing a simple phrase.

1.5.2 Part II: Reconstructing German locative phrases

To ground the modeling efforts in sufficient knowledge of a real spatial language system, I decided to reconstruct a part of German spatial language – German locative phrases. The second part of this book reconstructs the syntax and semantics of German locative phrases. The part starts out with an in-depth look at German locative spatial language as a natural language phenomenon. Chapter 5 gives more examples of the syntactic variety and the connection to the space of conceptualization strategies supported in German locative phrases. This sets the scope for the reconstruction effort, but also identifies a number of processing issues that the reconstruction has to deal with in order to be successful.

1.5.2.1 Spatial semantics

The following chapter details the operationalization of spatial semantics. Chapter 6 the basic semantic building blocks of German locative phrases and discusses how they work together to make up the complex semantics of spatial scenes.

1.5.2.2 Syntactic processing

A close look at German locative phrases reveals a number of interesting phenomena. Most importantly it uncovers the tight relationship between spatial syntax and spatial semantics. Chapter 7 explains how FCG can be used to model the tight connection between the words and grammatical relations observed in German locative phrases and the world of spatial semantics. These mappings are interesting because they pose particular challenges to the organization of linguistic processing. The re-use of the same spatial categories in different strategies for conceptualizing reality and their syntactic expression requires sophisticated mechanisms for dealing with many-to-many mappings in language. Another important issue is how to deal with the case system of German. All of these aspects of linguistic processing are discussed in Chapter 7.

1.5.2.3 Conceptualization of spatial scenes

Spatial scenes do not come a priori labeled, categorized and construed. Agents have to autonomously conceptualize reality given the particular communicative goal they have. Chapter 8 deals with the problem of conceptualization which is the problem of how to construct semantic structure that is helpful in reaching communicative intentions. The chapter gives an overview of different factors influencing the conceptualization of spatial scenes and compares different implementations of spatial conceptualization.

1.5.2.4 Integrating syntactic and semantic processing

The last chapter of this part reports on the integration of syntax, semantics and conceptualization. One of the issues that can be studied in an approach like mine is SEMANTIC AMBIGUITY which refers to the fact that natural language is often ambiguous with respect to the precise interpretation of a phrase. But humans are very strong in communicating even though language only encodes hints at how to conceptualize reality. The key is that humans integrate the sparse information communicated in utterances with knowledge about the current context of the interaction. Chapter 9 explains how one can operationalize this process of disambiguation through the context using the conglomerate of systems for linguistic and semantic processing as well as perception.

1.5.3 Part III: Spatial language evolution

Finally the book turns to evolution in the third part. The organization of this part orients itself along the stages of complexity introduced earlier. There are two parts on single-word utterance systems, followed by a chapter on multi-word utterance systems. The part closes with a chapter on the evolution of grammatical structure.

1.5.3.1 Acquisition and formation of basic spatial category systems

The first chapter in this part explains how the basic building blocks of spatial language – spatial relationships and corresponding words – become shared in populations of agents. This corresponds to complexity stage one – single words. The goal of the chapter is to define the language strategies necessary for forming single-word spatial language systems.

Single-word spatial language systems are built by a particular strategy of conceptualizing reality which includes a priori commitments to certain reference objects, frames of reference and perspectives on the scene. The chapter shows how a language strategy which is a combination of a particular strategy for conceptualizing reality plus the necessary invention operators for basic spatial categories build the language systems that allow agents to communicate successfully. Language strategies are tested in two scenarios – ACQUISITION and FORMATION. In acquisition a learner agent has to pick up the spatial language system spoken by a tutor. In formation all agents start from scratch and progressively develop categories and lexical items.

The most important influence on what kind of language system emerges is the language strategy. The chapter details different language strategies necessary for building proximal, projective and absolute systems which encompass dedicated invention, adoption and alignment operators as well as the different conceptualization strategies. The success of the learning operators and the conceptualization strategy is tested in experiments where populations are fitted with a particular strategy. The resulting languages spoken by individual agents are analyzed with respect to communicative success and how similar they are to each other.

Another important factor influencing the emerging language system are environmental conditions. The chapter studies the impact of environmental conditions systematically by manipulating environmental features such as global landmarks or the statistical distribution of objects.

Obviously, natural languages support many conceptualization strategies at the same time. German, for instance, simultaneously has a proximal, a projective and an absolute system. So one can ask what happens when agents are simultaneously operating different strategies. I hypothesize that agents need additional cognitive mechanisms for choosing between different strategies and that choosing a strategy can be realized using the discriminative power of each strategy in a particular context. When an agent has to invent a new category they use the strategy that is most discriminating using a new category. Experiments show that this principle allows agents to build multiple language systems at the same time. Lastly, the chapter also studies the impact of different environmental layouts on formation of language systems for interacting strategies.

1.5.3.2 Origins and alignment of spatial conceptualization strategies

Chapter 11 deals with the emergence and alignment of conceptualization strategies. When one compares different languages of the world it becomes clear that many languages differ in the kinds of conceptualization strategies they support. Some languages solely use an absolute system, others can use intrinsic and relative systems and so on and so forth. Consequently, the evolution of spatial language is intricately connected to the origins and evolution of spatial conceptualization strategies. The chapter shows that conceptualization strategies are organized in a process of recruitment, selection and self-organization.

To explain conceptualization strategies from the viewpoint of the theory of linguistic selection is to explain (a) how different conceptualization strategies are created and (b) how they are selected for in communication. Competition is an important aspect of selection. Obviously environmental conditions and communicative success are main influences on which strategies are selected for because they are more successful. The chapter proposes alignment operations that update and track the score of conceptualization strategies so that agents can locally align in their interactions. I show that these operators lead to global convergence of the population on using single conceptualization strategies. The chapter studies competition of different strategies for landmarks and frames of reference and shows that with the right alignment strategy agents can agree on using a particular conceptualization strategy while co-evolving a lexicon and ontology of spatial relations at the same time.

Besides selection the theory has to explain how conceptualization strategies are created. This is were the idea of recruitment comes into play. Conceptualization strategies are assemblies of cognitive operations. For instance, an absolute strategy consists of a particular way of applying spatial categories plus the computation of a global landmark. Recruitment is the process of drawing from the pool of cognitive operations and assembling and packaging them so that the complete structure for conceptualization can be scored and the score updated and tracked. In a second set of experiments creation and competition of strategies are studied together.

1.5.3.3 Multi-word lexical systems for expressing landmarks

Single-word utterance systems are limited in how much information can be conveyed in them. Upon hearing a single term it is hard to decide what conceptualization strategy was it part of. Which landmark is used? Which perspective did the speaker have in mind? These are questions that cannot be decided by just looking at a single word, unless of course the word is known and always refers to the same landmark and the same conceptualization strategy. When we look at human language we see a lot of re-use of spatial relations. Absolute, projective and proximal relations in German can be used with different landmark objects. Chapter 12 examines what mechanisms are needed for agents to mark landmark objects using lexical items while at the same time co-evolving a lexicon and ontology of spatial relations. Once these mechanisms are in place success of such extended lexical systems can be studied and compared to systems which only support a single conceptualization strategy.

1.5.3.4 Grammar as a tool for disambiguating spatial phrases

The part on language evolution of this book is concluded by Chapter 13 that examines the role and evolution of grammatical language.

Lexical systems which are all systems studied up to this point in the book, have considerable shortcomings. One can study the effect grammar has by removing grammatical knowledge from the German locative grammar implemented for this book. The results presented in Chapter 13 show that agents operating a German locative system without grammar have significantly lower communicative success. I show that environmental conditions and diverging perspective on the scene can increase the drop in communicative success. The lack of grammar increases semantic ambiguity of phrases which means that the number of possible interpretations of a phrase escalates. As a consequence, the number of wrongly interpreted topics enlarges as well.

Given such a clear communicative advantage for having grammar, one can study the necessary operators that enable agents to develop a grammar for disambiguating spatial phrases. This is the topic of the second part of Chapter 13 which reports on the precise implementation of these operators. I test the operators in multi-agent experiments which prove that the hypothesized invention, learning and alignment operators allow agents to become increasingly more successful in communication because they develop an effective grammatical communication system.

Part I

Spatial language games and technical background

2 Grounded spatial language games

Language does not occur in a vacuum. Spoken language occurs in physical, situated interactions when two interlocutors meet with specific communicative intentions. This chapter explains the basic social interactions at the center of the approach to language. Physical robots meet in communicative encounters and try to reach communicative goals within real world settings. Taking such a radical approach to the study of language is grounded in a number of social and perceptual mechanisms. Here I look at the prerequisites for the computational models discussed later in this book.

Figure 2.1 shows such an encounter of two humanoid robots in which one of the robots, the speaker, has the goal of drawing the attention of the hearer to some object in the environment using language. Such interactions are called LANGUAGE GAMES (Steels 2001). Language games are routinized interactions between two members of a population. The game combines a particular script for the interaction, the linguistic information transfer and extra-linguistic feedback about the success of the interaction. Here is an example of a language game called the SPATIAL LANGUAGE GAME:

1. The language game starts by randomly drawing two agents from the population. One agent is randomly assigned the role of speaker, the other is assigned the role hearer.

2. The agents establish joint attention and perceive the scene.

3. The speaker chooses an object from the perceived context as the object he wants to draw the attention of the hearer to.

4. The speaker produces an utterance that he thinks draws the attention to the object.

5. The speaker passes the utterance to the hearer.

6. The hearer interprets the utterance and tries to find the object that the speaker might have in mind.

7. The hearer points to the object he thinks the interaction was about. If he was unable to interpret a topic, he signals this by shaking his head.

8. The speaker interprets the pointing. If the object pointed to by the hearer is correct, he signals this by noding. If the hearer pointed to the wrong object or did not point at all, the speaker points to the topic he wanted to draw the attention to.

Figure 2.1: Example scene. Two robots autonomously perceive and act in an office environment that contains different types of objects. Both robots autonomously create world models reflecting the state of the environment (see bottom left and right schematics), that include objects with spatial and color properties, the carton boxes as well as the robots.

To study language in a real world setting requires to fully spell out all components involved in the interaction. Besides social mechanisms agents need operational systems for perceiving the world, as well as the construction and interpretation of utterances. Figure 2 shows a schematic view of the systems involved in production and parsing, conceptualization and interpretation. Both agents independently process sensorimotor data stemming from the onboard cameras and proprioceptive sensors in order to construct world models of the environment (Spranger 2008; Spranger, Loetzsch & Steels 2012). Based on the particular communicative goal and the current state of the world represented in the world model, the speaker conceptualizes a meaning which is then rendered into an utterance by the language system. The hearer parses the utterance to determine its meaning and interprets it with respect to his current model of the world in order

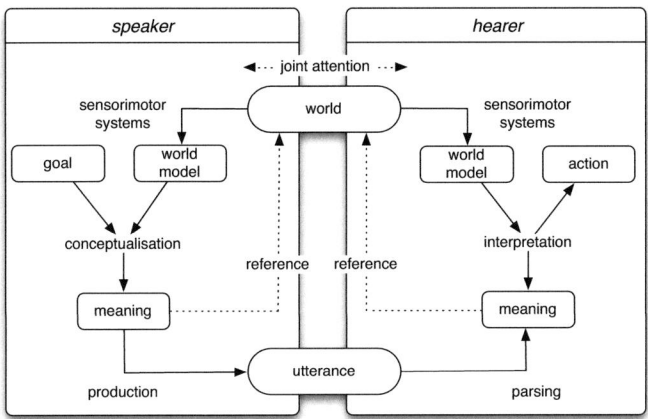

Figure 2.2: The semiotic cycle is a model of situated communicative interactions between two interacting agents.

to infer the speaker's communicative goal and, for instance, perform a desired action. The system used for conceptualization and interpretation are explained in detail in Chapter 3. The system for producing and parsing utterances is treated in Chapter 4. The following sections focus on the necessary prerequisites for language production, parsing and evolution in terms of social mechanisms and perceptual processing.

2.1 Perception

The environment that robots interact in is equipped with four kinds of objects that were carefully chosen to pick out special features relevant for spatial language: blocks, boxes, wall markers and the robots themselves (see Figure 2.1).

Blocks Are the colored brick like objects. They are typically of the same color. Agents perceive these objects as having a certain distance from their egocentric coordinate systems originating in the robot's body.

Boxes The environment also features card boxes which have particular markers on their sides. These markers are perceived by the sensorimotor systems as distinct sides of the object. The perceptual systems perceive them as having a particular distance and orientation with respect to the robot's coordinate system.

Wall markers Figure 2.1 shows that the same markers used for the carton boxes can also occur on the wall. Cardboard boxes introduce a geocentric orientation on the scene.

Robots Robots also establish the position of the interlocutor in each interaction. Every robot tracks the position and orientation of the other robot in his environment.

Before a language game starts the robots perceive their environment. The robots are endowed with perceptual systems for recognizing and tracking the objects in their environment. These systems continuously build up WORLD MODELS of the environment consisting of sets of objects. The objects are characterized by continuous real-valued features such as color, position and orientation but also width, height and length. The perceptual system also provides a basic grouping of objects into classes such as robots, blocks and boxes and wall markers. The following is the world model built by the agent to the left in Figure 2.1. It includes the other robot (robot-2), the landmark (box-1) and the colored blocks (obj-265, obj-266 and obj-268):

```
((robot-1 :type robot :x 0.0 :y 0.0 :orientation 0.5)
 (robot-2 :type robot :x 1461.65 :y -351.24 :orientation 0.9)
 (box-1 :type box :x 513.0 :y 891.67 :orientation 0.36
        :width 320.0 :height 450.0 :length 310.0)
 (obj-265 :x 1454.74 :y 248.72 :z 0.0 :width 59.75
          :height 235.99
          :average-y 128.0 :stdev-y 26.49 :min-y 51.0
          :max-y 199.0 :average-u ...)
 (obj-266 :x 285.0 :y 549.02 :z 0.0 ...)
 (obj-268 ...)
 (box-wall :orientation 0.36))
```

Each robot constructs perceptual representations of the objects in its immediate surroundings from the raw sensations streaming from the robot's sensor. Each type of object in the environment is tracked by a dedicated perceptual system. In general, processing of the different object classes is a three step process. First, low-level vision routines process raw camera images to yield basic PERCEPTS – these are connected regions that differ from the background of the environment or are related to the patterns distributed on the boxes and wall markers. Second, these regions are tracked in subsequent camera images. In order to do so, the vision system needs to establish a correspondence between an internal MODEL and the image regions that refer to the same physical object, a process known in robotics as ANCHORING (Coradeschi & Saffiotti 2003). I use state estimation techniques from robotics, e.g. Kalman filters (Kálmán 1960), for maintaining such persistent models. Third, the vision system fuses information from the proprioceptive sensors of the robot the visual information to encode a set of visual properties about each object. In this particular setup these properties are the position and orientation of objects, an estimated width and height and color information. In the experiments discussed in this book only position and orientation are relevant. Most importantly, the perceptual systems only track objects on the ground. The position and orientation of objects is encoded in a two dimensional *egocentric* coordinate system which has its origin between the two feet of the robot facing to the front of the robot. Spranger (2008) gives more detail on the perceptual systems.

The experiments reported on in later sections require that agents play many language games. In order to speed up the process of a game and in order to do repeatable, manipulatable experiments, data from spatial scenes such as the one in Figure 2.1 are recorded and stored. The output of the perception system of more than 800 spatial scenes with different spatial configurations has been collected and can be accessed by artificial software agents without the agents required to run on physical robots. A spatial language game can be enacted on such stored scenes as if robots were perceiving the scene at the very moment they are playing a particular language game.

Figure 2.3 shows different spatial scenes. Each spatial scene consists of a world model for each of the two robots recorded from the position of each robot. Scenes are grouped into data sets with similar characteristics with respect to perspective on the scene, the number of objects and the availability of boxes and wall markers. For instance, in some data sets the perspective of interlocutors is similar (see Figure 2.3 for examples from one data set), i.e., robots are looking at the scene from the same position and there are few objects. Figure 2.4 shows examples from different data sets.

2.2 Social mechanisms

Language games require a number of social mechanisms to be in place. Joint attention, turn-taking behavior, pointing and other non-linguistic feedback are mechanisms at the heart of the social interaction. Crucial social mechanisms required for these interaction are considered prerequisites for studying the evolution of language. They constitute the background against which communication and evolution of communication take place.

In joint attentional scenes (Tomasello 1995), interlocutors are jointly attending

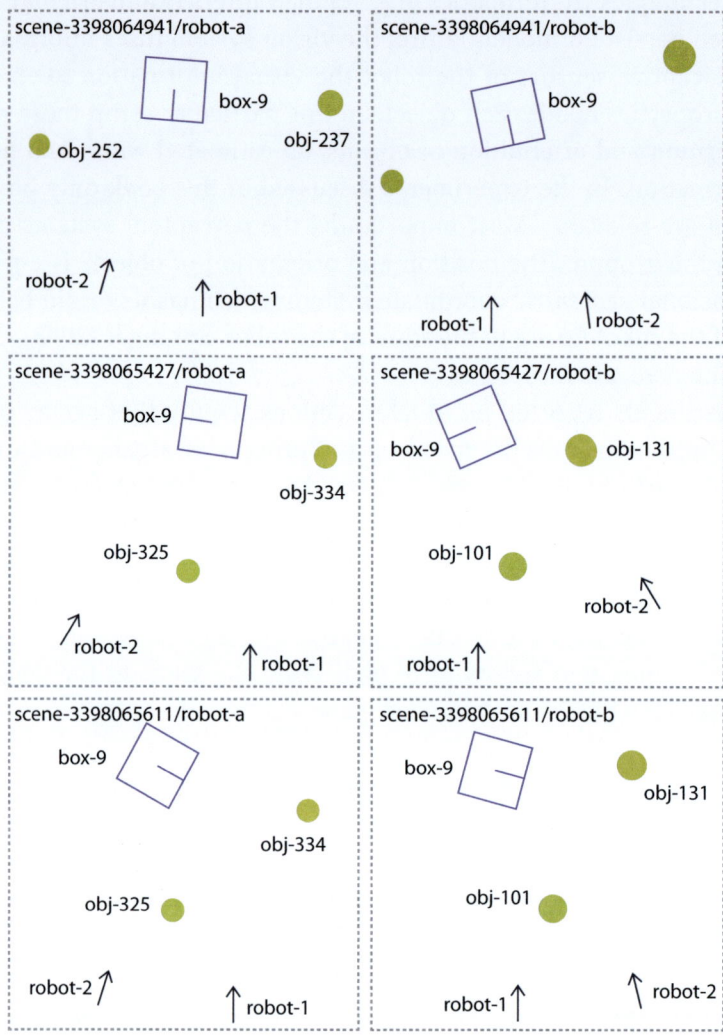

Figure 2.3: Example world models from a spatial data set called space-game-2. Left the world model of robot *a* is shown. To the right the world model of robot *b* is shown. All scenes share similar properties. In this data set robots share a similar perspective on the scene. The actual position of the robots varies across different scenes, but is always similar. Similarly, every scene has a box landmark and two yellow blocks in it. However, the actual position of the box and its orientation, as well as the position of the objects change in every scene.

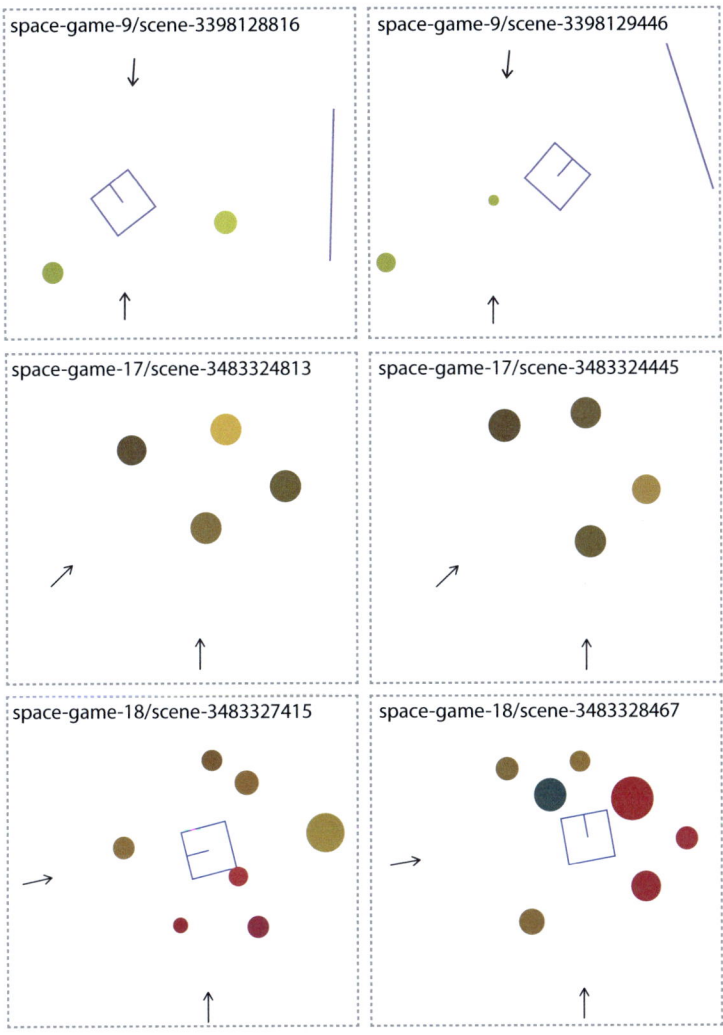

Figure 2.4: Example scenes from different spatial data sets. Each row shows scenes from a particular data set (the world model of robot *a* is always shown). The first row shows a data set which features a global landmark (space-game-9). The middle row shows scenes of a data set without global landmark and without box (space-game-17). Lastly, a data set which features many objects is shown (space-game-18).

to some object for some reasonable amount of time. Establishing joint attention in robotic experiments means that two robots taking part in a language game must (1) share a physical environment, (2) attend to a set of objects in their surrounding, (3) track whether the respective other robot is able to attend to the same set of objects and (4) be able to manipulate attention by pointing to distal objects and perceiving these pointing gestures. Joint attention is monitored by an external computer program, that has access to the world models of both interacting robots. This system initiates the interaction between two agents as soon as both agents observe the same set of objects. Spatial scenes are manipulated by a human experimenter to find spatial setups in which joint attention is possible, the program monitors whether robots are seeing the same set of objects and informs the experimenter whether the robots jointly attend to the same set of objects.

Social interactions have to be structured, so that agents can interpret the signals they exchange. For instance, if the hearer points before he has received the utterance, the speaker will have a hard time understanding the gesture. However, if the hearer points after receiving the utterance, the speaker can assume that this is the response to his speech act. Language games are coordinated by behavioral scripts. Every agent in the population knows the language game script and individually reacts to changes in the environment and actions of the other robot. For example the speaker triggers the action of pointing to the intended topic when the hearer signals that he did not understand the utterance. The scripts are implemented in the form of finite-state machines: actions are performed depending on the current state in the game flow, the perception of the environment and the history of the interaction.

In order to be able to learn and form spatial language systems, robots need non-linguistic means of conveying information, such as pointing to an object or conveying notions of success, failure and agreement in communication. For demonstration purposes robots are equipped with pointing gestures but in the communicative interactions underlying the results presented in this book, robots use a different mechanism in order to avoid further difficulties stemming from uncertainties in pointing (see Steels & Kaplan 1998 for a discussion of the impact of such uncertainties on the performance in language games). When a robot wants to point to an object in the environment, he directly transmits the coordinates of the intended object to the interlocutor. Since robots model object positions in their own (egocentric) coordinate systems, additional steps have to be taken to interpret these coordinates. Most importantly the robot has to know the position and orientation of the robot that is pointing. With this information robots transform the coordinates into their own coordinate system and interpret the pointing by choosing the closest object to the pointing coordinates in their world model. Similarly, robots directly exchange other non-linguistic feedback, for instance agreement and disagreement in communication by exchanging signals whose meaning is shared. Moreover, linguistic utterances are directly passed between interlocutors.

3 Embodied cognitive semantics with IRL

Artificial agents trying to achieve communicative goals in situated interactions in the real-world need powerful computational systems for conceptualizing their environment. In order to provide embodied artificial systems with rich semantics reminiscent of human language complexity, agents need mechanisms for both conceptualizing complex compositional semantic structure, but also for actively reconstructing semantic structure in interpretation of ambiguous utterances. Furthermore, the system must be open-ended and allow agents to adjust their semantic inventories in order to reach their goals. This chapter presents the computational system called Incremental Recruitment Language (IRL) that allows agents to represent and process complex conceptualizations of spatial scenes. The work presented here is based on substantial previous work. Key ideas of the IRL system have been laid out by Steels (2000b), with progress reported by Steels & Bleys (2005), Van den Broeck (2008), and recently by Spranger, Loetzsch & Pauw (2010) and Spranger et al. (2012).

3.1 Procedural semantics

In order for a hearer to interpret an utterance, he has to apply the meaning conveyed in the linguistic structure to his perception of the context. Consequently, a speaker who uses language to achieve a certain communicative goal wants the hearer to execute a program (Johnson-Laird 1977), i.e. a set of operations that allow the hearer to, for example, discriminate an object in the environment or perform an action. Thus we model semantics, i.e. what it is a speaker wants the hearer to execute, as a program linking operations and data. Let us start with an example. Suppose a speaker utters the phrase *der rote Block* ('the red block') with the intention of making the hearer point to an object. In this case, the phrase encodes a program, i.e., set of operations, that are supposed to lead the hearer to identify the object in question. Presumably the hearer of this utterance has to filter the context for blocks first, followed by the application of the color category red, in order to arrive at the set of red blocks, which is used to compute the topic consisting of a single entity. A possible program, also called IRL-NETWORK, is shown in Figure 3.1. This network explicitly represents the chain of the four operations get-context, apply-class, apply-color and apply-selector by linking their arguments through variables (starting with ?). The network also includes the color category red, the object class block and the selector unique which are introduced via so called BIND STATEMENTS, as in (bind color-category ?color red). We collectively refer to concepts, categories etc. as SEMANTIC ENTITIES.

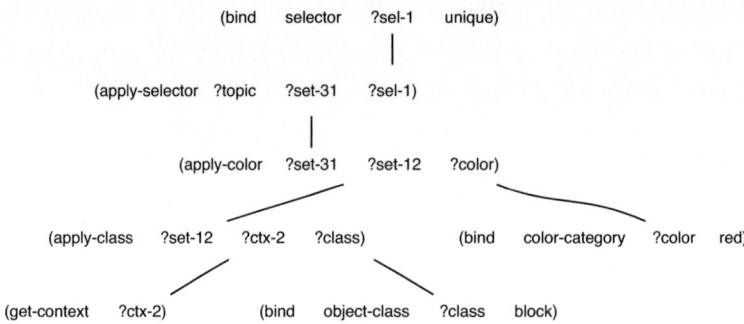

Figure 3.1: Semantic structure underlying the utterance *der rote Block* ('the red block').

IRL-networks consist of two types of nodes :

Cognitive operations also called SEMANTIC OPERATIONS, are the algorithms used in conceptualization. They encode a particular cognitive function such as categorization using a color category, applying a selector or applying an object class and many more as will be shown later in this book for the domain of space. Cognitive operations are identified by their name, e.g. apply-color, and they have a set of arguments which can be linked to other operations or semantic entities via variables (starting with ?).

Semantic entites is the general term for referring to prototypes, concepts and categories that are used by cognitive operations. Besides such long-term data, semantic entities can also be discourse representations, the representation of the current context and data exchanged between cognitive operations. They are introduced explicitly in the network via bind-statements which are special operations for retrieving the actual data representation using a pointer or shorthand notation for it. For instance, the statement (bind color-category ?color red) encodes the access to the color category red which is a prototype represented using values for different color channels.

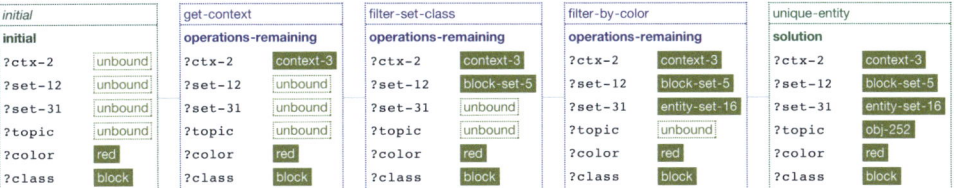

Figure 3.2: Progressive evaluation of the network in Figure 3.1 on the context shown in Figure 2.1. From left to right, each node represents a step in the evaluation process. From top to bottom, the evaluated operation, the node status, and the current list of bindings of each node are shown. A consistent solution with bindings for all variables is found in the last node, and the value obj-252 is indeed a unique red block (compare Figure 2.1).

3.2 Evaluation

A program such as the one in Figure 3.1 is *evaluated* by a speaker to test the semantic structure with respect to the particular communicative goal, or by a hearer in order to interpret an utterance. Evaluation is a process which cycles over the network and progressively computes values for variables, a process called BINDING. When the network in Figure 3.1 is evaluated the following happens. First get-context gets the current world model from the perceptual processes that are monitoring the environment for events and objects and binds it to the variable ?ctx-2. This is followed by the evaluation of the apply-class operation which computes a similarity score for every object in the context with respect to the object class block. This yields the set of objects from the context with each object scored using the computed similarity. The set is bound to the variable ?set-12. Because this variable is linked to the operation apply-color, the set bound to the variable ?set-12 is further processed using the color category red. apply-color first computes a similarity score for every object in the input set to the color category red which is multiplied with the similarity score the object already has from the application of the class block. This yields a new set of objects with multiplied similarity scores. The set is bound to the variable ?set-31. Lastly, apply-selector checks the objects in ?set-31, finds the object with the highest similarity score and binds it to the variable ?topic which is the referent[1] of the phrase *der rote Block* ('the red block'). Figure 3.2 gives an idea how variables get progressively bound when the IRL-network is evaluated.

This is only one example how such a network can be evaluated. As Steels (2000b) has argued, language requires that semantic structure does not encode control flow, but rather data flows in all directions and is computed wherever possible. For this, operations need to be able to function in different directions with varying input-output parameters. For instance, the operation apply-class, which has three arguments, applies a class such as block to an input set, when the class is explicitly represented in the network. But in case this class is not introduced via a bind statement in the network, the operation can also provide this information, effectively turning this argument into an output argument. This MULTIDIRECTIONALITY of operations proves important for dealing with missing items, for instance due to partial parsing of an utterance, but it is also needed when constructing semantic structure.

3.3 Conceptualization and interpretation

There are two scenarios in which agents autonomously compose semantic structure like the one just described in Figure 3.1. First, speakers have a particular communicative goal and need to construct semantic structure, for instance, for singling out the particular topic they want to draw attention to. This process is called CONCEPTUALIZATION. In the second scenario, hearers use information parsed from the observed utterance and their knowledge about the current context of the interaction to actively reconstruct meanings from the potentially partial structures parsed by the language system. We call this process INTERPRE-TATION. Both cases are equally important and they both conceive the process of building semantic structure as a heuristically guided search process, that explores the space of possible IRL-networks driven by the agent's particular communicative goal and the information available to him.

In conceptualization, in other words while "planning what to say" (Steels & Bleys 2005), a speaker searches for an IRL-network that, when executed by the hearer, will reach a particular given communicative goal in a particular context. IRL-networks are constructed by assembling basic building blocks, in particular, cognitive operations packaged into chunks into more and more complex semantic structures. Each assembled structure is immediately tested by evaluating it

---

[1] Note that the word "object" here refers to an agent's private representation of things he has perceived in the world and only indirectly refers to the physical object which is the referent.

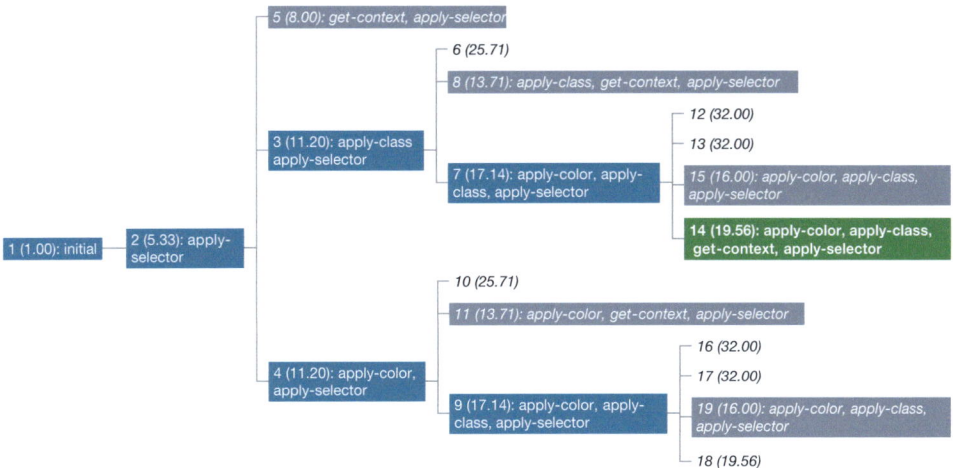

Figure 3.3: The search tree for finding the semantic structure seen in Figure 3.1. From left to right, nodes represent progressively growing programs combined from several chunks, which are each tried out and in some cases lead to solutions (green nodes).

which assesses its compatibility with the current communicative goal and the perceived context. Figure 3.3 shows an example of such a search process that has produced the program in Figure 3.1 for discriminating the red block in Figure 2.1. The search process for "good" semantic structure is guided by many different heuristics, one being that the structure can be expressed using the language system available to an agent. Others are more focused on the particular character of the communicative goal. If the goal is to discriminate an object in the environment, then it is beneficial to use more discriminative categories, i.e. categories that enlarge the distance between the similarity of the topic and the similarity of all other objects in the context.

Search is also applied when an agent perceiving an utterance tries to interpret it. The semantic structure an agent parsed from an utterance is often incomplete and semantic entities, cognitive operations and links can be missing in the network. Interpretation is a flexible, active process by which agents use search to add missing items to the network. Networks are immediately evaluated to see if they find a referent for the parsed utterance. The search process is constrained by the partial meaning parsed from the utterance and the kinds of semantic structures that are appropriate in the current context. The same scoring mechanisms as for conceptualization ensures that only a structure that is discriminating for a particular object (implicitly assuming that the speaker constructs structure based on these principles) will be considered and the best of all possible results is chosen as the interpretation of an utterance.

3.4 Chunking

Search spaces quickly become intractable because the number of possibilities for composing semantic structures increases exponentially with the number of cognitive operations. A look at language is helpful here. Grammar can be analyzed as a sophisticated tool that highly structures human language in order to manage not only the search space of possible syntactic structure (Steels & Wellens 2006) but perhaps more importantly the vast space of possible conceptual structures. Parts of meaning that are covered by a particular part of language can be stored as a chunk and then used as an basic atomic unit in composition. Ready-made semantic structure dramatically reduces the search space. If a structure like the final structure in Figure 3.1 is constructed from scratch using simple operations, the search tree would have a search depth of three (essentially one step in depth per operation). However, every time an operation is added to a program, it can be linked to the current structure in multiple ways, which leads to an explosion of nodes on every layer of depth. Hence, the system soon has to deal with a wide search tree, where every node will be executed and tested against the context. Consequently, using chunking dramatically increases the performance of the system, even in simple examples.

Chunks have an important role in the study of language because they package strategies for conceptualizing reality. Chunks allow to research how cognitive operations form strategies for conceptualizing reality, how these strategies can be adapted by agents and how strategies become conventionalized. For studying conventionalization, chunks have scores. This allows to track the success of each strategy with respect to the communicative goals, e.g. discriminative power of a strategy, but also with respect to communicative success. Strategies for conceptualizing reality are tightly linked to language. For instance, one can image that the chunk in Figure 3.4 which is extracted from the network in Figure 3.1 could be the semantics expressed by a determined adjective noun phrase construction. One important claim is that the structure in language – in particular in grammar – is tightly connected to the conceptualization of reality underlying every utterance. So the exemplary facts that in English, noun phrases have determiners, or that in Russian, all verbs are marked for aspects, suggests that these languages require speakers to conceptualize reality in a certain way and mark these conceptualizations in language.

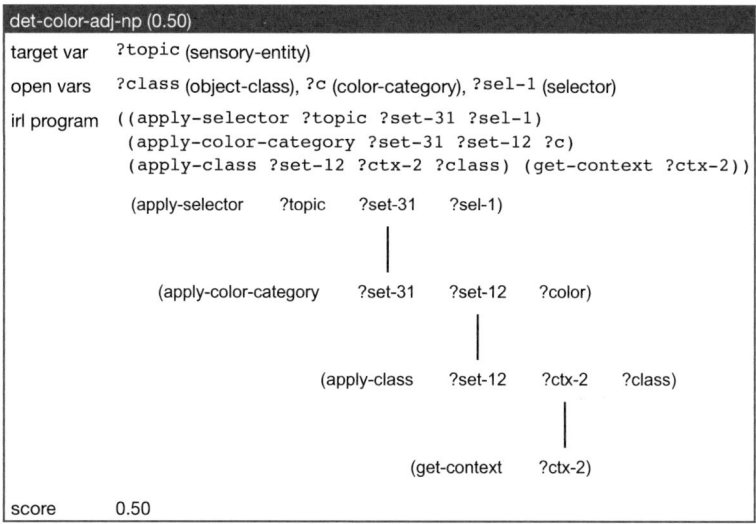

Figure 3.4: Chunk representing the meaning of a determined color-adjcctive noun phrase. Chunks consist of an IRL-network, plus additional information used for processing: a target variable and open variables. These variables are typed (see brackets for type information) and they are used in conceptualization and interpretation for combining chunks to larger structures. The target variable of a chunk can be linked to the open variable of another chunk. Which selector is used, which object class and which color category are, is mostly determined by evaluating the network which yields bindings for the variables. Since the corresponding variables are open variables the information can also be provided by other chunks or in interpretation by the actual lexical items observed in the utterance. Chunks also have a score which can reflect the degree to which they are conventional ways of conceptualizing reality.

3.5 Grounding

Another important issue is grounding. There are now many proposals of how agents can ground lexicons and categorical systems in sensorimotor interaction with the environment (Billard & Dautenhahn 1998; Vogt 2002; Steels 2008) and IRL is designed to allow such insights to be applied straightforwardly. For instance, the implementation of the operation for apply-color is in part based on findings about how basic color categories can be grounded in the sensor data streams of digital cameras (Steels & Belpaeme 2005; Bleys et al. 2009). Similarly, other grounding mechanisms such as for events (Siskind 2001; Steels & Baillie 2003) are easily instantiated in IRL operations.

One of the main claims in this book is that agents co-evolve syntax and semantics. Chunks are one way in which agents can shape strategies for conceptualizing reality. Another is related to the semantic entities themselves and the fact that the number of prototypes and categories and their particular representation is not fixed. For instance, there is now abundant research in the formation of basic color categories (Steels & Belpaeme 2005; Belpaeme & Bleys 2007) and how agents can invent, adopt and shape their inventory of color categories based on the environment they are facing. These insights into adaptive categories, but also names and individuals can be incorporated into IRL, which provides mechanisms for the creation and adaptation of categories in semantic structure.

3.6 Discussion

IRL is a powerful system that for the first time allows to study complex semantic phenomena that go beyond purely lexical studies. IRL is a general system for representing the procedural semantics of utterances. It establishes a link between perception and language by providing a mechanism for representing the meaning of utterances, finding and interpreting the meaning of utterances. Moreover, IRL is designed to allow language processing to be a flexible, adaptive process which can be extended by new cognitive operations, new chunks, and new categories at any moment. Moreover, IRL provides mechanisms for tracking the success of semantic material such as chunks and categories.

The oldest and in some sense most similar system to what I have presented here is Winograd's SHRDLU (Haddock 1989; Winograd 1971), However, SHRDLU misses the key aspects of grounding, active interpretation and conceptualization as a search process. Other work such as those by Bailey, Feldman & Narayanan (1997) and Siskind (2001) focus mostly on lexical meaning. Some approaches have taken more general approaches e.g. to event structure (Narayanan 1999) but stay mostly tied with that particular domain. One of the few approaches talking about objects and events in the same framework is Roy's (2005), which is comparable to ours, but so far has been a theoretical proposal only.

4 Construction Grammar with FCG

Construction Grammar posits that linguistic knowledge is organized in the form of "constructions" (Goldberg 1995; Croft 2001) which are mappings of semantics and pragmatics to syntax, i.e. words and grammar, but also phonology, prosody or intonation. Typically, Construction grammarians take a functional view on language and analyze every piece of language as a tool for communication and in terms of the syntactic and semantic function it performs. The theoretical framework of Construction Grammar is important for this book, because it integrates semantics with syntax and opens up ways for understanding the acquisition and evolution of language as a tool for solving communicative problems in which all elements of processing from semantics to syntax can be used as a tool for solving these problems.

Every part of an utterance has meaning and a semantic function. The meaning of a lexical item is the reference to the category, prototype or concept that it refers to. Its function is how it is used both in the semantic structure underlying the phrase and in the syntactic structure of the phrase. The following two examples include the word *rot* ('red') but they use the word in completely different syntactic and semantic structures.

(1) der rote Block
    'the red block'

(2) Rot ist eine Farbe
    'red is a color'

In (1) *rot* ('red') is used to modify the set of objects denoted by the word *Block* ('block') whereas in (2) the statement is about the color itself. We can precisely capture these differences in semantic function using cognitive operations and IRL (an structure for (1) can be found in Section 3). The semantic function is coupled to a particular expression in syntax. In (1) the color is expressed as an adjective which signals its use as a modifier. In (2) the color is expressed as a noun and signals that the subsequent verb phrase is a fact about the color itself. In production, the speaker can therefore choose to express the category as an adjective if the category is linked to the corresponding cognitive operation (e.g. `apply-color`). In parsing, when he observes a color adjective this allows him to infer that he is supposed to modify a set of objects using that operation. Which set of objects the color adjective modifies is determined by the larger syntactic and semantic context. For instance, in (1) the adjective is part of an adjective noun phrase that indicates which set is modified by the color category namely the set of blocks. From the viewpoint of the adjective noun phrase the adjective has the semantic function of providing a modifier and in particular of modifying the set of objects denoted by the noun. Of course, other adjectives, such as spatial adjectives can have the same function within an adjective noun phrase. The modified set is then input to another operation namely the operation `apply-selector` which is marked by the determiner. So what we can see already in these simple examples are mappings from semantics to syntax and back, where every aspect of syntax, i.e. words and grammatical relations have a specific effect on the semantic interpretation of the phrase. Vice versa, the speaker can use all the potential of syntax to communicate precise semantic distinctions that he wants to convey. The key item for analysis is the function of items both in syntax and semantics. These dependencies between syntax and semantics can be easily operationalized using FCG (De Beule & Steels 2005; Steels, De Beule & Neubauer 2005).

Throughout this book language processing is implemented in FCG, a computational implementation of Construction Grammar. FCG is (1) a formalism that provides a notation for specifying constructions, (2) a an engine that processes linguistic structure by applying constructions, in order, to produce utterances or parse meanings, and (3) a set of design principles for organizing the grammar and linking grammar to representations of semantics, in particular, to semantic structure formalized using IRL.

4.1 Linguistic processing

Linguistic processing encompasses both production and parsing of utterances. In production, FCG starts from a conceptualized meaning and tries to translate as much as possible of the semantic structure conceptualized by IRL into syntactic structure, i.e. words and grammatical relations using constructions in the linguistic inventory. In parsing this process is reversed and the construction inventory is used to recover as much semantic structure from an utterance as possible. Processing is organized around the TRANSIENT STRUCTURE which acts as a blackboard representing the current state of processing. Constructions work like rules – if a construction is applicable, i.e. if conditions for its application are met, the construction can change the transient structure. Over time the transient structure accumulates information provided by the different constructions that have applied until some end state is reached, for instance, no construction can apply anymore.

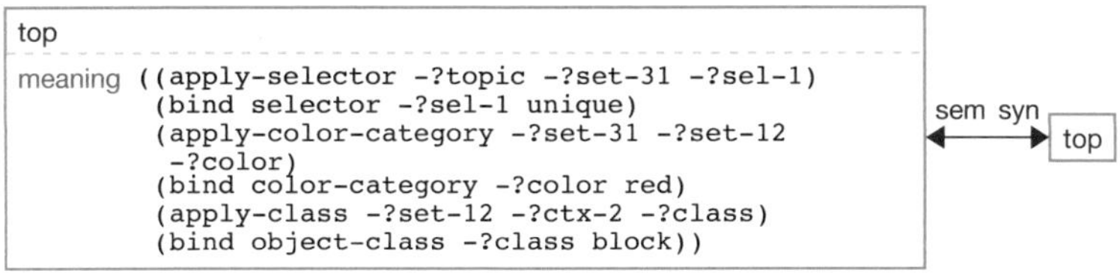

```
top
meaning ((apply-selector -?topic -?set-31 -?sel-1)
         (bind selector -?sel-1 unique)                   sem syn
         (apply-color-category -?set-31 -?set-12                   top
          -?color)
         (bind color-category -?color red)
         (apply-class -?set-12 -?ctx-2 -?class)
         (bind object-class -?class block))
```

Figure 4.1: Initial transient structure which contains only the meaning to be expressed in the top-unit of the semantic pole (left). There is no hierarchy yet and the syntactic pole (right) is empty.

4.1.1 Transient structure

The transient structure has two poles: a semantic and a syntactic pole. Information regarding meaning is accumulated on the semantic side, information about words and grammatical relations are gathered on the syntactic side. Information is organized into units identified by a unit-name. Units consist of attribute-value pairs. In order to represent constituent structure, units can form hierarchies in which some units are hierarchically linked to other units effectively building tree like structures. In the beginning of processing the transient structure is filled with information either from the conceptualization processes, e.g. in production, or from the utterance observed, e.g. in parsing. Subsequently, constructions change the transient structure by adding new units, introducing hierarchy, changing the value of attributes or by introducing new attributes. Figures 4.1 and 4.2 show the transition from an initial transient structure which only contains a single unit, called "top-unit" on each side to a final transient structure with hierarchical organization of units and many more features. The initial structure only contains a meaning on the semantic side. The final structure contains, among other things, strings and syntactic word order constraints which can be used to build an utterance, a process called RENDERING. Figures 4.1 and 4.2 show graphical representations of the list representation (s-expression) used in processing. The following restates the initial transient structure as s-expression.

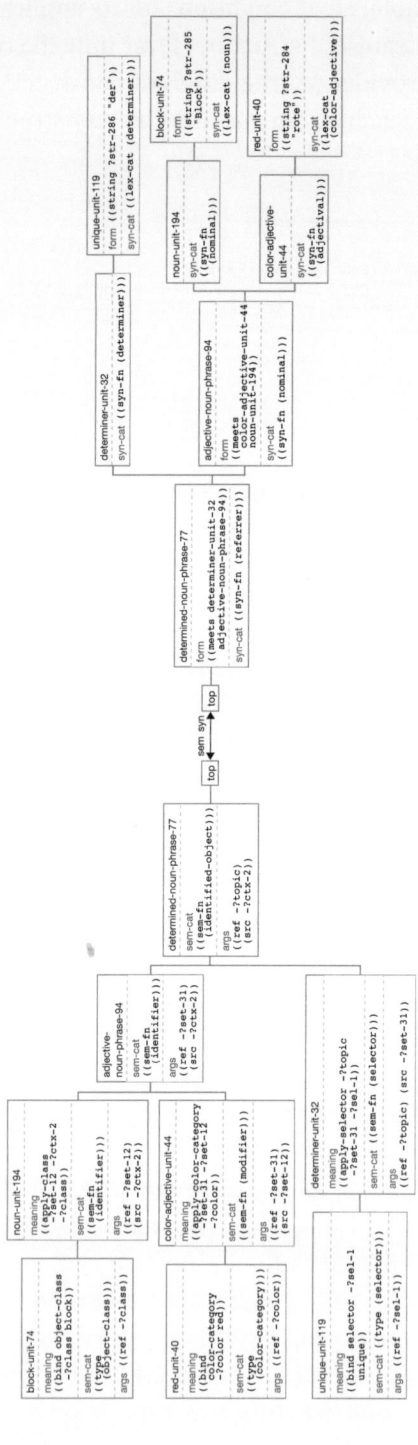

Figure 4.2: Final transient structure after many constructions of a simplified German grammar have been applied. The structure consists of units which are hierarchically organized starting from the top-unit. The meaning to be expressed is distributed over various units on the semantic side. Units feature semantic and syntactic categorization (sem-cat and syn-cat) which was build up in processing to organize constituent structure and allow for high-level constructions to abstract from individual items. On the syntactic side units have form features consisting of strings providing words and, so called "meets constraints" which introduce word order.

```
((top
  (meaning ((apply-selector -?topic -?set-31 -?sel-1)
            (bind selector -?sel-1 unique)
            (apply-color-category -?set-31 -?set-12 -?color)
            (bind color-category -?color red)
            (apply-class -?set-12 -?ctx-2 -?class)
            (bind object-class -?class block)))))
<-->
((top))
```

The top shows the semantic pole. The bottom, after the <-->, shows the syntactic pole. Both poles have one unit (the top-unit). On the semantic side the top-unit has one attribute, the meaning attribute which has an IRL-network in list form as its value. The following shows the final structure in the same representational format.

```
(...
 (color-adjective-unit-44
  (meaning ((apply-color-category -?set-31 -?set-12 -?color)))
  (sem-subunits (red-unit-40))
  (sem-cat ((sem-fn (modifier))))
  (args ((ref -?set-31) (src -?set-12))))
 (red-unit-40
  (meaning ((bind color-category -?color red)))
  (sem-cat ((type (color-category))))
  (args ((ref -?color))))
 ...
 (top (sem-subunits (determined-noun-phrase-77))))
<-->
(...
 (color-adjective-unit-44
  (syn-subunits (red-unit-40))
  (syn-cat ((syn-fn (adjectival)))))
 (red-unit-40
  (form ((string ?str-284 "rote")))
  (syn-cat ((lex-cat (color-adjective)))))
 ...
 (top (syn-subunits (determined-noun-phrase-77))))
```

Only parts of the complete final structure are shown, in particular, three units on each pole are shown the red-unit-40, color-adjective-unit-44 and top. In contrast to the initial transient structure, meaning is distributed across different units. Notice that which unit is subunit of another is coded by a special attribute called syn-subunits on the syntactic pole and sem-subunits on the semantic pole. Compare this with Figure 4.5 which shows the hierarchy in the final structure. For example red-unit-40 is a subunit of color-adjective-unit-44.

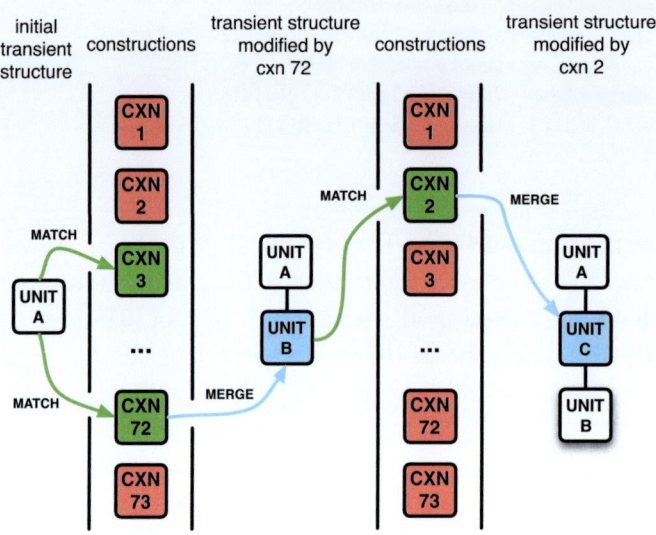

Figure 4.3: This figure shows a schematic view on construction application (Figure adapted from Steels 2011b). Starting from the initial transient structure (left) all constructions in the set of constructions are tested whether they match with the structure. Two constructions match with the initial transient structure. If a construction matches it can merge new information. Construction 72 adds unit C. After the structure has been changed, the process continues and all constructions are checked whether they merge with the transient structure modified by construction 72. Because construction 72 has applied, the transient structure is in a state such that construction 2 can now apply. This was previously not the case. Construction 2 is depending on information provided by construction 72. Subsequently, construction 2 further changes the transient structure and so on and so forth. Often multiple constructions from the set of constructions can apply. For example, construction 3 could also change the initial transient structure. This poses a general problem in processing which is solved by using a search algorithm described later in this section.

4.1.2 Constructions

Constructions are organized in the same way as transient structures. They consist of two poles and the data in each pole are organized in terms of units, attributes and values. FCG supports bi-directional constructions which means that the same construction is used in production and parsing. The difference between production and parsing is how the syntactic and semantic pole of a construction is used in each case. In production the semantic pole is used to check the applicability of the construction. In parsing the syntactic pole is used. Applicability of a construction is checked using a mechanism called MATCHING. Matching is based on the well studied concept of UNIFICATION which is a computational process for equating two terms in this case the semantic or syntactic pole of the construction with the corresponding pole of the transient structure. If matching succeeds, the construction can change both poles of the transient structure, a process called MERGE, because it fuses information. The precise inner workings of these two fundamental operations are described in Steels & De Beule (2006). The most important fact is that matching in FCG mainly relies on variables, which in FCG (and in IRL) start with ?. In computational terms constructions specify (1) under which conditions they apply and (2) if they apply how the structure should be changed.

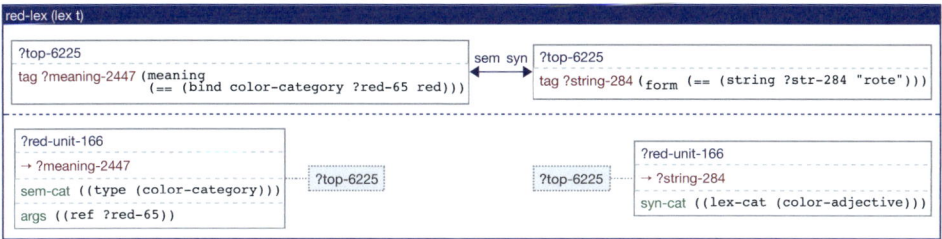

Figure 4.4: Schematic representation of a construction. The two poles of the construction are shown. The top shows the tagged and matching parts of the construction. The bottom shows the hierarchy building part of the construction.

Figure 4.4 shows an example of a lexical construction that maps the color category red onto the string *rote* ('red') (Figure 4.5 shows what happens when this construction is applied to the initial transient structure). The following shows the low-level list representation of the construction schematically depicted in Figure 4.4

(3)

```
((?top-6143
  (tag ?meaning-2381
    (meaning (== (bind color-category ?red-57 red)))))
 ((j ?red-unit-158 ?top-6143)
  ?meaning-2381
  (sem-cat ((type (color-category))))
  (args ((ref ?red-57)))))
<-->
((?top-6143
  (tag ?string-251 (form (== (string ?str-251 "rote")))))
 ((j ?red-unit-158 ?top-6143)
  ?string-251
  (syn-cat ((lex-cat (color-adjective)))))))
```

The top displays the semantic pole followed by the syntactic pole after the `<-->`. In production the construction requires the meaning `(bind color-category ?red red)` to be present. If this is the case, the construction merges the information on the syntactic side, in particular the stem, into the transient structure. Additionally, this construction builds hierarchy. It introduces a new unit which is a subunit of the top-unit and which is used to collect information for this particular lexical item. Already this simple construction uses the four basic ways in which constructions interact with the transient structure:

Variables and matching Constructions inevitably contain many variables. Already the unit names in the transient structure are changing every time a new utterance is parsed or a new meaning is produced. But also, just to give another example, variables in the meaning linking cognitive operations are different every time IRL conceptualizes. Using a variable in one part of the construction and repeating it in another can lead to changes in the transient structure triggered by matching and merging (Steels & De Beule 2006). (3), for instance, uses matching and merging by re-using the variable in the meaning `?red-57` in the `args` attribute. Whatever this variable binds to in processing the re-occurring variable will make sure that the data is available in both places.

Hierarchy Hierarchy is built using a special operator called the "J-operator", which changes the transient structure to include a new unit (De Beule & Steels 2005). The new unit can have units that are already present in the transient structure as children. A construction can therefore easily change the hierarchical structure of the complete pole. The J-operator syntax is:

(4)

```
((J ?new-unit ?parent (?child-1 .. ?child-n))
 (new-attribute new-attribute-value))
```

In the example construction the J-operator is used on the semantic and on the syntactic side. It introduces new units on both sides and adds information to this unit (in Figure 4.4 the parts pertaining to the J-operator are shown below the dotted line). Notice that the name of the new units is equal.

Movement Constructions can *tag* attributes and their values in order to move them around. In this example construction, the tag-operator moves the bind statement pertaining to the color category from the top-unit to the newly created unit. The tag operator takes the following form:

```
(?unit (tag ?tag-variable (attribute attribute-value)))
```

The operator binds whatever follows the variable ?tag-variable to the variable. If the variable is used in a J-unit, i.e. a unit with a J-operator, in another part of the construction, this denotes the place where (attribute attribute-value) will be moved. The example construction has tag operators on the semantic side for moving the bind statement to the new semantic unit. Similarly, on the syntactic side the operator is used to move the string *rote* to the new syntactic unit.

4.1.3 Search

Constructions are organized in a pool of constructions. In principle, constructions compete for access to the transient structure in processing. More than one construction can typically apply to the transient structure and the question is how to organize the process if there are multiple constructions that want to change the transient structure. In the absence of a priori rules to prefer one construction over another, each construction that can apply to the transient structure, is tried in a different branch of a heuristically guided search process. In other words, instead of having competing constructions change the same transient structure, the structure is copied and each potentially applying construction is applied to a copy without necessarily influencing the other. Naturally, this leads to different branches in processing, in which each branch computes a particular parsing or production result. Search is represented using a search tree

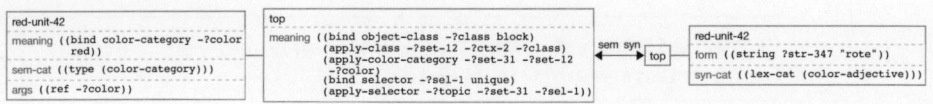

Figure 4.5: Transient structure after the lexical construction applied. The construction has introduced two new units using the J-operator. One on the semantic side and one on the syntactic side. Both units have the same name `red-unit-42`. The construction introduced the string *rote* on the syntactic side and the bind statements used for triggering the construction has been moved moved using the tag-operator from the top-unit to the new semantic subunit. The construction also added new semantic and syntactic categories (`sem-cat` and `syn-cat`) that can be used by subsequent constructions.

in which each node contains a transient structure. The initial node contains the initial transient structure. Leaf nodes contain final structures. The search process itself can be manipulated. For instance, it is possible to remove and refrain from processing duplicate nodes which contain the same transient structure and the order of following a particular branch can be influenced by how successful one predicts the branch to be. Figure 4.6 shows an example search tree for production of the utterance *der rote Block*.

Figure 4.6: FCG search tree which produces *der rote Block* given the IRL-network shown in Figure 3.1.

4.1.4 Design layer

In order to design grammars it has proven beneficial to abstract from the low level processing layer of FCG and add a representational layer that connects high level linguistic analysis with the processing engine of FCG. The idea is to allow re-occurring problems in grammar design to be solved using TEMPLATES – without having to resort and copy the code needed for describing a construction in the basic list notation. Templates are a general mechanism for expressing DE-SIGN PATTERNS, i.e. solutions that can be re-used to deal with the same problem occurring in different situations. For instance, all grammars implement phrasal constructions. One of the main semantic functions of phrasal constructions is to introduce variable equalities for linking constituents. A template encapsulates the solution to the problem of linking constituents in a way that the solution can be re-used in other phrasal constructions of the same grammar, but ideally also for phrasal constructions in other grammars. Templates are defined similar to functions. They have a name and a set of arguments which are specific to the template.

(5)

```
(template-name  construction-name
 :argument-1    value-1
 :argument-2    value-2
 ...
 :argument-n    value-n)
```

Let us consider an example. I redefine the lexical construction introduced earlier, using a template called `def-lex-skeleton`.

(6)

```
(def-lex-skeleton red-cxn
 :meaning (== (bind color-category ?cat red))
 :args ((ref ?cat))
 :string "rote")
```

If this template is executed it translates into the low-level list representation in (3).

4.2 Open-ended language evolution with FCG

Besides the obvious requirement of computational formalism for linguistic processing for computational experiments, FCG has a number of features that make it an optimal choice for studies in language evolution. FCG is not fixed to a certain set of constructions, a particular grammar layout, a particular set of meanings, or even a particular set of semantic and syntactic categories. FCG solely provides dedicated mechanisms for processing language but makes no actual claims about how a particular phenomenon should be processed in language. This allows different solutions to be explored by grammar designers. But, most importantly, it allows artificial agents to invent different constructions for solving a particular problem in communication, track their success and adapt them until the agents have conventionalized a solution to their particular problem. Language is not a fixed system, but rather a system negotiated by its users to reach communicative goals in a decentralized manner. The fact that there are different solutions to solving the same problem therefore requires formalisms that are designed to be open to change syntactic and semantic categorization, and evolve meaning structure and new constructions. FCG is such a formalism.

From a computational perspective, FCG provides an easily manipulatable data representation, which makes inventing new constructions, changing and adapting semantic and syntactic categories, and introducing hierarchy or movement of data relatively easy. As in Construction Grammar the *unified* nature of representation is important. There is absolutely no difference in terms of representation and processing between lexical, functional or phrasal constructions. Hence, FCG supports research into how constructions can change from lexical to grammatical constructions, which is of interest for the study of the influence of the grammaticalization processes on language evolution (Traugott & Heine 1991).

Another important argument for the use of FCG is its robust behavior in parsing and production. The search process for construction application and the bi-directional nature of constructions allow agents to produce as much of the meaning as they can when they are speaker. In parsing, the same process allows agents to recover as much of the semantics of a phrase as they possibly can. This is a prerequisite for any kind of grounded language learning let alone language evolution. Agents have to get as much information as possible from the different systems, such as perception and conceptualization, but also language processing. If agents would have to deal with a grammar engine that essentially gives up on processing as soon as an agent encounters a phrase that he thinks is unconventional, learning the new unconventional phrase can never occur or is significantly hindered. Whereas if the grammar engine provides as much information as possible, agents have a much better shot at guessing underlying meaning and making sense of what was conveyed to them. Subsequently, they can better represent the new parts of an utterance versus parts they already know. Modeling this whole process as a search process is an immense advantage of FCG. Agents can track what changes when they apply other constructions and explore different possible parse and produce results, in order to identify problems in language processing.

The last point with respect to the advantage of keeping information from the search process that governs linguistic processing is important, in particular for the main problem studied in this book: conventionalization. In order for agents to realize that constructions are competing for the same string, the same grammatical structure or the same meaning, it is vital to fully explore the search process.

If there are multiple ways of producing an utterance for a meaning, for instance because there are multiple words to express the same category, then the search can recover all of them. Together with a mechanism for tracking success of constructions, the search can choose the best one of them. After the interaction the agent can then update the constructions used and those that he could have used, for instance, by rewarding successfully used constructions and punishing unsuccessful or unused constructions. Constructions are equipped with a score that allows agents to update their inventories by scoring constructions according to their success in communication. If scores get too low agents can remove the affected constructions.

4.3 Discussion

There is no question that this is a short, in many ways too short, introduction to FCG. FCG has been under continuous development since 1998 and it has developed into a mature system which allows to research complex language phenomena such as Russian aspect (Gerasymova & Spranger 2010; 2012). The complexity of natural language has without doubt left its mark on the system and many design choices in the system are not immediately obvious, unless one takes the scope of the research program into account. Recently several book projects (Steels 2011b; 2012) attempted to communicate the full scope of FCG research performed in the last decade. The interested reader is referred to these efforts to get a broader introduction.

Part II

Reconstructing German locative phrases

5 German locative phrases – an introduction

To appreciate the complexity of spatial language one just needs to consider a particular human language such as German. The following chapters detail an elaborate reconstruction effort which targets locative German phrases (parts of this reconstruction effort have been published in Spranger & Loetzsch 2011). I specifically focus on the processing of German locative phrases in a whole systems approach encompassing the perception, conceptualization, as well as production and parsing of spatial phrases. Before we jump to the implementation and the specific challenges in modeling such a complex phenomenon, this introduction overviews German spatial relations and highlights the syntax and semantics of German locative phrases, as well as the close interaction of syntax and semantics. The claim is that important aspects of the syntactic structure of an utterance, i.e. the lexical items and the grammatical relations between them, work together to convey semantic structure, i.e. meaning. Vice versa, the varied syntactic devices in German spatial language allow to express subtle differences in the conceptualization of spatial scenes. The German spatial language system serves as a beautiful example of how syntax connects to the extraordinarily rich world of spatial semantics.

The literature distinguishes several classes of spatial relations available in German. Among them are projective, proximal and absolute relations (see Figure 5).

Projective relations – sometimes also called DIMENSIONAL TERMS (Eschenbach 2004; Herskovits 1986) – in German comprise the class of six items referring to spatial dimensions *vor* ('front'), hinter ('behind'), *über* ('above'), *unter* ('below'), *rechts* ('right'), *links* ('left') (Tenbrink 2007; 2005b; Wunderlich & Herweg 1991). Traditionally, and for reasons of distinct syntax and semantics the class of projective relations is further divided into FRONTAL (*vor* and *hinter*), LATERAL (*links* and *rechts*), HORIZONTAL (comprising lateral and frontal relations), and VERTICAL RELATIONS (*über* and *unter*).

Proximal relations are part of the larger class of topological relations that structure space with respect to proximity, contact and inclusion (Grabowski &

Weiss 1996). For this book proximal relationships such as *nah* ('near') and *fern* ('far') are important.

Absolute relations refer to cardinal directions, for instance *nördlich* ('north'), *westlich* ('west'), *östlich* ('east') and *südlich* ('south').

Spatial relations take different syntactic forms in German. All of the projective terms, for instance, can be expressed in different lexical classes, most prominently as adjectives, adverbs and prepositions. For example, the projective term *vor* can appear as adjective as in (1), as adverb as in (2) and as preposition as in (3).

(1) der   vordere   Block
     the.NOM front.ADJ.NOM block.NOM
     'The front block'

(2) der Block   vorne
     the block.NOM in the front.ADV
     'The front block'

(3) der   Block   vor   der   Kiste
     the.NOM block.NOM front.PREP the.DAT box.DAT
     'The block in front of the box.'

The different lexical classes carry with them different syntactic functions, e.g. adjectives can function as modifiers in determined adjective noun phrases, prepositions are followed by noun phrases and in German govern case. But each lexical class is also connected to a different semantic interpretation. In particular, there is a tight connection between the lexical class and specific spatial construal operations that govern how precisely the spatial relation is to be applied. The meaning of a projective category when used as an adjective is to filter objects (Tenbrink 2007), whereas when used as preposition the meaning is to construct a region (Klabunde 1999). For instance, the following phrase (4) uses the projective category front to construct a region to which one is asked to put a chair. Unlike in the adjective case, the region is not used to modify or filter, rather the region is necessarily empty in order for the chair to be put there.

(4) Stelle den Stuhl vor   den Schrank!
     Put   the chair front.PREP the cupboard
     'Put the chair in front of the cupboard!'

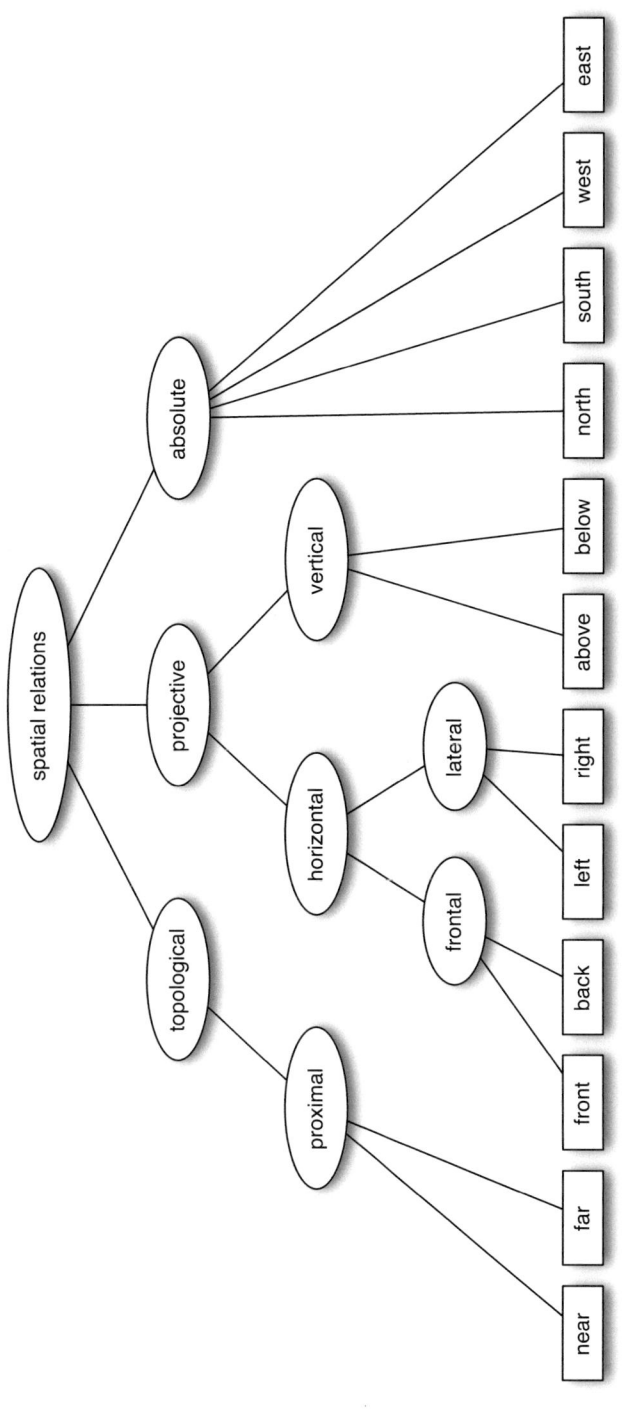

Figure 5.1: Taxonomy of spatial relations discussed in this book. The rectangular items refer to the spatial terms used for denoting the relations. Since in German spatial relations can be expressed in different lexical classes and word forms, English equivalents are used as placeholder.

Another important difference between spatial adjectives and spatial adverbs and prepositions is the potential for REFERENCE OBJECTS or LANDMARKS. Example (3) relates a LOCATED OBJECT, also called "figure" (Talmy 2000) and "trajector" (Vandeloise 1991) to a reference object, also called "landmark" (Vandeloise 1991), "relatum" (Tenbrink 2007) or "ground" (Talmy 2000). If a spatial term is used prepositionally as in (3), both the spatial relation, in this case *vor*, and the landmark *Kiste* ('box'), are expressed in the prepositional phrase itself.

A third possible lexical class, in which spatial relations partake, are adverbs. Spatial adverbs can be accompanied by a prepositional phrase, as in (5)–(6):

(5) der   Block   vorne   in   der   Kiste
     the.NOM block.NOM front.ADV of.PREP the.DAT box.DAT

'The block in the front of the box'

(6) der   Block   links   von   der   Kiste
     the.NOM block.NOM left.ADV of.PREP the.DAT box.DAT

'The block to the left of the box'

The prepositional phrases *in der Kiste* and *von der Kiste* both introduce a landmark which, via the spatial term, relates to the figure, in this case *der Block*. The two different prepositions *in* and *von* denote whether the relation referred to by the spatial term is INTERNAL to the landmark or EXTERNAL. In the case of *von*, the spatial region denoted by the projective adverb, e.g. *links* ('left'), is external to the landmark, whereas in the case of *in* the region lies within the landmark. The projective adverbs *links* ('left') and *rechts* ('right') can be followed both by *von* and *in* prepositional phrases, hence they can have an internal and external reading. The projective adverbs *vorne* ('front') and *hinten* ('back') can only be extended by *in* prepositional phrases. The vertical projective adverbs *oben* ('above') and *unten* ('below') elicit internal readings. Again differences in semantic processing are syntactically marked, in the case of adverbs by prepositional phrases that complement the adverb.

The last important component of spatial language considered in this book is perspective marking. The following two example feature perspective markers. In (7) an adverb is perspective marked, in (8) a prepositional phrase is perspective marked.

(7) der   Block   vorne   von   dir   aus
     the.NOM block.NOM front.ADV from.PREP the.DAT box.DAT

'The block in front from your perspective'

(8) der   Block   links   der   Kiste   von   dir
     the.NOM block.NOM left.PREP the.GEN box.GEN from.PREP your.DAT
     aus
     perspective
     'The block to the left of the box from your perspective'

Perspective on a scene is important for particular interpretations of spatial phrases, because it influences how the spatial scene and in particular the landmark is conceptualized.

These few examples from German locative phrases show that we can analyze the syntax of spatial language fruitfully in terms of its spatial semantics. This resonates with theories of syntax which put the direct mapping of syntax to semantics at the core of language processing, such as Construction Grammar. The tight relationship between syntax and semantics is an important claim in this book which underlies the reconstruction efforts, and also the evolution experiments.

The first question I am focusing on is how to organize language processing. That is, how semantics is encoded in words and grammar – and vice versa. However, this is not the full story. One needs to ground language in perception. Speakers need to be able to plan what they are going to say based on their communicative intention. Hearers must have machinery for interpreting the utterance based on the spatial context. This widens the question from how to organize the syntax and semantics interface to how to organize processing in a large array of systems comprising perception, conceptualization, interpretation and also processing of syntax. In particular, one has to identify the cognitive operations underlying the semantics of German locative phrases and how these operations are used in conceptualization of spatial scenes, as well as how conceptualization interacts with the perception of spatial scenes. The following section examine three main questions. First, what is the meaning of phrases such as *der Block links von der Box von dir aus* ('the block left of the box from your perspective', see (8)) and how can we formalize the semantic structure of these utterances? What are the cognitive primitives that are necessary for modeling the semantics of spatial phrases in particular? Second, how does semantic structure get translated into words and grammatical relations and back? And thirdly how can agents autonomously conceptualize spatial scenes given communicative goals and how can agents interpret semantic structure recovered in parsing so that success in communication can be achieved?

6 Spatial semantics

So what is then the meaning of a phrase such as *der Block links von der Kiste von dir aus* ('the block left of the box from your perspective')? Figure 6.1 shows an IRL-network that agents autonomously construct to conceptualize a particular spatial scene. The structure consists of a set of cognitive operations that involve, for example, the construction of regions, the identification of landmarks, the application of perspective transformations and so on. But of course the network also contains references to spatial categories, selectors, and other semantic entities that are processed by cognitive operations. The following sections identify and describe the cognitive operations and the semantic entities underlying locative utterances.

6.1 Representing spatial relations

The semantics of spatial relations is the subject of ongoing debate. The key question is whether there is something like a SEMANTIC CORE of spatial relations, i.e. a core meaning that abstracts from discourse situations as far as possible (Tenbrink 2007), and what that semantic core should be. For many scholars, the semantic core of spatial relations is related to geometric properties (Herskovits 1986; Eschenbach 1999; Tenbrink 2007) in particular prototypical axis (directions) and distances defined using tools like lines, points, vectors, half-planes, etc. (Levinson 1996). Particularly, projective relations, e.g. *vor* ('front') have been studied in this respect and certainly the class of absolute relations, e.g. *nördlich* ('north'), can be conceived in these terms. For instance, Herskovits (1986) describes the meaning of the spatial relation *in front of* as graded concept with the frontal axis as the focal region. This conception links to another important property of spatial language namely its inherent vagueness (Hall & Jones 2008). Many of these proposals are rooted in a strand of psycholinguistic research that is concerned with prototypes and prototypicality effects (Roach 1978). Here, prototypes or prototypical points in the sensorimotor space are used as representations for spatial categories (for a similar approach to color, see Bleys 2010). For instance, the projective term *links* ('left') can be interpreted for objects which relate to the ref-

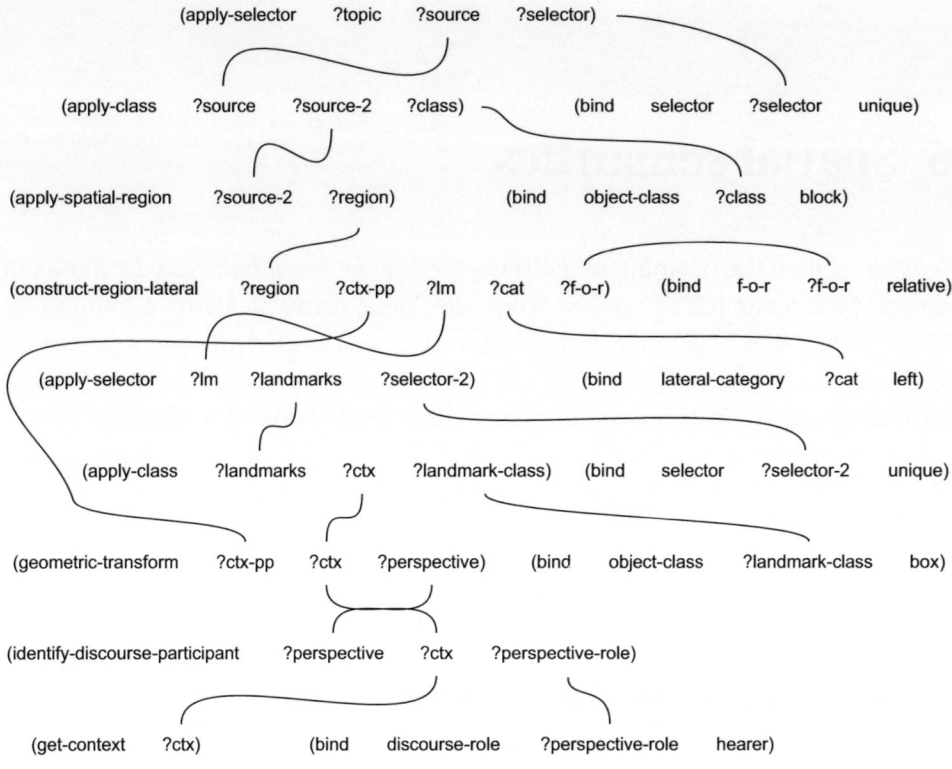

Figure 6.1: An IRL-network representing the meaning of the phrase *der Block links von der Kiste von dir aus* ('the block left of the box from your perspective')

erence object by an angle of 90° (prototypical left angle). The more the angle between the target object and the reference system deviates, the less acceptable the spatial relation becomes (Tenbrink 2005a; Herskovits 1986; Gapp 1995).

In this section I focus on the geometric properties of spatial relations and combine them with the prototype approach to spatial categorization. There are two features of the sensorimotor space which are of particular importance for spatial categorization: distance and angle. Two objects always have a certain distance from each other, and if there is a coordinate system available which supports rotation also angles between objects can be measured. Consequently, from a computational point of view, there are two important category types for representing the geometric properties of the German spatial relations discussed in this book angular-category, which represent prototypical angles and proximal-category, which represent prototypical distances (see Figure 6.2 for an overview).

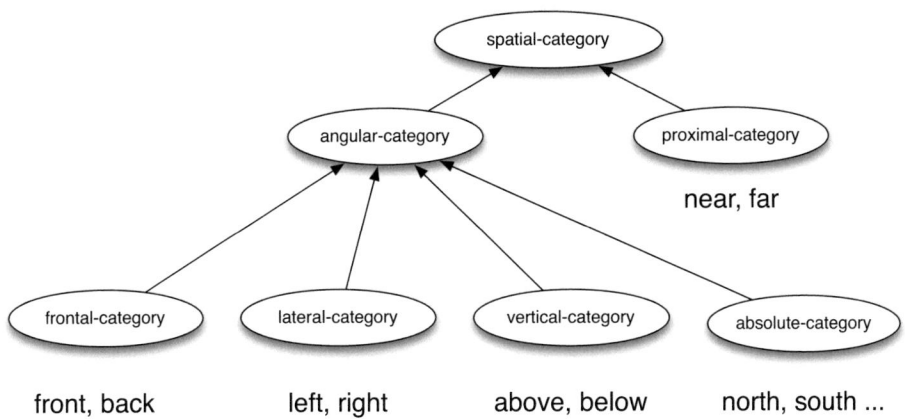

Figure 6.2: Category type hierarchy used in semantic processing

6.1.1 Angular relations

The core semantics of spatial relations is represented using functions that map a particular input location to the applicability degree of a particular category. For prototype based spatial categories degree of applicability amounts to similarity in some spatial dimension, e.g. in the angular dimension for angular relations. Projective and absolute relations are examples of angular categories, with a focal region around the denoted axis. For instance, frontal categories have a high degree of applicability along the frontal axis. Whereas lateral categories have a high degree of applicability along the left and right axis. Similarly, absolute categories have high values of applicability in their respective direction (see Figure 6.1.2 for an overview). In other words, for angular categories, similarity of some location to the category depends on the distance of angles. In order to get a similarity function $sim_a \in [0, 1]$ the angle distance is wrapped in an exponential decay envelope and weighted by a σ which steers the steepness of the exponential decay. High values for σ correspond to a slow decay in similarity the bigger the angular distance, whereas low values for σ correspond to a sharper decline in similarity. Consequently, the following equations defines the degree of applicability given a location l and an angular category c, as the angular distance between c and l, weighted by σ and run through an exponential decay.

$$sim_a(l, c) \quad := \quad e^{-\frac{1}{2\sigma_c} d_a(l,c)} \tag{6.1}$$

$$d_a(l, c) \quad := \quad |a_l - a_c| \tag{6.2}$$

In this definition a_l denotes the angle of the position of location l to the coordinate center and a_c denotes the prototypical angle of the category c. Given this definition, one can go ahead and define angular categories, in particular I need to define the prototypical angle for each angular category and the σ. Examples of definitions of angular spatial relations are depicted in Figure 6.1.2.

6.1.2 Proximal relations

Proximal relations relate to some prototypical distance. Two relations are modeled: near and far. The only difference to the definition of angular categories is that proximal relations rely on the distance channel.

$$\operatorname{sim}_d(l, c) \quad := \quad e^{-\frac{1}{2\sigma_c} d_d(l,c)} \tag{6.3}$$

$$d_d(l, c) \quad := \quad |d_l - d_c| \tag{6.4}$$

In this definition d_l denotes the distance of the location l to the coordinate center and d_c denotes the prototypical distance of the category c.

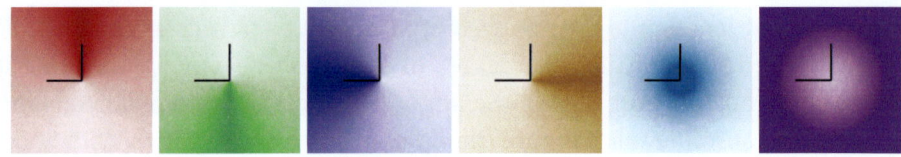

Figure 6.3: Degrees of acceptability shown for prototypical representation of frontal and lateral projective categories. From left to right front, back, left, right, near and far are shown. The opacity of each color denotes acceptability for a particular location in space (x-axes and y-axes each run from -2000.0 to 2000.0). Front, for instance, shows a strong acceptability along the x-axes. Definitions of categories are $a_{\text{front}} = 0.0$, $a_{\text{back}} = \pi$, $a_{\text{left}} = \frac{\pi}{2}$ and $a_{\text{left}} = -\frac{\pi}{2}$ and $\sigma_{\text{front}} = \sigma_{\text{back}} = \sigma_{\text{left}} = \sigma_{\text{right}} = 1.0$. For absolute categories the same definitions exist with north being defined like front and so forth. The two proximal categories near and far are defined with $d_{\text{near}} = 0.0$, $a_{\text{far}} = 2000.0$ and $\sigma_{\text{near}=700.0}$ and $\sigma_{\text{far}} = 1200.0$.

6.2 Applying spatial relations

Prepositionally and adverbially expressed spatial relations denote SPATIAL RE-
GIONS which are always related to some reference object. For instance, in the
phrase *der block links der Kiste* ('the block to the left of the box') an object *der
Block* ('the block') is related to the landmark *die Kiste* ('the box') via the spatial
category *links* ('left'). The information about which category is used and which
landmark is referred to is packaged in a spatial region. In order to represent the
difference between the construction of a region as for instance denoted by the
prepositional phrase *vor der Kiste* ('in front of the box') and the application of
that region to filter objects, as in the phrase *der Block vor der Kiste* ('the block
in front of the region'), in other words in order to represent spatial relations,
spatial processing is split into two distinct semantic operations. One operation
constructs the region and packages the particular landmark and the particular
spatial category, the other applies the region as a spatial relation to the objects
available in the context.

6.2.1 Spatial regions and spatial relations

Proximal regions are computed based on the distance prototype of the corresponding category and the landmark. The semantic operation `construct-region-
proximal` therefore constructs a specific region based on a spatial category and a
landmark. The right image in Figure 6.4 shows an example of a proximal region.

Semantic operation   CONSTRUCT-REGION-PROXIMAL

description	Computes a proximal region based on the landmark.
arguments	`?spatial-region` (of type spatial-region)
	`?source-set` (of type entity-set)
	`?landmark` (of type point)
	`?category` (of type proximal-category)

The other operation needed for applying a region is called `apply-spatial-region`.
This operation computes the similarity of every object in the context, given a
region constructed, for instance by the operation `construct-proximal-region`. For
the case of a proximal region, this involves (1) transforming the context so that
the landmark is at the center of origin of the coordinate system and (2) applying
the similarity function defined in Equation 6.3. This operation in many ways acts
as a classifier such as the semantic operations for `color` and `object-class` described
in Chapter 3. For each object in the source set the similarity of this object to the
spatial region is computed, based on the constituents of the region, e.g. which

category and which landmark was used to define the region. This similarity is combined with the other computed similarities for the object (see Chapter 3 for description). The operation `apply-region-filter` is general enough to be applicable to all regions, including projective and absolute regions whose description is to follow.[1]

Semantic operation APPLY-SPATIAL-REGION

description	Applies a spatial region, by computing the similarity of the region with every entity in `?source-set`.
arguments	`?target-set` (of type entity-set)
	`?source-set` (of type entity-set)
	`?region` (of type spatial-region)

An example of the interplay of the operations `construct-region-proximal` and `apply-region-filter` for a spatial scene can be seen in Figure 6.4. The following table summarizes the similarities computed when applying the region to the context (Figure 6.4 left).

object	distance (mm)	similarity
robot-1	1041.02	0.48
robot-2	1224.53	0.42
box-1	0.00	0.00
obj-266	419.97	0.74
obj-265	938.99	0.51

6.3 Frames of reference

Projective and absolute relations are defined in terms of focal directions. Consequently, for these kinds of relations the rotation of the landmark is an important issue determining the precise applicability of these relationships. For example, what is considered the front direction of a landmark has a direct effect on what is considered a frontal region. It turns out that there is considerable amount of choice when it comes to how to define the rotation of the landmark. The combination of a coordinate system, in particular its rotation, with a landmark is called REFERENCE SYSTEM. Reference systems have been dealt with in great

---

[1] This operation can be very general because its implementation defers different methods of computing similarity for different category types using the method dispatching facility of lisp.

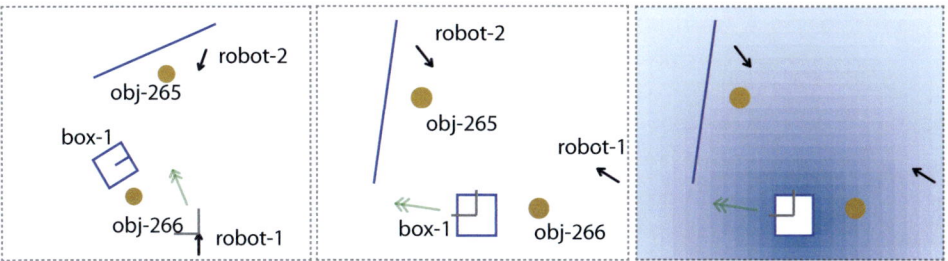

Figure 6.4: When a region is applied, first, the context (left figure) is transformed so that the landmark is at the origin of the coordinate system (middle figure) which is followed by the application of the spatial relation (right figure). Here, these steps are depicted for the category near and the landmark box-1.

detail in cognitive semantics and psycholinguistics under the term FRAME OF REFERENCE. Levinson (1996; 2003) identifies three possible frames of reference: INTRINSIC, RELATIVE and ABSOLUTE, all of which denote a particular way of construing a landmark for spatial relationships involving direction. In German all three frames of reference are possible.

Intrinsic frame of reference The intrinsic frame of reference is an object centered coordinate system, meaning that projective categories are applied to the reference object based on particular sides of the object, which are construed as front, back, left and right. Hence, those objects that have something that can be considered as their front (with other sides, identifiable as well, e.g., left, right and back) are eligible to be used as landmarks with an intrinsic frame of reference. Examples of such objects are television sets, where the front is the screen, or houses, where the front is the main entrance or street access, and so forth.

Relative frame of reference The relative frame of reference is a perspective based coordinate system. (See Figure 6.5 for a graphical explanation.) Instead of relying on intrinsic features of the reference object for determining the particular layout of the coordinate system, the rotation of the coordinate system is determined by its angle to an explicitly or implicitly given perspective. Hence, the front of an object is induced by the particular perspective on the scene. For example, *vor dem Baum* ('in front of the tree') implicitly refers to a perspective, because trees do not have an intrinsically

determined front, and it is the position of the observer together with the
position of the tree that designates the precise region denoted as front.

Absolute frame of reference Absolute frames of reference construe the landmark
using an external rotation. Neither intrinsic properties nor the perspective
on the landmark determine the layout of the coordinate system, but rather
geocentric features of the environment, for instance cardinal directions as
in *nördlich* ('north') or the direction of gravity as in *über* ('above') govern
what the precise layout of the reference system is.

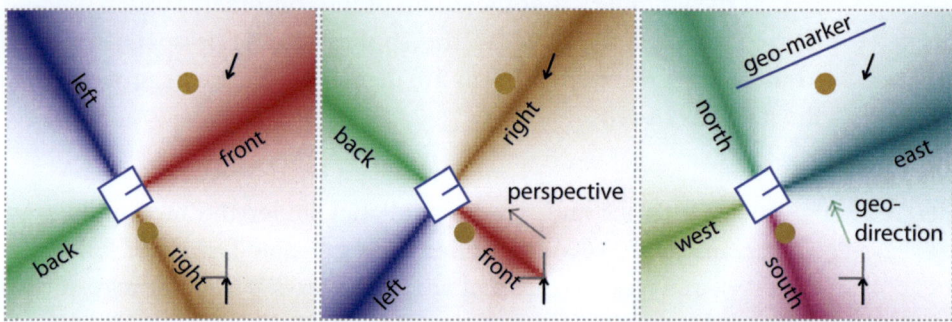

Figure 6.5: Frames of reference have a profound effect on spatial relations. In
all three pictures spatial relations are shown with box-1 as reference
object. The left figure shows the landmark construed with an intrinsic
frame of reference which orients the coordinate system such that the
front of the landmark (little blue line in the landmark) corresponds to
the frontal spatial relation with left, right and back projective relations
aligned accordingly. The middle figure shows the same landmark, but
with a relative frame of reference constructed from the perspective
of robot robot-1 which entails that frontness corresponds to a region
between the perspective and the landmark. Left and right in relative
frames of reference are aligned not with respect to front, but rather are
parallel to the left and right side of the perspective robot-1. The right
figure shows an absolute frame of reference applied to the landmark
box-1. Cardinal directions are aligned based on a geocentric direction
induced on the scene by a marker.

The differences in processing frames of reference are captured using distinct
semantic operations. In other words, absolute relationships, such as *nördlich*

('north') or *über* ('above') demand other semantic operations as relative and in-trinsic ones. For instance, processing of phrases involving absolute regions, e.g. *nördlich* ('north'), is represented using the `construct-region-absolute` operation, which takes a landmark and transforms the context with respect to the land-mark, subsequently applying a rotation that follows from a geocentric direction. Some of the spatial scenes recorded by the robots feature a geocentric marker on the wall. The direction towards this marker defines the direction to the north. Figure 6.5 gives an example.

Semantic operation CONSTRUCT-REGION-ABSOLUTE

description	Computes an absolute region based on the landmark and the absolute frame of reference which must be available in source set.
arguments	`?spatial-region` (of type spatial-region)
	`?source-set` (of type entity-set)
	`?landmark` (of type point)
	`?category` (of type absolute-category)

Frontal prepositions, e.g., *vor* ('front') and *hinter* ('back'), can have both intrin-sic and relative readings. Both readings are incorporated into a single operation, which construes the landmark both in relative and intrinsic way signified by an additional parameter of type `f-o-r` (frame of reference) to the operation. For the relative reading the perspective on the scene additionally influences the layout of the region. The viewpoint on the scene constrains front regions in such a way that only those locations which are between the perspective and the landmark have a high degree of applicability.

Semantic operation CONSTRUCT-REGION-FRONTAL

description	Computes a frontal region based on the landmark and the relative or intrinsic frame of reference.
arguments	`?spatial-region` (of type spatial-region)
	`?source-set` (of type entity-set)
	`?landmark` (of type point)
	`?f-o-r` (of type f-o-r)
	`?category` (of type frontal-category)

Vertical relations can be construed with an absolute, relative or intrinsic frame of reference. In the case of absolute frames of reference the orientation is derived from gravity. For the purpose of this book only absolute frames of reference readings are implemented in the operation `construct-region-vertical`.

6.4 Internal and external regions

Another line of processing distinctions can be made between internal and external relations. *North* and *south*, but also prepositional use of *front*, e.g. *vor*, are referring to external regions, that is the region lies outside of the landmark. Internal regions on the other hand lie inside the reference object. Adverbs such as *vorne* ('front') denote such regions inside the landmark. Consequently, they require separate treatment and there is a specific operation for handling the internal processing of frontal relations construct-region-frontal-internal.

Semantic operation CONSTRUCT-REGION-FRONTAL-INTERNAL

description	Computes an internal frontal region based on the landmark and the relative or intrinsic frame of reference.
arguments	?spatial-region (of type spatial-region)
	?source-set (of type entity-set)
	?landmark (of type point)
	?f-o-r (of type f-o-r)
	?category (of type frontal-category)

Internal lateral regions are not clearly marked in syntax. While lateral prepositions clearly denote an external region, lateral adverbs can be used more varied which becomes apparent since they can be complemented both by *von* headed prepositonal phrases, as well as *in* headed prepositional phrases. In other words, the interpretation of an adverb depends on the complement. If there is no complement both readings internal and external are possible.

Semantic operation CONSTRUCT-REGION-LATERAL

description	Computes an internal frontal region based on the landmark and the relative or intrinsic frame of reference.
arguments	?spatial-region (of type spatial-region)
	?source-set (of type entity-set)
	?landmark (of type point)
	?f-o-r (of type f-o-r)
	?category (of type frontal-category)
	?region-layout (of type region-layout)

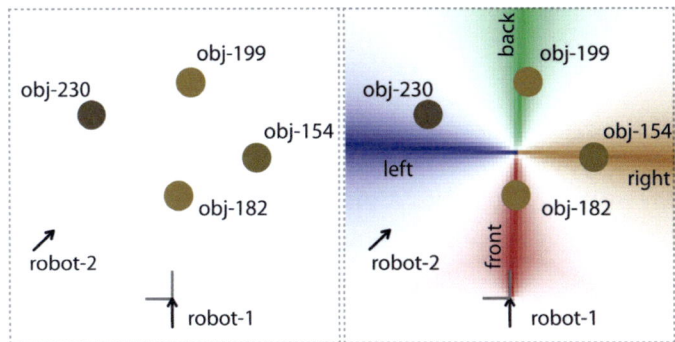

Figure 6.6: Group-based reference requires computing a landmark based on a group of objects. The centroid of the group of objects, in this case all blocks in the context, is construed using a relative frame of reference. Consequently, object obj-182 could be described in German as *der vordere Block* ('the front block').

6.5 Group-based reference

The semantics of German spatial adjectives is best understood in terms of group-based reference.[2] In order for a group of objects to function as a reference object, the group needs to be construed as a landmark object, and in particular its position needs to be established. One way of computing a position for a group of objects, is to use the spatial centroid (center of mass) of the group as the position of the reference object. Additionally, a frame of reference, in other words a rotation, needs to be chosen. This choice depends on the spatial relation. For absolute relations the frame of reference is determined by an absolute frame of reference. In the absence of intrinsic features of the group of objects, a relative frame of reference seems to be the natural choice, as a spatial group of objects has no intrinsic front without including further constraints. Together, the centroid and the respective frame of reference sufficiently describe the reference system in order for spatial relations to be applied.

Semantic operation   APPLY-SPATIAL-CATEGORY-GROUP-BASED

description	Applies the spatial category based on a group-based landmark.

---

[2] Recent evidence (Moratz & Tenbrink 2006) points to more variety in interpretation. For the purpose of this book, however, I choose to model group-based semantics only.

arguments   ?target-set (of type entity-set)
             ?source-set (of type entity-set)
             ?category (of type spatial-category)

Group-based reference offers a technical challenge of how to compute the group used for reference in the first place. Given that all objects in the context are scored by successive operations, how can a group of objects be established, in order to compute the spatial centroid? For instance, in phrases like *der linke block* ('the left block'), the spatial adjective is part of a noun phrase, which primarily denotes the type of objects that constitute a set, namely the set of all block which relates to the group that the reference should be based on. The implementation of the semantic operation apply-spatial-category-group-based relies on a well-known clustering algorithm called *k*-means) (Lloyd 1982) in order to find the group of objects in the input set. The scores of all objects in the input set are used to divide the input set into two groups and all elements in the group with the higher score centroid are used to compute the spatial landmark.

6.6 Perspective marking

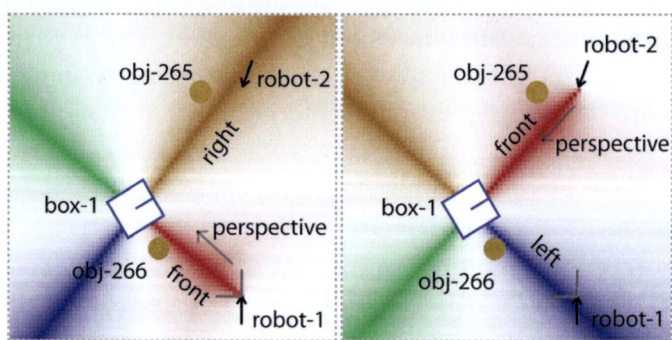

Figure 6.7: The two figures show the influence perspective has on relative frames of reference. The left figure shows the landmark box-1 when construed with a relative frame of reference from the perspective of robot-1. In this configuration object obj-266 is in front and object obj-265 is to the right. Whereas when the same landmark box-1 is construed with a relative frame of reference from the perspective of robot-2 it is object obj-265 which is in front, whereas object obj-266 is to the left.

The perspective of relative frames of reference is sometimes explicitly marked by speakers. In the example *der Block links von der Kiste von dir aus* ('the block left of the box from your perspective'), the speaker choose to provide a perspective *von dir aus* ('from your perspective'). Only relative interpretations of a spatial phrase can be perspective marked. The perspective itself marks the position of the viewpoint, and therefore also the view direction, i.e. rotation.

Intrinsic frames of reference computationally behave very similar to perspective-marked relative frames. Some argue therefore, that an intrinsic reference system is in essence a conflated relative reference system that coincides with the perspective on the scene (Levinson 1996). Hence, intrinsic reference systems are never perspective marked, since they already include position and orientation. However, perspective marking is only compatible with relative frames of reference and excludes intrinsic the usage of intrinsic or absolute frames of reference. On the other hand, relative reference systems always explicitly or implicitly mark perspective, since they cannot be conceived without since by definition relative reference systems always construe the world from a perspective (see Figure 6.7).

Perspective on a scene is changed by an operation that transforms a complete spatial context as if it had been perceived from a particular viewpoint.

Semantic operation GEOMETRIC-TRANSFORM

description	Transforms the context to be viewed from a particular perspective. Notice that perspectives require both a particular point of view but also a rotation.
arguments	?transformed-context (of type sensory-context)
	?context (of type sensory-context)
	?perspective (of type pose)

6.7 Discussion

6.7.1 Functional constraints

Purely geometric accounts of spatial semantics have been criticized on the basis of psycholinguistic studies that reveal for many spatial relations, that additional functional constraints influence their applicability. Studies in particular for topological relations, including *in* and *on*, but also for projective relations such as *over* and *under* (Coventry, Prat-Sala & Richards 2001) as well as *in front* and *behind* (Carlson-Radvansky & Radvansky 1996) have led to new proposals (Coventry et al. 2005) as to how to include functional considerations into the semantics of spatial terms (see also Coventry & Garrod (2004) for an overview). For instance, whether or not an umbrella is *over* a person depends on the direction of rain which can come from different angles. I do not account for functional constraints for two reasons: (1) because it requires detailed functional models of objects which as of now are rarely available in robots and (2) the current model theoretically can incorporate such models once they become available. In order to acquire functional knowledge, such as that chairs are for sitting, tables are used to put things on and so forth, robots need to interact robustly and repeatedly with objects of this kind, in particular using complex interactions in which objects take on functional roles. Many of these skills, e.g. basic actions such as sitting, are contemporary research fields in robotics and still need to see significant progress before they are generally available. On the other hand, functional approaches to semantics are typically committed to conceive the application of spatial relations in terms of degree of applicability. In other words, functional models are essentially mappings of locations and landmarks to some number representing the degree in which some relation is deemed acceptable. This is precisely the basis of the semantics advocated in this chapter. Semantic operations compute degrees of applicability. Consequently, once a functional model can be established in terms of similarity, it can readily be incorporated into the current model by exchanging semantic operations.

6.7.2 Contextual factors

Besides functional constraints, contextual factors affect the applicability of spatial terms. For instance, for proximal relations: PROTOTYPICAL SIZE (Gapp 1994), but also OBJECT SALIENCE (Regier & Carlson 2001), and OBJECT INTERFERENCE (Kelleher & Costello 2009) seem to play a role. Just to give an example, the prototypical size factor can explain why the proximal region *nahe des Gebäudes* ('near the building') is larger than that of *nahe dem Apfel* ('near the apple') (example adapted from Gapp 1994) by the difference in typical size of buildings and apples. Constraints such as the prototypical size, as well as the influence of object salience, are easily integrated into the model, but just as for functional constraints do not affect the basic assumptions of the model. The third constraint – the object interference constraint – refers to the interference by other objects that are for instance closer than the related object. Such constraints are better treated under the problem of how to choose spatial relations which is inevitably connected to the particular communicative goal. For instance, in a discrimination task other categories might be more relevant for the task than in object location description tasks. Such processes are dealt with in detail in Chapter 8.

6.7.3 Other modeling approaches

Spatial semantics is an important and vibrant research area. Many different proposals are currently being made. Some suggest the use of formal ontology engineering (Bateman, Tenbrink & Farrar 2007; Bateman 2010; Bateman et al. 2010) as a tool for enhancing spatial language interpretation by artificial systems. Others suggest to use formal reasoning techniques and representations (Freksa 1991; Cohn & Hazarika 2001). The system presented in this book can benefit from these extensive approaches in the sense that the detailed modeling of spatial representation and spatial reasoning could enhance our modeling approach. On the other hand, in this book modeling serves the goal of establishing basic concepts, e.g. spatial relations, so that we can later study their evolution. This is the reason why more elaborate modeling approaches are avoided. Engineering robust and extensive solutions for the processing of spatial language is a valid goal in itself, but it is only one aspect of this book.

6.7.4 Summary

This chapter gave an account of the semantic core of German spatial relations in terms of geometric constraints, frames of reference and perspective. Spatial relations have been defined as graded categories, whose application is governed by semantic operations. It remains to be shown (1) how conceptualizations of a scene given a concrete communicative goal are achieved (a problem that can be summarized in how and which spatial relations should be chosen), (2) how spatial categorization fits into larger semantic structures for spatial phrases such as *der Block links von der Kiste* and (3) how these semantics interact with language in production and parsing of spatial phrases.

7 Syntactic processing

The syntax of German locative phrases mirrors the complexity of spatial semantics. The main task of syntactic processing is to allow agents to express themselves by translating semantic structure into proper German syntax and back. This chapter reports on the syntactic processing of German locative phrases using Fluid Construction Grammar. It provides an overview of the mapping from semantics to syntax and zooms in on different aspects of the implementation for dealing with complicated syntactic phenomena such as the German case system.

Syntactic processing of German spatial language is primarily a problem of orchestrating intertwined information processing. Great care has to be taken to ensure that the ordered application of constructions in production and parsing of spatial utterances can proceed efficiently,without excessive branching in search. In many cases information needed for processing is spread in the semantic structure to be produced or in the utterance to be parsed. For instance, lexical constructions might able to decide on word stems based on semantic entities in the semantic structure, but already the decision which lexical class to use for expressing some lexical item in production requires a larger broader of the semantic structure to be produced. Even more so, in order to decide on the actual word form including German morphology, a whole array of syntactic information is to be considered. For instance, case, gender and number marking of spatial adjectives in prepositional noun phrases requires collection of information from the noun about its grammatical gender, and from the preposition about the required case. This chapter shows how advanced techniques in FCG can be applied to organize efficient processing while allowing grammar designers to build extendable and concise grammars.

This chapter starts by presenting the general ideas behind the design of the grammar (Section 7.1) and identifying core issues that have to be resolved in order to arrive at an operational system. The remaining Sections 7.2–7.5 show how to deal with these issues.

7.1 Overview of syntactic processing

One of the main problems of syntactic processing in a system that is integrated with procedural semantics such as IRL is the problem of how semantic structure such as IRL-networks are expressed in language. The following are the two main ideas originally presented in Steels & Bleys (2005).

Lexicon Lexical constructions directly map semantic entities to content words.

Grammar Grammatical constructions broadly speaking encode the cognitive operations and the links between them and semantic entities. Consequently, grammar provides information on how semantic structure is combined (Steels 2011a) by modulating the syntactic expression of the lexical items through grammatical markers, word order, morphology, etc.

German requires fine grained distinctions of constructions in order to facilitate and coordinate processing. The grammar is organized into certain types of constructions each providing different information (see Steels 2011a for the original idea).

Lexical Constructions These constructions map semantic entities to stems and back. Hand in hand with morphological constructions they are responsible for the expression of lexical items. Lexical constructions introduce lexical units in the transient structure that are used to assemble information necessary for decisions on the lexical class and the word form of the semantic entity in production. In parsing these units gather information required for the semantic interpretation of a semantic entity in the surrounding semantic structure. Lexical constructions introduce abstractions into the transient structure that allow to go from concrete semantic entities to the class they are in. For instance, *links* ('left') is a lateral spatial category such as *rechts* ('right'). Both behave similar in semantics as well as in syntax. Lexical units introduce such type information to allow hierarchy in processing to take advantage of this information.

Functional Constructions This class of constructions is related to how a particular semantic entity is used in processing. For instance, in parsing, when a spatial relation is observed as an adjective, this licenses the introduction of the cognitive operation apply-region-group-based which represents how the spatial category is supposed to be applied. Consequently, functional constructions handle and process lexical classes and map them to particular cognitive operations. These constructions introduce functional units into the transient structure, which assemble all information related to lexical classes. On the semantic side these units gather information related to the output and input of the cognitive operation. This information is particularly used by phrasal constructions to combine functional units into larger phrases. There are functional constructions for determiners, nouns, spatial adjective, spatial adverbs and prepositions.

Phrasal Constructions These constructions, as the name suggests, are organizing both larger syntactic structure, i.e. phrases, and larger semantic structure by linking functional units. For instance in parsing, when observing a spatial adjective and a noun in the correct German word order, the adjective-noun-phrase construction links the processing of these items on the semantic side. In turn, the new constituent can be further combined with determiners which happens when the determined-noun-phrase construction applies. Phrasal construction do the work of processing grammatical relations between constituents.

Morphological Constructions Certain constructions deal exclusively with morphology. They are responsible for determining and processing word forms, i.e. the string, for expressing lexical items. In German the concrete form of a lexical item is often determined by the larger syntactic structure. For instance, a spatial adjective such as *links* ('left') in a determined adjective noun phrase has to agree with the gender and the number of the noun and with the case of the determined noun phrase. This requires that in production the form of a lexical item is determined when this information is available, which requires that constructions such as the determined-noun-phrase construction have supplied this information. In parsing, morphological constructions function as word form recognizers.

Semantic Constructions Lastly, there is a special type of constructions which is only used in parsing for handling semantic ambiguity. They are discussed in detail in Section 9.2.

Figure 7.1 shows the sequence of construction application in production and in parsing. In processing, the constructions are part of a large pool of constructions, which are applied based on which construction can apply at a specific point in time. Syntactic processing proceeds bottom-up which means from the lexical items to the phrasal level. For instance, phrasal constructions require functional units to function which in turn depend on lexical constructions. In every step information is assembled in hierarchical units, e.g. lexical units, which expose

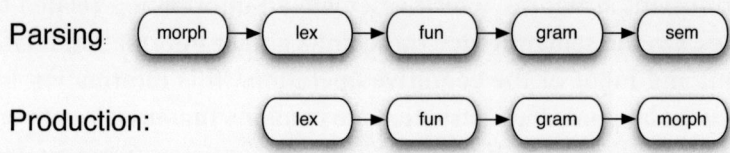

Figure 7.1: Construction application in the German spatial language grammar discussed in this chapter. In parsing, morphological constructions apply first followed by lexical and grammatical constructions. Finally, the semantic constructions important for handling semantic ambiguity apply. In production, these constructions are not applied. In contrast to parsing, morphological constructions apply in production at the very end in order to decide on the actual form used in the utterance.

new information, in order for constructions to use this information. This process can also be understood as a process of gradual categorization and assembly of constituents into larger structure both on the syntactic and on the semantic side. For instance, lexical constructions abstract from the concrete semantic entity such as the spatial category left and provide information about the semantic type so that functional constructions can use this information and apply to groups of spatial relations.

The following three sections look in more detail at the implementation of different constructions such as lexical and functional (Section 7.2) phrasal constructions for landmarks and landmark complements (Section 7.3) and high-level phrasal constructions (Section 7.4). The chapter concludes by discussing how to deal with the German case system (Section 7.5).

7.2 Lexical classes – lexical and functional constructions

In German the same spatial relation can be expressed using different lexical classes (adjective, adverb or preposition). The following shows an example of the spatial relation front expressed as adjective (1), adverb (2), and prepositions (3) which are repeated here for convenience from Chapter 5.

(1) der   vordere   Block
    the.NOM front.ADJ.NOM block.NOM

'The front block'

(2) der Block   vorne
     the block.NOM in   the front.ADV
     'The front block'

(3) der   Block   vor   der   Kiste
     the.NOM block.NOM front.PREP the.DAT box.DAT
     'The block in front of the box'

Lexical classes are an example of a many-to-many mappings. Every German spatial relation discussed in this book can be expressed in different lexical classes. Vice versa, every lexical class has a number of relations that are part of it. For instance, the spatial relations front, back, left, can all be expressed as adverb. However, not all spatial relations can be expressed as adverbs. The proximal relations *nah* ('near') and *fern* ('far') do not occur in adverbial form.[1] Table 7.2 gives an overview of lexical classes and associated forms. The table shows that different groups of spatial relations partake in different lexical classes. For instance, all spatial relations except for proximal relations such as near and far can be expressed as adjectives. Projective relations such as up, front and left can be expressed as adverbs. Only vertical and lateral relations can also be genitive prepositions, whereas frontal relations can only be dative prepositions. Vertical relations can be both genitive and dative prepositions.

The problem of choosing a lexical class in production and finding the lexical class in interpretation is solved by a careful setup of the interaction of functional and lexical constructions. I use a particular design pattern called ACTUAL-POTENTIAL.[2] The design pattern allows to store possible lexical classes in the form of potentials for each lexical item directly in the lexical units of the transient structure. Subsequent functional constructions can constrain their application based on the potential of the lexical item, consequently, ruling out non standard usage, e.g., expressing proximal relations as adjectives. The same is used on the semantic side, where the semantic type hierarchy of the semantic entity is stored as a list of potentials.

The actual-potential technique allows to distribute decision making across lexical and functional constructions by separating the specification of options (po-

---

[1] Linguistic analysis is made difficult by diverging vocabulary in linguistics and different usages of the same term by different schools. I use the term adverb here for spatial relations such as *vorne* ('front') that can be followed by prepositional phrases and used as postmodifiers on determined noun phrases e.g. *der Block vorne in der Kiste* ('in the front area of the box').

[2] The pattern is inspired by earlier work on argument realization (van Trijp 2008) which is also a many-to-many mapping problem.

Table 7.1: Lexical Classes and word forms for German spatial relations (adapted in part from Tenbrink 2007). This by no means is an exhaustive list of spatial relations, lexical classes or lexical forms in German spatial language, but it is the part of German relevant for this book. Items marked with * seem to be possible, but due to being unconfirmed in the reviewed literature are omitted.

Relation	Adjective	Adverb	Preposition [POSS]	Preposition [DAT]
up	*ober*	*oben*	*oberhalb*	*über*
down	*unter*	*unten*	*unterhalb*	*unter*
front	*vorder*	*vorne*	–	*vor*
back	*hinter*	*hinten*	–	*hinter*
right	*recht*	*rechts*	*rechts*	–
left	*link*	*links*	*links*	–
near	*	–	–	*nahe*
far	*	–	–	*fern*
north	*nördlich*	*	*	*nördlich*
south	*südlich*	*	*	*südlich*
west	*westlich*	*	*	*westlich*
east	*östlich*	*	*	*östlich*

tentials) from the *actual* decision. Possible choices are explicitly stored in the form of disjunctive potentials in the transient structure thereby signaling to subsequent constructions which choices are possible which allows subsequent constructions to constrain their application by observing potentials and triggering only when the right potentials are present. Before we jump to the application of the actual-potential design pattern, we need to consider the lexical and functional constructions that are involved.

The fact that Examples (1)–(3) refer to the same projective category front is expressed by the lexical construction for the spatial relation front. The construction maps the reference to the spatial relation onto the word stem *vor*. The following template shows the lexical construction for the category front:

(4) ─────────────────────────────────

```
(def-lex-cxn
(def-lex-skeleton front-cxn
  :meaning (== (bind frontal-category ?cat front))
```

```
:args ((ref ?cat))
:stem "vor"))
```

Lexical constructions capture the similarity of different syntactic and semantic usage scenarios of the same category. They encode that no matter how the lexical item is used in the larger semantic and syntactic structure it refers to the same semantic entity, e.g. spatial relation.

Functional constructions map a particular lexical class to syntactic and semantic properties thereby elevating lexical items to constituents in grammatical structure. On the semantic side, functional constructions trigger on semantic operations used in conceptualization. On the syntactic side, the constructions provide syntactic functions and syntactic classes in order for grammatical constructions to be able to build grammatical structure out of functional units. Below are the skeletons for the functional constructions of spatial adjective, frontal adverbs and frontal prepositions:

(5)
```
(def-fun-cxn spatial-adjective
 :meaning (== (apply-spatial-category-group-based
                ?target ?source ?category))
 :args ((ref ?target)(src ?source)(cat ?category))
 :sem-function (modifier)
 :syn-function (adjectival))
```

(6)
```
(def-fun-cxn frontal-adverb
 (def-fun-skeleton frontal-adverb
  :meaning (== (construct-region-frontal-internal
           ?target ?source ?landmark ?category ?f-o-r))
  :args ((ref ?target)(src ?source)
          (cat ?category)(landmark ?landmark))
  :sem-function (modifier)
  :sem-class (region internal-region relative-region)
  :syn-function (adverbial)
  :syn-class (adverb)))
```

(7)
```
(def-fun-cxn frontal-preposition
 (def-fun-skeleton frontal-preposition
  :meaning (== (construct-region-frontal
           ?target ?source ?landmark ?category ?f-o-r))
  :args ((ref ?target)(src ?source)
          (cat ?category)(landmark ?landmark))
```

```
:sem-class (angular-relationship)
:syn-class (angular-preposition)))
```

These constructions introduce constructional meaning, e.g. `construct-region-frontal`, together with semantic and syntactic potentials. One is the functional role of the unit in the larger syntactic structure, here denoted by `syn-function`. Aside from these two constructions, there are a number of other important functional constructions. In particular the difference in semantics of lateral and frontal adverbs, but also between projective, topological and absolute relations are each captured by separate functional constructions (see Table 7.2 for an overview).

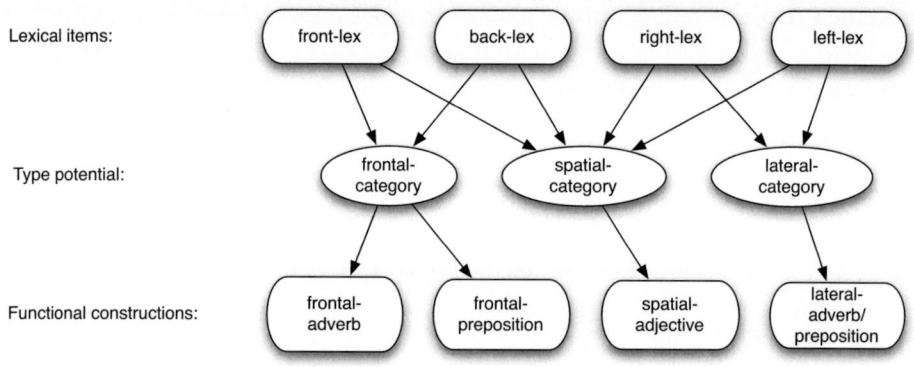

Figure 7.2: Subset of the mapping of lexical items to functional constructions.

7.2.1 Encoding type and lexical class potentials

In order to solve the many-to-many mapping problem, lexical and functional constructions are extended using the *actual-potential* design pattern on the syntactic and semantic pole of constructions. Lexical constructions merge semantic and syntactic potentials into lexical units. This information is used by functional constructions to constrain their application. On the semantic side, the `type` constraints are rooted in the type hierarchy of spatial relations, whereas on the syntactic side, the lexical class `lex-cat` potential encodes which functional constructions can apply. The constraints take the form of disjunctive lists of potentials. For example, since all angular categories, i.e. projective and absolute categories, can be used as adjectives, the lexical constructions for these categories feature the `type` potential `angular-spatial-category`, as well as the syntactic `lex-cat` potential `spatial-adjective`. The adjective construction constrains itself to only apply

Table 7.2: Overview of a subset of the functional constructions of the German grammar. The three columns lex-type, lex-cat and operation show the requirements for each construction. The four columns sem-functions, sem-class, syn-functions and syn-classes detail the syntactic and semantic functions and classes that the constructions introduce.

name	lex-type	lex-cat	operation	sem-functions	sem-classes	syn-functions	syn-classes	examples
spatial-adjective-cat	spatial-category	spatial-adjective	apply-spatial-category-group-base	modifier	–	adjectival	–	*linke, rechte, vordere, hintere*
frontal-adverb	frontal-category	frontal-adverb	construct-region-frontal	modifier	relative-region, frontal-region, region	adverbial	frontal-adverb, adverb	*vorne, hinten*
frontal-preposition	frontal-category	frontal-preposition	construct-region-internal	–	angular-relationship	–	angular-preposition	*vor, hinter*
spatial-preposition-cat	spatial-category	spatial-preposition	construct-region-proximal	relationship	–	preposition	–	*an*
lateral-adverb-preposition	lateral-category	lateral-adverb-preposition	construct-region-lateral	modifier	relative-region, angular-relationship, ...	adverbial	lateral-adverb, angular-preposition, ...	*links, rechts*
noun-cat	object-class	noun	apply-object-class	identifier	–	nominal	–	*Block, Kiste*
article-cat	selector	article	apply-selector	determiner	–	determiner	–	*der, die, das*

to lexical units that have this potential thereby licensing the application of the spatial adjective construction. The lexical units for proximal relations, such as near and far do not have these potentials, hence, the adjective construction cannot apply. Other fine-grained distinctions can be modeled as well. Lateral and frontal projective categories differ in how their corresponding adverbs behave syntactically and semantically which necessitates two functional constructions, one for lateral adverbs and one for frontal adverbs. Consequently, the potentials in frontal category units differ from lateral ones. They feature the type frontal-category, where lateral lexical constructions (i.e. for left and right) provide the type potential lateral-category (see Figure 7.2 for type potentials of projective lexical constructions and Figure 7.3 for lex-cat potentials)

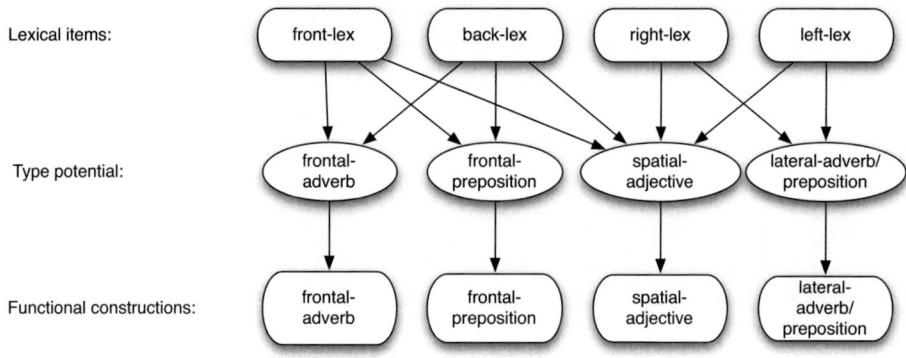

Figure 7.3: Subset of the mapping from lexical items to functional constructions.

7.2.2 Technical realization

The actual-potential design pattern is easily implemented using a dedicated template for extending lexical constructions. Example (4), for instance, is supplemented by the following two templates which introduce potentials on the semantic and syntactic side.

(8)

```
(def-add-potential front sem sem-cat type
 (angular-spatial-category
  projective-category
  frontal-category))
(def-add-potential front syn syn-cat lex-cat
 (spatial-adjective frontal-adverb frontal-preposition))
```

These two templates specify the type and lex-cat potentials and directly translate into attributes in the front lexical construction:

(9)
```
(...
(J ?front-unit ?top ()
  ...
  (sem-cat
   (==
    (type
     ((actual ?type-value)
      (potential
       (angular-spatial-category
        projective-category
        frontal-category)))))
   ...)
...)
<-->
(...
(J ?front-unit ?top ()
  ...
  (syn-cat
   (==
    (lex-cat
     ((actual ?lex-cat-value))
      (potential
       (spatial-adjective
        frontal-adverb
        frontal-preposition))))
   ...))
...)
```

Importantly, the template def-add-potential not only adds the potential attribute but also an attribute called actual. This attribute, as we will see in the next paragraphs, is automatically set to a variable in the lexical construction and is used to store which type attribute is used. If one of the potentials is picked up, for instance by a functional construction, the actual attribute is also set.

The information stored by the lexical construction in the transient structure allows functional constructions to choose the potential in which they are interested and to constrain their own application. This process can be seen in an extended version of the functional spatial adjective construction:

(10)
```
(def-require-potential spatial-adjective
  ?cat-unit sem sem-cat
  type angular-spatial-category)
```

```
(def-require-potential spatial-adjective
  ?cat-unit syn syn-cat
  lex-cat spatial-adjective)
```

In order for the spatial adjective construction to apply, these templates express that certain potentials need to be present in the transient structure. More precisely, the type potential angular-spatial-category and the lex-cat potential spatial-adjective need to be there.

The template for spatial adjectives translates into the following feature structure (for illustrative purposes, only the semantic side is shown here):

(11)
```
(...
 (?cat-unit
  (sem-cat
   (==
    (type
     ((actual angular-spatial-category)
      (potential
       (==! angular-spatial-category))))
     ...))
  ...)
```

This construction can only apply if the type potential of the lexical constituent in the transient structure imperatively includes angular-spatial-category. Additionally, it requires the actual attribute to be angular-spatial-category or a variable. There are two things to note here: the use of the ==! operator for potentials and the handling of the actual attribute. The ==! operator only unifies and never merges, which means that neither in production nor parsing can a missing potential be merged. The specified potential always has to be present, in this case on the semantic side, but for the lex-cat potentials, the case is vice versa on the syntactic side. Consequently, choosing a potential does not change the potential in the transient structure. The second feature, the actual attribute, must be equal to angular-spatial-category or a variable in order for the spatial adjective construction to apply. If the attribute is a variable, then that variable is bound to angular-spatial-category, and hence the application of the spatial adjective construction modifies the transient structure and sets the value attribute to the required potential. Of course, the corresponding potential also has to be present for the construction to apply in the first place (see Figure 7.4)

This split into value and potential and the ability to interact via these two attributes is not only interesting for grammar designers who can track the application of constructions by tracing the actually chosen potential, but it also

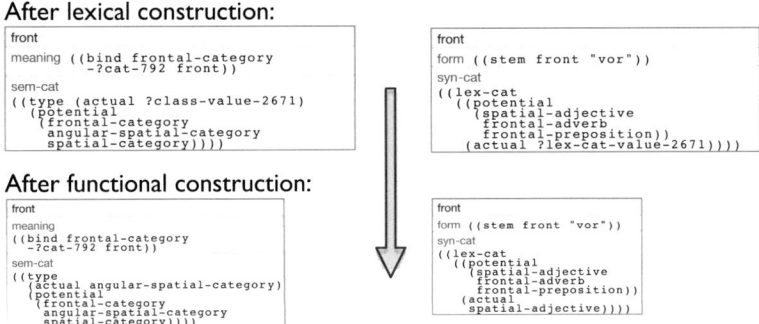

After lexical construction:

```
front

meaning ((bind frontal-category
          -?cat-792 front))

sem-cat
((type (actual ?class-value-2671)
    (potential
       (frontal-category
        angular-spatial-category
        spatial-category)))))
```

```
front

form ((stem front "vor"))

syn-cat
((lex-cat
    ((potential
       (spatial-adjective
        frontal-adverb
        frontal-preposition))
     (actual ?lex-cat-value-2671)))))
```

After functional construction:

```
front

meaning
((bind frontal-category
   -?cat-792 front))

sem-cat
((type
   (actual angular-spatial-category)
   (potential
      (frontal-category
       angular-spatial-category
       spatial-category)))))
```

```
front

form ((stem front "vor"))

syn-cat
((lex-cat
    ((potential
       (spatial-adjective
        frontal-adverb
        frontal-preposition))
     (actual
       spatial-adjective)))))
```

Figure 7.4: Interaction of lexical constructions with functional constructions in production of *vordere* ('front'). The arrow signifies the order of application. Left, the vordere unit on the semantic side of the processed transient structure is shown. Right, the syntactic unit is shown. The transient structure actually contains more units, and the units themselves contain more features, but everything has been shortened for illustrative purposes. The top row shows the lexical unit after the application of lexical constructions, which have equipped the lexical unit with potentials for type on the semantic side, and lex-cat on the syntactic side. Both of these potentials have no value assigned to them yet. It is only after the application of the functional construction of spatial adjective that both have values assigned to them, spatial-category for type and spatial-adjective for lex-cat.

plays an active role in processing. In parsing, the lexical class of a word is decided by morphological constructions. The morphological constructions apply first when parsing an utterance and they provide a value for the actual attribute. For instance, when observing the form *vorne*, the morphological construction responsible for the string *vorne* triggers and adds the information to the transient structure, namely that an adverb was observed in parsing (see Figure 7.5 for a schematic overview).

7.2.3 Discussion

Handling the many-to-many mapping problem in lexical class choice in principle also has other solutions. In particular, one could rely on the search process of FCG in order to branch into all possible lexical classes for a particular lexical

After lexical constructions:

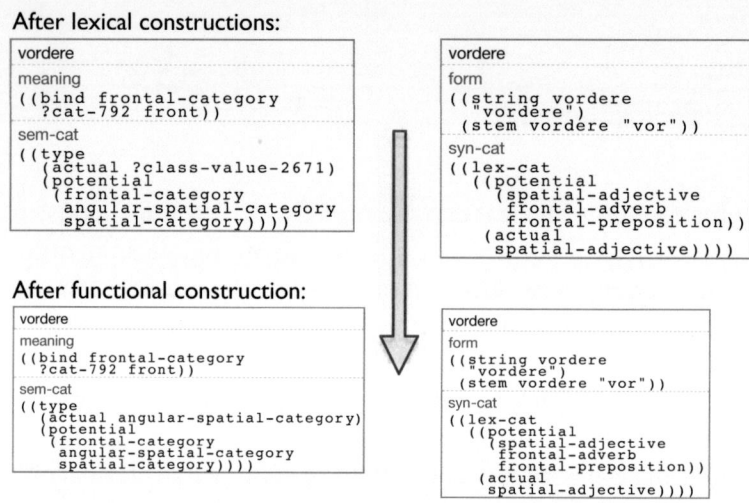

After functional construction:

Figure 7.5: Interaction of lexical constructions with functional constructions in parsing *vordere* ('front'). Lexical constructions apply before functional constructions. The vordere unit on the semantic side of the processed transient structure is shown on the left. The syntactic unit is shown on the right. The transient structure actually contains more units, and the units themselves contain more features, but everything has been shortened for illustrative purposes. The top row shows the lexical unit after the application of morphological and lexical constructions. The parsed string unambiguously allows for a decision to be made on the lex-cat value, and hence the value is set on the syntactic side. It is the functional construction that picks one of the potential types on the semantic side and fills its value attribute.

item, and cut branches until only the one relevant for the current purpose, e.g. for the meaning produced, survives. This solution requires one lexical constructions for each possible lexical class and for each category. This leads to excessive branching in search. The solution presented in this chapter does not require branching in search and is thus more efficient. Another solution to this problem is to code the interaction of lexical items and lexical classes in a holistic fashion, which means that every possible combination of lexical class and lexical item is represented by exactly one construction. This solution does depend on branching of search, but demands grammar designers to hand code many constructions (for the case discussed in this chapter more than 30 combined constructions are needed). The solution presented in this chapter leads to a concise grammar, with much fewer constructions (less than 20 lexical and functional constructions).

7.3 Landmarks and complements – adverbial and prepositional constructions

Chapter 5 contains a number of examples of landmark and perspective marking in German spatial phrases. Most importantly I concluded that in spatial prepositional phrases the landmark is always part of the prepositional phrase. This contrasts with adverbs which allow landmarks to be expressed optionally using prepositional complements. Additionally, we have seen in Chapter 6 how spatial semantics chiefly relies on particular semantic operations and linking of semantic structure. Consequently, there are two important questions related to processing landmarks and perspective in adverbial and prepositional phrases: (1) how to deal with optional elements in a concise way, and (2) how to achieve linking. In this section I explore the solution to these problems for projective categories, in particular projective adverbs and projective prepositions.

Let us first consider the extension of projective prepositions using a landmark. The construction handling projective and absolute prepositions is called angular-pp-phrase. It has two constituents (see Table 7.3). The first constituent is one that has the semantic class angular-relationship and the syntactic class angular-preposition (see Table 7.2 and in particular the semantic and syntactic function attributes of all projective prepositional constructions frontal-preposition, lateral-preposition and vertical-preposition) functional construction). The second constituent is the landmark. For the landmark there are only functional constraints. Whatever is supposed to act as the landmark needs to be some kind of reference (semantic) and referring-expression (syntactic). How is the linking precisely achieved? When we look at the prepositional construction in (7), we see that it

Table 7.3: Syntactic and semantic mappings of constructions governing prepositional and complemented adverbials. Syntactic and semantic functions and classes for the two constituents (*c1* and *c2*) are shown. To the right the newly introduced syntactic and semantic function and classes are shown.

cxn	c1 syn-function	c1 syn-class	c2 syn-fn	c2 syn-class	syn-functions	syn-classes	examples
angular-pp-phrase		angular-preposition	referring-expression		adverbial		[vor] [der Kiste], [links] [der Kiste]
lateral-region-landmark-marked	adverbial	adverb	referring-expression		adverbial		[links] [von mir]
relative-region-perspective-marked	adverbial		referring-expression				[vor der kiste] [von mir aus], [links] [von mir aus], [links von der Kiste] [von mir aus]

cxn name	c1 sem-function	c1 sem-class	c2 sem-fn	c2 sem-class	sem-functions	sem-classes	examples
angular-pp-phrase		angular-relationship	reference		modifier	region, relative-region	[vor][der Kiste], [links][der Kiste]
lateral-region-landmark-marked	modifier	lateral-region	reference		modifier	region, relative-region	[links] [von mir]
relative-region-perspective-marked	modifier	relative-region	reference		modifier	region	[vor der Kiste] [von mir aus],[links] [von mir aus], [links von der Kiste] [von mir aus]

features the variable ?landmark connected to the landmark slot of the respective operation. Since FCG cannot rely on variable names as they might change, the variable is repeated in the args feature, clearly marked in the attribute landmark. This means that the angular-pp-phrase construction can unify with this specific argument, which is for this purpose. Let us look at the template to understand the linking.

(12)

```
(def-phrasal-cxn angular-pp-phrase
 :constituents
 (def-constituent
  :syn-class angular-preposition
  :sem-class angular-relationship
  :args ((landmark ?landmark)))
 (def-constituent
  :syn-function referring-expression
  :sem-function reference
  :args ((ref ?landmark)))
  :syn-function adverbial
  :sem-function modifier)
```

Linking is achieved by explicitly unifying the corresponding args in the structure, using the variable ?landmark. The variable occurs both in the ?ref argument of the reference constituent and the landmark argument of the angular-relationship constituents.

For adverbs the linking with landmark works similar to prepositions. However, there are important differences in syntax between prepositions and adverbs. Let us consider the example of lateral adverbs. Lateral adverbs can be extended by landmarks, but the has to be marked using a *von* prepositional phrase. The construction handling the landmark augmentation of lateral adverbs is shown below. In addition to linking, this construction introduces the preposition *von*.

(13)

```
%\begin{footnotesize}
%\begin{verbatim}
(def-phrasal-cxn lateral-adverb-landmark-marked
 :constituents
 (def-constituent
  :syn-function adverbial
  :syn-class lateral-adverb
  :sem-function modifier
  :sem-class lateral-region
  :args ((landmark ?landmark)))
 (def-constituent
```

```
    :syn-function referring-expression
    :sem-function reference
    :args ((ref ?landmark))
    :preposition "von")
   :syn-function adverbial
   :sem-function modifier)
 %\end{verbatim}
 %\end{footnotesize}
```

These two constructions show how to solve parts of the complexity puzzle of the interaction of syntax and semantics, i.e. the linking issue, while at the same time they deal with the syntactic differences for adverbs (in this case only lateral adverbs are discussed, but similar constructions exist for vertical and frontal adverbs) and prepositions. Moreover, the two constructions also prevent frontal adverbs from being landmark-augmented by any of the two constructions, since frontal adverbs do not have the angular-preposition potential. Also they cannot be extended using the lateral landmark marking scheme, since they are not of class lateral-region. Other constructions deal with *in* prepositional phrases and frontal adverbs.

7.4 Linking everything together – high-level phrasal constructions

The previous section looked at prepositional and adverbial constructions. But there is more. Particularly, there are important constructions which only care about the syntactic and semantic functions of their constituents, and hence are widely applicable and underlie the ability of the grammar to build and parse complex recursive utterances involving many complemented phrases. Phrasal constructions have two constituents. The unification of constituents is based on the actual-potential design pattern. The constructions require their constituents to provide certain semantic and syntactic function potentials, while providing new potentials for semantic and syntactic functions themselves. All of them also introduce a particular word order and a particular linking of the arguments of their constituents and the meaning they express. They internally link the arguments of constituents while providing new arguments themselves. Hence, in production these constructions express particular linkings in the semantic structure using a particular word order. Vice versa, in parsing they introduce links in the semantic structure when observing a particular word order of their functional constituents.

Table 7.4: Mapping of syntactic functions (phrasal constructions). All phrasal constructions have two constituents and all build hierarchical structure by subsuming the two constituents (*c1* and *c2*) into a new unit. Columns *c1 syn-fns* and *c2 syn-fns* show the syntactic function potential expected from constituents. The column *syn-fns* details the syntactic function potential of the new unit. All constructions shown here introduce word order and require the first constituent *c1* to meet the second constituent *c2*, i.e. *c1* has to be exactly before *c2*.

cxn	c1 syn-fn	c2 syn-fn	syn-fns	examples
adjectival-nominal-phrase	adjectival	nominal	nominal	[linke] [block]
determiner-nominal-phrase	determiner	nominal	referring-expression	[der] [block]
referring-expression-adverbial-phrase	referring-expression	adverbial	referring-expression	[der block] [links], [der block] [vor/an...]
preposition-referring-expression-phrase	preposition	referring-expression	adverbial	[an][der kiste]
possessive	referring-expression	referring-expression	referring-expression	[die linke Seite] [der Kiste]

The simplest example of such a construction is the adjectival-nominal-phrase, which allows agents to build large adjective noun phrases (see Steels 2011a for the original idea). Tables 7.4 and 7.5 detail the semantic and syntactic functions of the constituents of all phrasal constructions, as well as the syntactic and semantic function potentials they introduce. The adjectival nominal construction maps a constituent with syntactic function adjectival and semantic function modifier and a constituent with syntactic function nominal and semantic function identifier onto a new unit. Hence, it builds hierarchy by introducing a new unit with two subunits – namely its two constituents. This new unit has the semantic function potential of identifier and the syntactic function potential nominal. There are a number of functional constructions providing such semantic and syntactic functions. Both color and spatial adjectives provide the semantic function modifier and the syntactic function adjectival. The semantic function identifier and the syntactic function nominal are provided by nouns. Hence, when encountering such constituents in production, for instance because noun and adjective functional constructions have provided suitable constituents, the construction will form a new unit with semantic function nominal and introduce the German word order, where adjectives always come before the noun. This new structure can itself be considered functionally equal to nouns, as it features the same syntactic and semantic functions. It therefore can be subject to modification through other adjectives. Finally, units that have the semantic function identifier and the syntactic function nominal, can be extended by determiners through application of the determiner-nominal-phrase, which results in a unit that encapsulates the semantic function reference and the syntactic function referring-expression and provides for all examples, where nouns or adjective modified nouns are determined using an article.

This explains how adjectival noun phrases can be build, but how do adverbial complement phrases discussed in the previous section get linked to referring expressions? This is solved by referring-expression-adverbial-phrase, which links constituents with the semantic/syntactic function reference/referring-expression (example *der Block* or *der grüne Block* and modifier/adverbial (example *links, links von der Kiste, vor der Kiste* ...) into a unit that not only syntactically introduces the word order, that the adverbial is behind the referring expression, but also links the meaning and adds the operation apply-region-filter. This construction, besides linking meaning of constituents, adds an operation that is applied to the output of the meaning of the adverbial phrase. Here, this operation is apply-region-filter, which filters the context given a particular region. It is important to understand, that this particular construction can be so general only because all

Table 7.5: Mapping of semantic functions of phrasal constructions. For every construction the semantic function potential that needs to be present for the two constituents *c1* and *c2* is shown, as well as the new semantic function potential provided (*sem-fns*). Some of the constructions add additional meaning with more complicated argument linking properties. All others however link the ref argument of constituent two (*c2*) to the source argument of constituent one (*c1*).

cxn	c1 sem-fn	c2 sem-fn	sem-fns	operation	examples
adjectival-nominal-phrase	modifier	identifier	identifier		[linke] [block]
determiner-nominal-phrase	determiner	identifier	reference		[der] [block]
preposition-referring-expression-phrase	relation	reference	modifier		[an] [der kiste]
referring-expression-adverbial-phrase	reference	modifier	reference	apply-region-filter	[der block] [links], [der block] [vor/an...]
possessive	reference	reference	ref	possessive	[die linke Seite] [der Kiste]

complements in the grammar compute regions. In other words all adverbial complements always denote a spatial region, be they prepositional phrases or adverbials or complemented adverbials. The referring-expression-adverbial-phrase construction, that handles all adverbial complements of determined nominal phrases, only needs to care about modifiers and hence, its generality is based on the fact that semantically all adverbial complements in this grammar compute regions while observing a particular word order. If there would be other possible complements, this construction would also need to specialize on the semantic type of the constituents.

7.5 Handling case

Case and gender agreement in German is an example of a highly distributed information processing task. The constraints on these syntactic features are contributed by many different constructions and thus have to be incrementally integrated in order to produce grammatical utterances in German. For instance, the grammatical gender of a prepositional determined adjective noun phrase is determined by the noun, as shown in the following example (*Block*, masculine).

(14)   hinter   dem   linken   Block
       behind.PREP the.DAT left.DAT block.DAT
       'behind the left block'

Alternatively, the case is governed by the preposition (*hinter*, requires dative). The determiner (*der*) and the adjective (*link*) have to be case and gender marked according to the information provided from these different sources, namely, both the determiner and adjective are used in their masculine dative forms (*dem* and *linken*). In other words, the concrete form of a projective adjective can only be fixed after the complete syntactic structure is processed. Along the way, information about which case to use (coming from the preposition) and about the gender (from the noun) need to be integrated. Consequently, the grammar needs to be set up such that sets of highly dependent constructions can interact for allowing a distributed decision on which forms to use when expressing a particular meaning. This includes mechanisms for (1) representing the state of information including its uncertainty, (2) moving information around in order to facilitate decisions and spread their effect, and (3) ways to postpone decisions until enough information is accumulated. The solutions presented for these problems naturally mirror the techniques discussed in the previous section. Logic variables embedded in feature matrices are used to represent uncertainty, percolation for moving information around and constructions of a particular type in order to postpone decisions.

7.5.1 Representing the state of information

Distinctive feature matrices (see van Trijp 2011) are a means to represent the current, possibly indecisive state of information in processing. They allow different constructions to independently contribute constraints on values of the syntactic, case and gender features until enough information has been collected. Hence, feature matrices function similarly to the logic variable used for representing uncertainty in the previous section, as they are a technique for accumulating information contributed by different constructions. Distinctive feature matrices extend the concept of logic variables and allow for the representation of dependencies between features in processing.

The way lexical items interact with the case gender agreement system is determined in part by the lexical item and in part by the word class. Nouns, for instance, have a particular gender and always need to be marked for case, which is governed by prepositions. Adjectives and articles agree in case and number with the phrase in which they are embedded, specifically with the noun. Consequently, the state of information for some word classes is initially constrained. While adjectives and articles have no constraints on case and gender, nouns already provide information about their gender, and prepositions about the required case. Distinctive feature matrices allow for the representation of such different states of information in the transient structure in a unified way by explicitly representing all combinations of possible feature values in a matrix. For our German example, this information is captured in a two dimensional matrix, where columns reflect the four German cases, and rows reflect the three grammatical genders. Every field in the matrix corresponds to a particular combination of case and gender, such as accusative-masculine, and every field can either be explicitly excluded (i.e. marked with a "–"), selected (i.e. marked by a "+") or in an unknown state of information, which is represented using variables i.e. marked with a "?").

Figure 7.6 shows the state of the transient structure after the application of lexical and functional constructions. It can be seen how the different states of information for articles, adjectives, prepositions and nouns are technically represented. The feature matrices for the spatial adjective (spatial-adjective-unit-334) and for the article (article-unit-334) are completely filled with variables. On the other hand, the feature matrix for the frontal preposition (frontal-preposition-unit-93) features a "–" everywhere but in the column representing the dative case, namely, the case it requires. On the other hand, the noun (noun-unit-334) is categorized based on its gender, and the feature matrix consequently has variables in the row for masculine and excludes all other fields.

7.5.2 Percolation and agreement – moving information around and unification

Given the setup of initial information by lexical and functional constructions, all subsequently applied constructions have to be able to move information around and to further constrain the information. Movement of information is done using percolation, and unification of feature matrices for agreement automatically

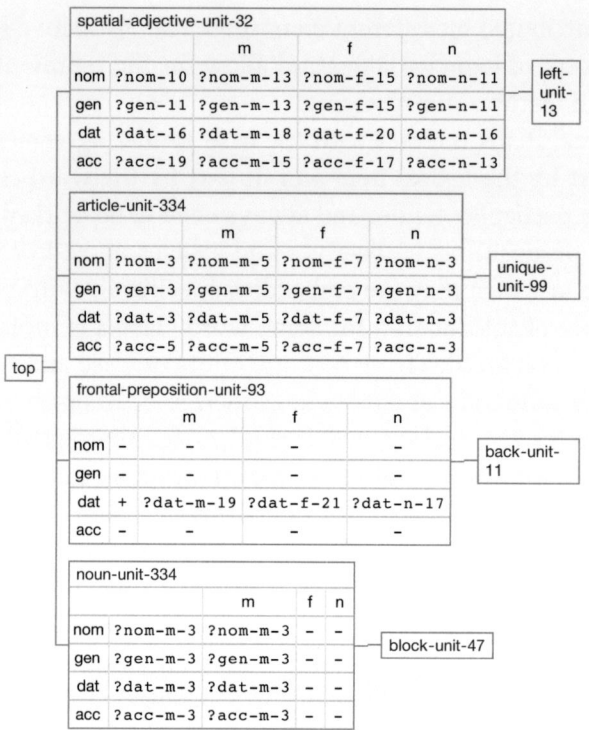

Figure 7.6: Transient structure after the application of lexical and functional constructions for production of *hinter dem linken Block* ('behind the left block'). For simplification, each unit is only shown with its distinctive feature matrix for case/gender agreement, if present. Furthermore, the feature matrices of the lexical units are identical to those of their parent units and are thus also not shown.

constrains the values in the feature matrices further and further.

Both percolation and unification are used together, for instance, by the `adjectival-nominal` construction (see Figure 7.7). In our example, this construction handles the adjective (`spatial-adjective-unit-334`) and the noun (`noun-unit-334`) as constituents. Apart from introducing German word order, this construction unifies the feature matrix of the adjective and the noun, which automatically constrains the gender possibilities for the adjective, in this case to masculine. In fact, through unification the two feature matrices are the same after the application of the `adjectival-nominal` constructions. Moreover, the newly created parent unit (`adjectival-nominal-phrase-43`) percolates this matrix up. This process is subsequently repeated, this time by the `determiner-nominal` construction, which has the same effect but this

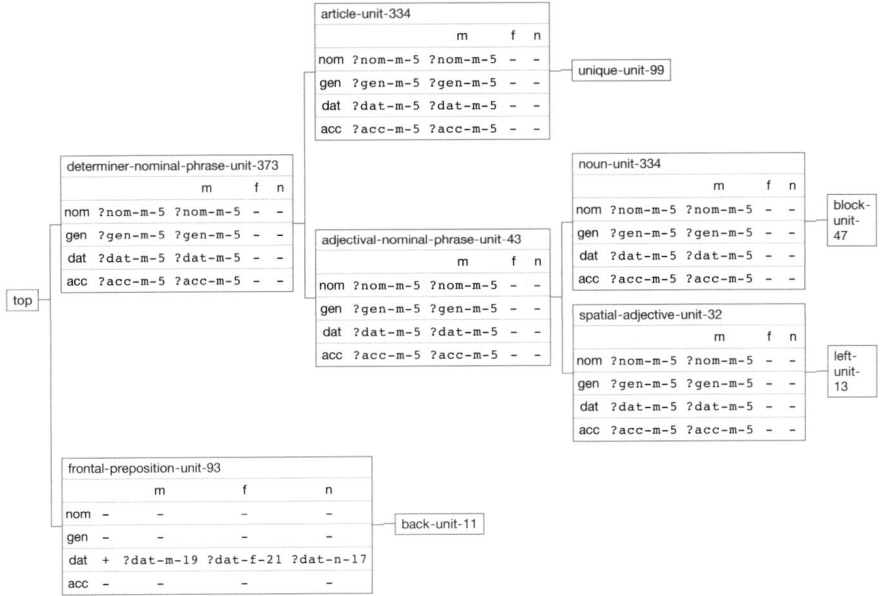

Figure 7.7: Gender agreement between the article, adjective and noun are en-
forced by the adjectival-nominal and determiner-nominal-phrase constructions applied to the transient structure in Figure 7.6.

time with its constituents being the article and the adjectival-nominal phrase,
which also constrains the article to be masculine. Percolation and unification
have essentially established the agreement between the article, the adjective and
the noun, while at the same time spreading the information about gender.

After the application of these two constructions, the decision on case is still
missing. Case is provided by the angular preposition, and agreement between the
preposition and the determined-nominal-phrase is established by the angular-pp-
phrase (see Figure 7.8). The angular-pp-phrase technically behaves very similarly to
the the determiner-nominal and the adjectival-nominal constructions: it unifies the
feature matrices of its two constituents (frontal-preposition-unit-93 and determiner-
nominal-phrase-unit-373). However, the effect is quite different in that now the
feature matrix of the article, the adjective and the noun is further constrained
in terms of case. Consequently, case and gender of this particular phrase are
ultimately decided.

For some phrases case is not established by prepositions but rather by the general grammatical structure. A prime example is when the utterance itself only
consists of a noun phrase, which then needs to be marked by the nominative case.

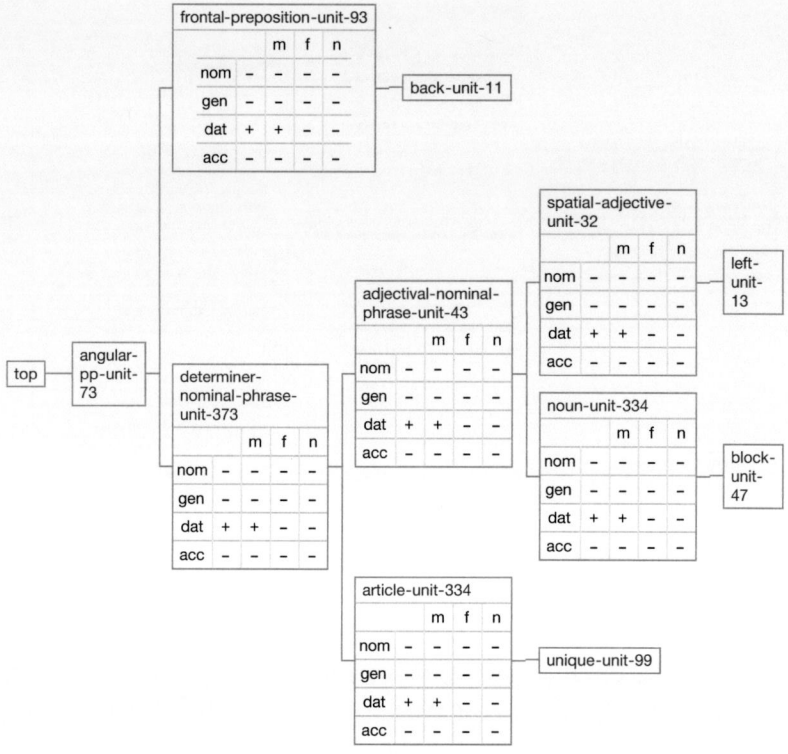

Figure 7.8: Case agreement after applying the angular-pp-phrase construction to the transient structure from Figure 7.7 while producing "hinter dem linken block".

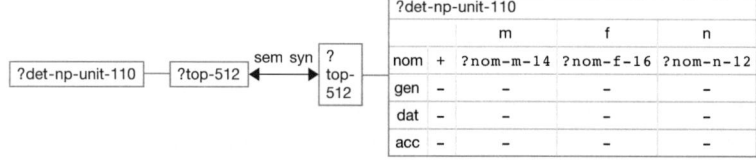

Figure 7.9: The referring-expression construction sets the case of a single determined-noun-phrase unit to nominative.

For example when meanings for utterances such as *der linke Block* ('the block to the left') are expressed, then there is no preposition that determines the case of the whole phrase by agreement. Rather, the referring-expression construction (see Figure 7.9) introduces the nominative case by unifying the feature matrix of the determined-noun-phrase unit with a matrix constraining the case to nominative.

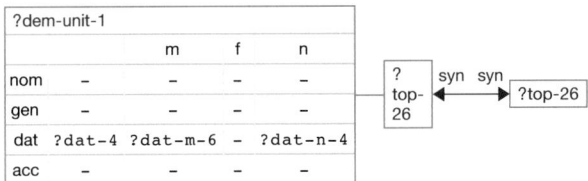

Figure 7.10: Distinctive feature matrix of the morphological construction that maps the string *dem* to masculine or neuter and dative articles. Note that since this is a morphological construction, both poles of the construction apply to the syntactic pole of a transient structure.

7.5.3 Postponing decisions

After the application of the `angular-pp-phrase` construction, all necessary information has been accumulated. Case and gender are decided, and hence all syntactic features for the particular word class in question are available to allow subsequent constructions to be able to decide the word form to be used. Morphological constructions are used here to represent this relationship between syntactic features and word forms. For example, for determiners there are six different articles in German that unevenly cover the 12 possible case-gender combinations, as shown in the chart below:

	m	f	n
nom	*der*	*die*	*das*
gen	*des*	*der*	*des*
dat	**dem**	*der*	**dem**
acc	*den*	*die*	*das*

For each of these forms, a separate morphological construction exists which decides on the form used to express the article based on the lexical class and the case-gender feature matrix. An example of such a morphological construction is shown in Figure 7.10. Since this construction has a variable in the dative masculine field, it matches with unit `unique-unit-99` in Figure 7.8. Similarly, other morphological entries add the strings *linken* to the `block-unit-47`, *Block* to the `block-unit-47` and *hinter* to `back-unit-11`.

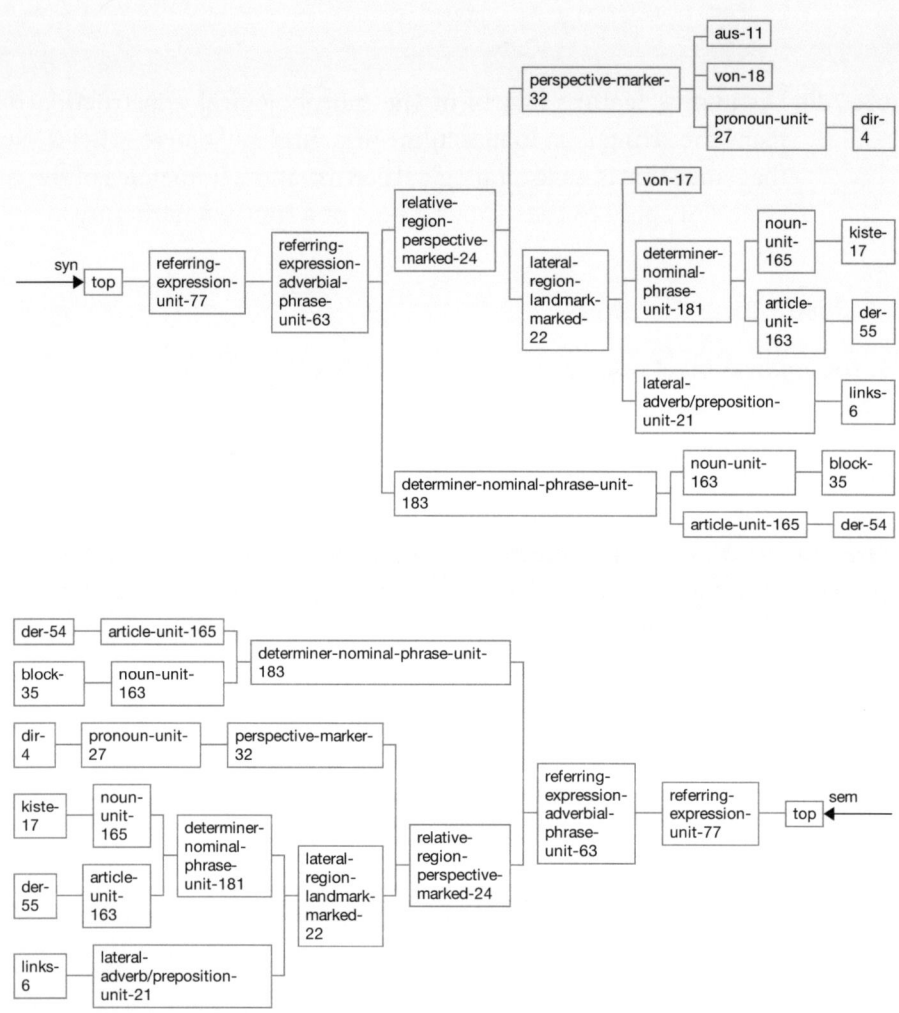

Figure 7.11: Parts of a final transient structure. The top shows the syntactic pole. The bottom shows the semantic pole.

7.6 Summary

Problems of intertwined information processing across multiple constructions and across different parts of transient structures often appear when dealing with complex, real world language. This chapter detailed how to tackle such problems using (1) adequate information representation techniques, such as logic variables, feature matrices and disjunctive potentials, (2) percolation for distributing information in the transient structure, and (3) special constructions which are needed to help postpone decisions until the state of information is ready. The techniques have proven to be sufficient for handling problems of syntactic indeterminacy, e.g. morphology and lexical class choice in German locative phrases. The discussed design patterns allow grammar designers to spread information processing across many constructions, leading to concise grammars, while facilitating efficient processing.

The grammar is powerful enough to deal with German locative phrases that include spatial relations, landmarks and even perspective. Figure 7.5.3 shows the final transient structure when an agent parses the phrase *der Block links von der Kiste von dir aus* ('the block to the left of the box from your perspective').

8 Semantic processing

In previous sections, I concentrated on how to represent the semantics of spatial relations. In this section I focus on how to conceptualize, i.e. how to choose a particular spatial relation, frame of reference, landmark or perspective in order to refer to some object in the environment. This chapter gives an overview of the factors influencing conceptualization (Section 8.1), followed by details of how conceptualization for spatial scenes can be implemented (Section 8.2). Lastly, I compare the approach favored in this book to another approach often used in modeling (Section 8.3). This last section also looks at the performance of the conceptualization machinery presented in this chapter.

8.1 Factors influencing semantic processing

A number of factors influencing the particular choice in a particular context have been identified by scholars. First, the communicative intention of the speaker plays a major role. Whether the speaker wants to describe the spatial position of an object or discriminate it with respect to other objects in the context or whether he is trying to give a route description (Tversky & Lee 1998), impacts on which spatial relations agents choose to express. Second, the context and in particular the presence and position of landmarks, their affordances with respect to frames of reference, the presence of geocentric reference systems and the perspective of the interlocutor all influence the choices agents make. Third, the available repertoire of spatial relations, frames of reference, as well as cultural factors are no less important. For instance, in some cultures social status governs the choice of perspective. How to talk about an object, in other words, how to conceptualize the world for reaching the particular communicative goal technically requires agents to choose semantic structure, including semantic operations and categories. Since we understand semantic structure as a program, the process of choosing appropriate semantic structure is essentially one of automatic programming, in which programs are constructed and tested based on their fitness for the particular task. The fitness or utility of some automatically constructed semantic structure is decided based on (1) the current communicative goal, e.g. to discriminate an object, (2) current spatial setup, in particular the position of objects, (3) available categories and concepts.

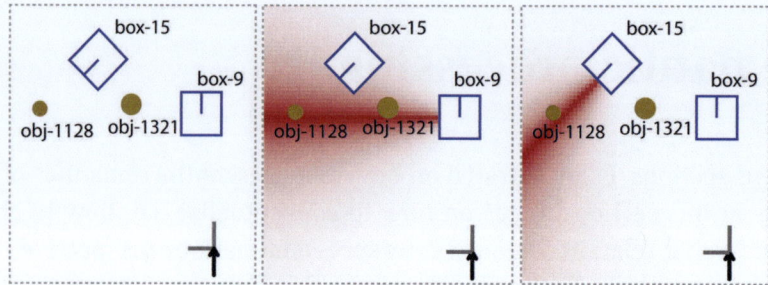

Figure 8.1: Difference between description and discrimination. The left figure shows the original context. The middle picture shows that object obj-1128 lies in the region described by "left of box-9" (intrinsic reading) with a high score. However, object obj-1321 lies pretty much in the same region of high applicability. In other words, "left of box-9" is not discriminating. The right figure shows an example of a discriminating spatial relation. "In front of box-15" (intrinsic reading) clearly discriminates object obj-1128 from obj-1321, as the score of both objects for this description varies significantly.

8.1.1 Influence of type of communicative goal – which vs where

Which communicative goal an agent is pursuing is an important driving factor in how he will conceptualize the world for reaching that goal. But it is not only the particular object an agent wants to talk about that makes a difference, but also the agent's intentions with respect to the object. For instance, there are important differences between descriptive and discriminating utterances. In discrimination scenarios, in answers to questions of the form *Welcher?* ('which') the hearer is required to distinguish, in other words identify, an object. This relies chiefly on the overall spatial setup including the position of other objects in the scene. *Wo?* ('where') questions, e.g. *Wo ist der Block?* ('where is the block'), on the other hand are asking for descriptions of the spatial relations an object takes part in. In psychological experiments spatial descriptions are elicited using contexts with only a single object (Levinson 2003). In description scenarios the applicability of a spatial relation is the important aspect, whereas in discrimination scenarios, the power to contrast the target object from the rest of the objects is more important (Tenbrink 2005a, see Figure 8.1 for an example). Agents in discrimination scenarios choose spatial relations and reference systems based on maximizing the distance to other objects (Herskovits 1986).

8.1.2 Influence of spatial contexts

Naturally, the spatial position of objects in the context has a direct effect on which spatial relations might be applicable for discriminating an object. This is based on the discussion of discrimination in the previous paragraph, but it also holds, somewhat trivially, because the position of an object with respect to another object determines the applicability of a spatial relation between the two. But there are of course other factors related to context that need to be taken into account. Examples are the presence or absence of landmarks for construing the world in relation to them and the availability of geocentric features which allow for the application of absolute frames of reference. Furthermore, landmarks without intrinsic features, such as trees who have no inherent front, prevent the application of intrinsic frames of reference, and lastly, available perspectives on a scene influence the layout of relative frames of reference on landmarks. In other words, the particular spatial setup has an effect on the space of possible or even desirable conceptualizations.

Figure 8.2: Spatial setup

8.2 Implementing spatial conceptualization

Implementing the conceptualization of spatial scenes is based on two computational steps. Semantic structure is, first, automatically combined and, second, it is ranked based on the particular communicative goal. We use a search algorithm (see Chapter 3) as a means to automatically combine simple semantic building

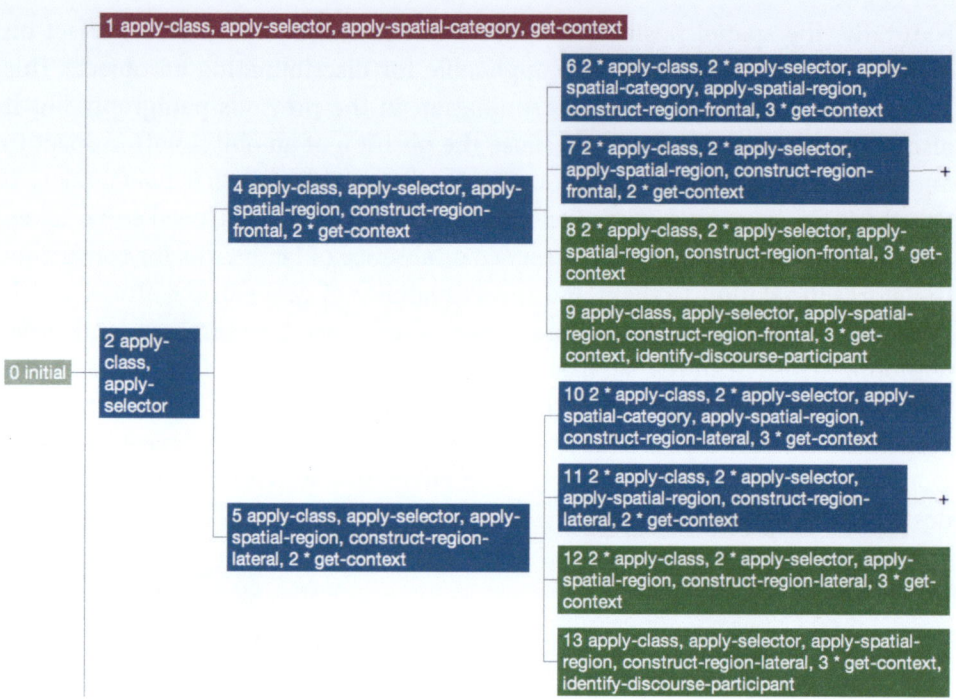

Figure 8.3: Part of the conceptualization search tree for the spatial scene depicted in Figure 8.2. Some conceptualizations are rejected (red node), because they do not work from the perspective of the hearer. This semantic structure in the red node in this figure corresponds to a determined spatial adjective noun phrase which is rejected because of the different perspectives of the two robots on the scene. Green nodes show successful conceptualizations. In total around 30 conceptualizations for the topic are found which differ in degree of applicability; some of them are more applicable than others.

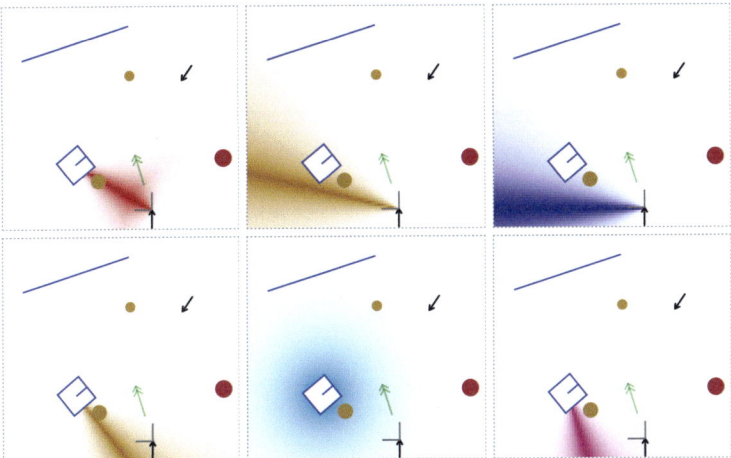

Figure 8.4: The search process in Figure 8.3 finds more than 30 different conceptualizations for object obj-266 in the spatial scene depicted in Figure 8.2. Some of them are depicted here in terms of regions that are described by the them. From left top to bottom right the figure shows the regions used to discriminate the target object. In the following, roughly corresponding utterances and discrimination scores for the particular semantic structure are shown.

    0.55 – *der Block vor der Box von mir aus*
         ('the block in front of the box')
    0.50 – *der Block rechts von mir von dir aus*
         ('the block right of me from your perspective')
    0.38 – *der Block links von mir* ('the block left of me')
    0.36 – *der Block rechts der Box* ('the block right of the box')
    0.30 – *der Block nahe der Box* ('the block near the box')
    0.23 – *der Block südlich der Box* ('the block south of the box')

blocks into more complex ones. Semantic structure assembled in the search process is immediately tried on the current context, given the specific target object and rated based on how well it fulfills the communicative goal.

8.2.1 Ranking of semantic structure

The scoring of semantic structure is guided by the communicative goal of the agent. For discrimination tasks, for example, the score of a particular semantic structure is mainly determined by how big the overall similarity of the target object is in contrast to the score of all other objects in the context. The DISCRIMINATION SCORE disc for the object o with respect to other objects O is computed by subtracting the maximum of all scores of the objects o' in O from the score s_o of o.

$$\text{disc}_{o,O} = s_o - \max_{o' \in O} s_{o'} \tag{8.1}$$

The discrimination score is computed by evaluating the particular semantic structure whose discrimination score is to be determined and more specifically by evaluating the semantic operation `apply-selector`. This operation singles out objects from sets of objects by choosing the object with the highest similarity score and binding it with its discrimination score $\text{disc}_{o_{\text{target}},O}$. For scoring semantic structure only the discrimination score of the target object of the semantic structure is of importance (see Figure 8.5 for an example of accumulating similarities over a semantic structure).

Besides the discrimination score, other factors can be incorporated into ranking semantic structure. For instance, one can include the scores of categories and semantic entities, whether or not the semantic structure also would work if applied from the perspective of the hearer, etc. The following is a non-exhaustive list of the factors that can be included into ranking semantic structure.

Score of categories and semantic entities Categories and semantic entities such as frames of reference can be scored to reflect how conventional a particular item is. This allows to model preferences for certain categories as, for instance, English native speakers show preference for lateral over frontal categories, but also allows to capture (Tversky, Lee & Mainwaring 1999) preferences for certain frames of reference. English speakers, for instance, have been observed to prefer the relative frame of reference over the intrinsic one (Levinson 2003), and German speaker seem to prefer the intrinsic over the relative frame of reference (Ehrich 1985). Although evidence

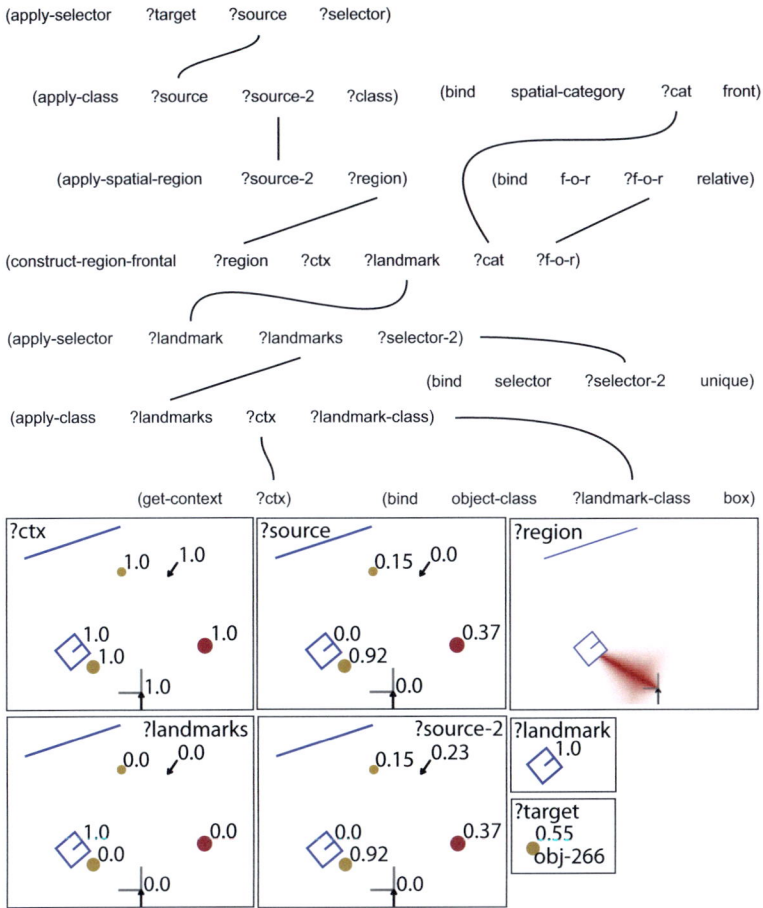

Figure 8.5: Evaluation of semantic structure and discrimination scores. The top figure shows a semantic structure which is evaluated. The bottom shows the bindings of variables resulting from evaluation. Objects have scores, and their scores are tracked and multiplied, which leads from the context where every object has a score of 1.0 to categorized sets such as the one bound to ?landmarks where the object class box has been applied which results in all objects having a score of 0.0 except for the box. Similarly, the region is applied (?source-2), followed by the application of the object class block (?source). Finally, the topic (?target) is identified.

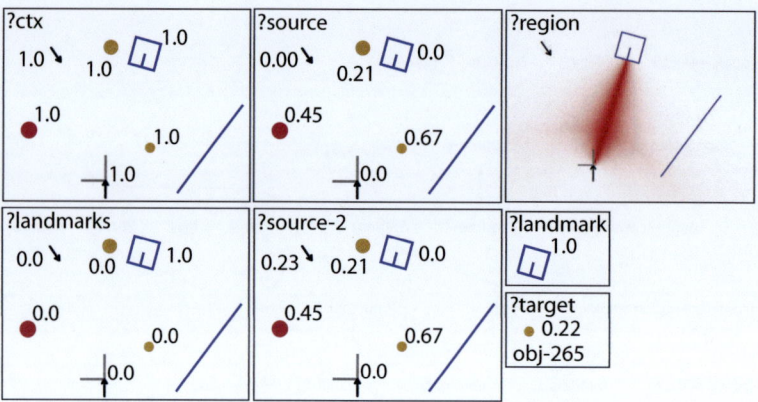

Figure 8.6: Predictive evaluation of the semantic structure shown in Figure 8.5. The speaker can test semantic structure how he thinks it would get evaluated by the hearer. In the case of the semantic structure shown in Figure 8.5 (top) the result of evaluation is object obj-265, which is different from the target of the semantic structure when evaluated from the perspective of the speaker (then it was object obj-266). In some sense this structure is ambiguous as to which object it refers to, since the semantic structure is not explicitly perspective-marked. On the other hand, the discrimination score of object obj-266 from the perspective of the speaker is much higher (0.55) than the score for object obj-265 from the perspective of the hearer. In other words, if this would indeed be the perspective of the hearer and not just a prediction, the agent could choose to interpret obj-265 to be the target object.

for these kinds of phenomena seems at least contradictory (see Miller & Johnson-Laird 1976 for reverse findings for English speakers) nevertheless the assumption that one frame of reference is conventionally selected more often is reasonable and can be incorporated into the scoring of semantic structure.

Score of chunks Chunks – the building blocks of semantic structure – are themselves scored entities. The score of chunks reflects how conventional or preferred a particular way of conceptualizing reality is. Languages, for instance, and their syntactic regularities clearly reflect certain preferred conceptual choices. For instance, in Russian, verbs always feature lexical

Aktionsarten which conceptualize every event in a way that highlights a particular aspect of that event, e.g. the beginning or the end or that it repeats, etc. The syntactic need to express these distinctions points to conceptualization strategies that are required to build correct Russian sentences. Such strategies can easily be expressed with chunks and their preference by scoring them accordingly (Gerasymova & Spranger 2010).

Perspective Choice In many situations speakers seem to prefer to conceptualize reality from the perspective of the hearer. Social status and cognitive abilities of the hearer (Mainwaring et al. 2003), as well as politeness (Schober 1993) and the question who is required to act (Tversky & Hard 2009) all have been observed to affect choice of perspective. Typically this entails that the perspective of the addressee or hearer is preferred over the perspective of the speaker. Choice of perspective is relevant for two cases of semantic structure. First, it is relevant for dealing with relative frames of reference and landmarks as in adverbial and prepositional phrases in which the perspective on the scene overtly controls the way the scene is conceptualized. The other one is less obvious and relates to semantic structures that covertly depends on perspective such as group-based reference systems. In principle there are two ways to incorporate perspective into the ranking of semantic structure both of which rely on the fact that the speaker immediately tries semantic structure from the perspective of the hearer. The first one is to outwardly reject semantic structure that does not evaluate to the desired target object when evaluated from the perspective of the hearer or any other desired perspective (see Figure 8.6 for an example of such a case). The other, more subtle one, is to compute the discrimination score of the semantic structure from the perspective of the hearer. In other words, while by default every agent uses his own perspective on the context to score semantic structure, the robot now uses the perspective of the interlocutor. To transform the context to the perspective of the hearer, each robot continuously tracks the position of the interlocutor and subsequently can use this information to evaluate semantic structure as he predicts the interlocutor would execute the structure. Of course, this is only a prediction in the sense that the speaker has no certainty about the position of the interlocutor in the spatial setup. Nevertheless, this is a hugely powerful device that can eliminate many misunderstandings in communication before they occur. It is important to realize that in many situations the choice of perspective has no or negligible effects which is mainly true for contexts where the perspectives of the interlocutors overlap sufficiently. Humans in such cases also do not mark perspective (Tenbrink 2005c). Additionally, there are ways to even out the effect of perspective by explicitly marking the perspective in the semantic structure using the perspective transform operation geometric-transform. Such semantic structure behaves like intrinsic or absolute spatial relations, since the perspective is part of the structure. For spatial adjectives this kind of marking of perspective seems to be impossible in the sense that it cannot be conveyed in language. In such cases a joint strategy by speaker and hearer, for instance, the choice to always conceptualize from the perspective of the hearer can be beneficial.

Length of semantic structure Speakers thrive to be efficient in how they communicate (Dale & Reiter 1995). The longer the semantic structure is for discriminating a particular target object, the more needs to be expressed in language. Length of semantic structure thus can be an important influence on the scoring of semantic structure. Typically long semantic structures are punished.

These and other influences are easily incorporated into the scoring function of semantic structure which is the crucial ingredient ultimately deciding which semantic structures from the vast space of possible semantic structures are worth considering. The other important ingredient in implementing conceptualization is governing how semantic structure is assembled in the first place. This process is one of automatic programming in which chunks of semantic structure are combined based on input-output arguments. Figures 8.3 and 8.4 show the conceptualization search tree and some results of conceptualizing semantic structure for object obj-266 in the spatial scene depicted in Figure 8.2.

8.2.2 Ready-made semantic structure

The size of chunks used in the conceptualization search process has a considerable influence on how elaborate the search process in conceptualization has to be in order to find suitable semantic structure for the particular communicative goal an agent might have. In order to handle the large space of conceptualization, chunks can reflect various degrees of ready-made semantic structure with some being very large covering complete utterances such as determined spatial adjective noun phrases, to smaller building blocks. How to choose the particular layout of chunks from the standpoint of designing a running system is a decision that depends on how flexible the system needs to be.

8.3 Categorization and discrimination

An important part of the complete machinery for discriminating an object in the environment is the problem of how spatial categories and relations themselves are applied. In computational modeling, discrimination is often conflated with categorization, or to be more precise, with a certain approach to categorization which can be called STRICT CATEGORY MEMBERSHIP (see Belpaeme & Bleys 2007 for an application of this approach to color). Categorization is understood here as strict membership in which a point in the sensorimotor space is categorized as belonging to the one category closest to him. For instance, an object is considered to be red, when red is the color category that is most similar to it. If this is the case the object is a member of the red category. Consequently, every point in the sensorimotor space belongs to precisely one category of the set of categories and the complete sensorimotor space can be decomposed into different sets of objects based on their category membership, a process known as Voronoi tesselation (Aurenhammer 1991, see Figure 8.7). Applying such an approach to discrimination, one needs to additionally define some criteria as to when a category c can be called discriminating object o from the context O. The strict category membership approach posits two requirements to be met.

Strict membership o is said to be a strict member of the category c, iff o is closer to c than to any other category from the repertoire of categories C. In order for c to be called to discriminate o, o has to be a strict member of c.

Discriminating category In order for c to be discriminatory, o has to be the only object from the context O that is a strict member of the category c.

Of course, the first criteria is a necessary condition for the second to apply, but in terms of objections that I will discuss following this approach, it makes sense to consider both of them separately.

There are two lines of arguments why such an approach to discrimination is wrong. First, there is accumulating evidence from natural language that is in conflict with both criteria. For instance, many scholars propose alternative principles particularly in conflict with the discriminating category criteria. Rather then requiring c to be the only category closest to o, they require that o is the closest object to c without further constraining the other objects in O and their relationship to c. So other objects in O can be strict members of c as long as they are not closer to c than o. In fact what seems to be driving people in their choice of categories in discrimination task seems to be most importantly the principle of GREATEST DISTANCE or greatest contrast which only requires the category to establish sufficient difference between the distance of object o and all other objects in the context. Such principles have been used generally to explain peoples behavior in object discrimination tasks (Hermann & Deutsch 1976) and also have been applied more specifically to spatial language (see the SHIFTING CONTRAST PRINCIPLE introduced by Herskovits 1986 and similar ideas in Freksa 1999). These insights primarily relate to criterion two. But one can also use them to attack the strict membership criterion. If humans really are looking for categories that establish high contrast, the assumption that o has to be closest to the category c in order for c to be even considered clearly has to be wrong. For instance, c might not be the category that is closest to o, however, if it establishes enough contrast between o and all other objects in the context it does not have to be. This seems to be the case for spatial language. Tenbrink (2005a), for instance, found that unmodified projective terms are frequently used by participants in a discrimination task for referring to objects that are far away from the prototypical axes. Now clearly in such tasks the linguistic material available to natural language speakers allows them to be much more precise about the actual spatial position in the sense claimed to be relevant by the strict membership criterion. In other words, speakers could choose to describe a spatial relation for objects based on smallest distance to some prototypical point, but they choose not to. So there seems to be some empirical evidence that speakers behave differently than claimed by these two principles.

The second line of arguments against the strict category membership approach to discrimination comes from computational modeling. In particular, we can compare the approach advocated in this book with the strict category membership to discrimination and show that it performs better in real-world scenarios. To be able to compare the two approaches we obviously need an implementation of both. I have already sketched the approach in the previous chapters, and I will sketch the implementational details of the strict category membership approach in the following paragraphs.

8.3.1 Strict category membership

Implementing such a notion of categorization has a profound impact on the processing of semantic structure. Instead of computing similarities and adding them to objects as in the lenient approach, categorization is implemented as a set of filter-operations which take some input set and filter the objects in the input set given a particular category which results in an output set only containing objects that are closest to that category (see Figure 8.8 for an example of semantic structure with filtering operations). When evaluating a semantic structure consisting

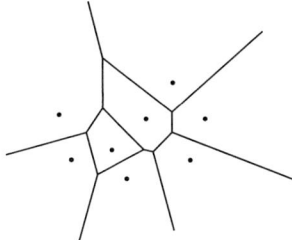

Figure 8.7: Decomposition of a metric space into different parts. Every point in the plane is categorized based on which centroid (black dots) it is closest leading to subsets of points where all points are closest to a particular centroid (Figure adapted from Aurenhammer 1991).

of such filter operations, the set of objects in the context progressively shrinks by applying subsequent filtering operations until one object is left, the topic or target of the semantic structure. For example, in the semantic structure shown in Figure 8.8, first get-context will introduce the set of objects perceived by the robot, followed by the filtering of blocks, which results in the set of blocks of the context. Afterwards, filter-by-spatial-category-group-based will compute the centroid of the group-based landmark, followed by the application of the spatial category left to that landmark, which results in the filtered set of "left blocks". The selector unique only checks whether the set of "left blocks" only contains one object and if that is the case outputs that object.

This way of modeling semantic structure bears some similarities with logic based approaches to semantics where, for instance, noun phrases denote a property that can be represented as a function from entities to truth values (see for example Barwise & Cooper 1981) – in other words, where noun phrases denote sets of objects for which the property holds. For instance the interpretation of *Ball* ('ball') denotes the set of all balls in the context which is the same as filtering the context for the set of balls. Such approaches are the dominant way of semantic analysis for instance in generative grammar and they are also applied by many scholars to the semantic analysis of spatial language (see Eschenbach & Kulik 1997 for an example). Consequently one is tempted to take such an approach to modeling the semantics of spatial language. However, there are some considerable problems associated with the category membership approach particularly when facing the problem of PERCEPTUAL DEVIATION.

While the target entity of the semantic structure in Figure 8.8 is essentially the same as, for instance, for a comparable structure using the approach advocated

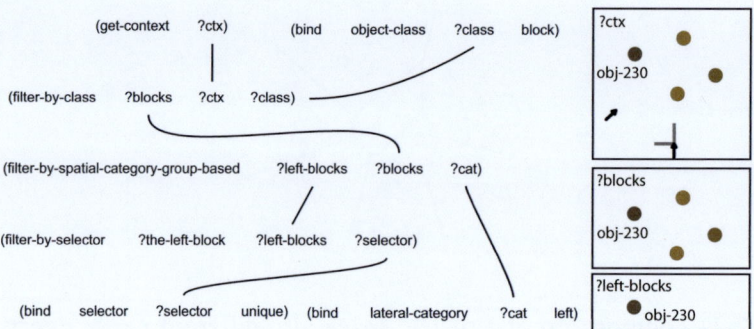

Figure 8.8: On the left side, the semantic structure of the phrase *der linke Block* ('the left block') with filter operations is shown. The images to the right show the progressive filtering of the set of objects in the context when the semantic structure is evaluated. The context ?ctx contains all objects perceived by the robot, whereas the set ?blocks contains all blocks filtered from the context and, finally, the set ?left-blocks only consists of the object obj-230.

in this book (see Figure 8.9), in many cases the category membership approach is bound to fail due to noise and uncertainty in the estimation of spatial distances and angles or other perceptual data channels such as color. The problem is that no two robots perceive the world in the same way. Colors, sizes, distances and angles are all estimated using complicated visual processing which is subject to noise and uncertainty, which makes for instance the distance of one object to another appear smaller for one of the robots in the scene. For instance, in Figure 8.2 object obj-266 (which is object obj-253 in the world model of the hearer) is smaller and more to the right of the box, than in the world model constructed by the hearer. In the case of strict category membership these sorts of perceptual deviations can lead to problems in interpretation. Even if grammar would allow for perfect transmission of a semantic structure, in other words, even if there would be no ambiguity or problems in linking when parsing a phrase like *der Block rechts der Kiste*, the evaluation of the underlying semantic structure can lead to misunderstanding, i.e. both robots think that the utterance is about different objects. The reason for this type of misunderstanding is the strict filtering of sets underlying interpretation of phrases in the category membership approach. While for the speaker the object in question, for instance obj-266 is still to the right of the box, this might not necessarily be true in the world model of the

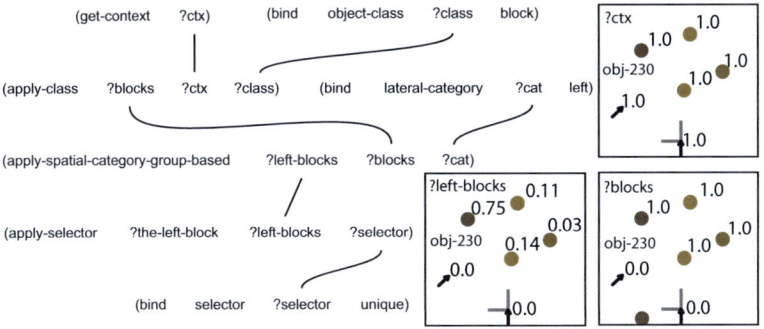

Figure 8.9: On the left side, the semantic structure of the phrase *der linke Block* ('the left block') with apply operations is shown. The images to the right show the application of semantic operations which leads to the bindings of the variables ?ctx, ?blocks and ?left-blocks with progressively changing similarity scores. For this example similarities are multiplied. First the operation apply-class is evaluated leading to scores of for all entities of type block and for all others. Next the spatial operation apply-spatial-category-group-based, which computes spatial similarities based on a landmark is executed. Consequently all objects in the ?left-block entity set are scored with indeed the left block object obj-230 having the highest overall score.

hearer, which can lead to no or false interpretations of the semantic structure. Consider Figure 8.10, where object obj-212 for the speaker is to the intrinsic left of the box, whereas it is to the intrinsic right for the hearer. Small estimation errors in judging distance and angle can thus lead to very different categorizations of the same object.

8.3.2 Lenient approach

In contrast to the strict category membership, the approach advocated in this book does not rely on category membership, but only considers similarities to categories without enforcing the strict membership criteria. In other words an object does not have to be closest to the category left in order to be categorized as left. Only one thing is important: the object needs to have a bigger similarity with left than any other object in the context (see Figure 8.9 which shows the accumulation of scores). From this fact alone one can predict that the le-

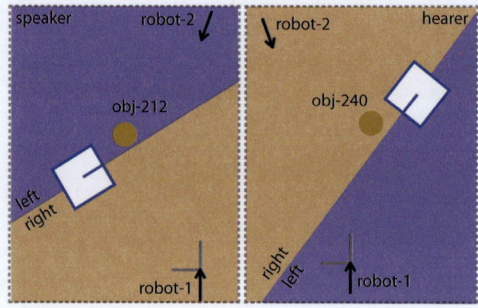

Figure 8.10: Example for perceptual deviation and impact on filtering operations

nient approach is better suited for dealing with perceptual deviation, as it is less restrictive in interpretation. But another prediction can be made as well. The approach is also less restrictive in conceptualization, in the sense that the strict category membership constraint is also not applied in finding a category to discriminate an object. Consequently, the lenient approach should also be able to find semantic structure in cases where the strict membership approach fails as its membership constraint cannot be met.

Figure 8.11 contrasts the example in Figure 8.10 from the viewpoint of strict and lenient discrimination. The top figure shows the similarity functions for left and right categories over the angle, from which the decomposition of the angular space show in the middle Figure follows. The particular similarity function of the two categories interact in the decomposition of the space. Object obj-212 is categorized by the speaker as being to the left, whereas the same object for the hearer which he knows as object obj-240 is to the right. When the speaker thus conceptualizes the object as left, the hearer has no chance of retrieving the object in the strict interpretation case. On the other hand, when applying a lenient discrimination scheme (bottom figure) there is no interaction between the categories left and right. The decision whether or not the hearer is able to discriminate the correct object depends on whether object obj-240 is indeed the most similar object to the category left (which it is in this case). To ensure that agents can always find the correct object, category similarity functions always span across the complete space. For instance, for the angular category left every angle has a similarity bigger than zero. For some angles similarity is small, but importantly it is never below zero.

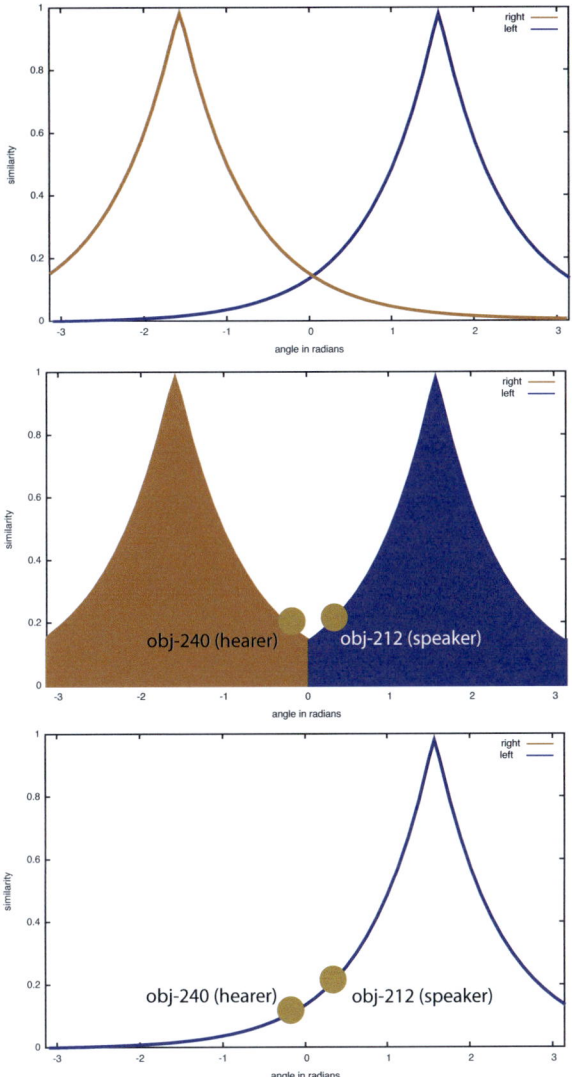

Figure 8.11: Lenient versus strict categorization. The first figure shows the similarity functions for left and right categories over the angle. The second figure shows the decomposition of the angular space using the strict approach. The third figure shows how the lenient approach uses the similarity function of the spatial category to retrieve the correct object.

8.3.3 Experimental setup

We can study the difference of the two approaches systematically by letting agents interact in controlled spatial scenes and see which of the two approaches performs better in a discrimination task. In order to to study only the effect of the particular implementation of semantic operations, I eliminate the influence of language using direct meaning transfer, in which the hearer is passed the semantic structure conceptualized by the speaker without going through production and parsing of syntactic structure. This is equivalent to having a language where sufficient information is provided in each utterance to decode the semantic structure intended by the speaker without uncertainty, ambiguity or loss of information. The particular interaction script used in the experimental setup is the following. Always two agents from a population interact. One is the speaker, the other the hearer. The speaker perceives the world, picks a topic and tries to conceptualize a semantic structure for reaching his communicative goal. If he is successful in finding semantic structure for discriminating the topic, he passes the semantic structure to the hearer. The hearer interprets the semantic structure by simply evaluating it. Afterwards he points to the object he thinks the semantic structure was about.

Thus, there are four different outcomes of the game.

Conceptualization failed After the speaker choose a topic, he has to conceptualize a semantic structure that discriminates the topic. This process fails, if the speaker cannot find any semantic structure that allows him to discriminate the object from all other objects in the context.

Interpretation failed After the speaker successfully conceptualized a discriminating semantic structure, the hearer interprets this structure by simply evaluating the semantic program. If this evaluation yields no result, the hearer is said to have failed.

Pointing failed When the hearer successfully interpreted the semantic structure passed to him by the speaker, he points to the topic he interpreted. The speaker then interprets whether the object pointed to is indeed the topic. If this is not the case then pointing failed.

Success The hearer pointed to the correct object and the game is a success.

We can compare the two approaches to categorization using two different sets of agents – one in which agents are equipped with a lenient implementation of semantic operations as advocated in this book, and a second where agents are equipped with category membership based semantic operations. Both agents were equipped with complex semantic structure, which allowed them to use group-based reference, landmarks, relative and intrinsic frames of reference together with proximal and projective spatial categories implemented as in the German space semantics discussed in Chapter 6. I test both populations and their respective success and failure on different sets of spatial scenes.

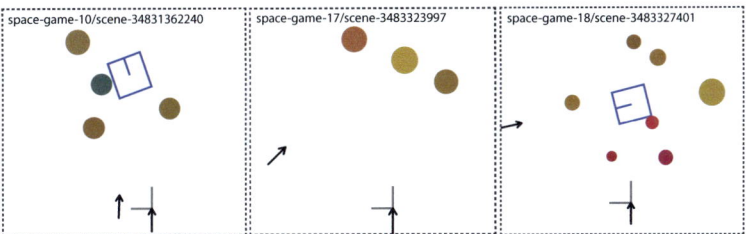

Figure 8.12: This figure exemplarily shows spatial scenes used for comparing lenient and strict categorization implementations. The left image shows an example scene from the data set labeled space-game-10 which consists of scenes with one landmark and two robots that can be used as reference systems. Spatial scenes in data set space-game-17 (middle image) consist of scenes without boxes. Only the two robots and group-based reference are available for conceptualizing the spatial scene. The right image shows an example from data set space-game-18 which features a box just as space-game-10, but in much more complex spatial layouts.

8.3.4 Results

The results in Figure 8.13 show a clear advantage for the lenient approach proposed in this book. The success in interaction for this approach to spatial categorization is consistently above 85% across various spatial scenes, whereas the success of strict categorization drops to 22% in the worst case (space-game-18) but consistently performs below 60% success showing the power of the lenient approach to deal even with very complex spatial scenes (see Figure 8.12 for some example scenes from the different spatial scenes). Notably, the lenient approach in almost all scenes is able to successfully conceptualize the spatial scene for the topic in question. Only few cases in data set space-game-18 are marked for failure in conceptualization. On the other hand, the strict approach shows enormous problems even conceptualizing for particular objects in particular scenes. Almost all cases of failure are either due to failures of conceptualization or failures of interpretation, where conceptualization as can be seen takes the major blame for failure.

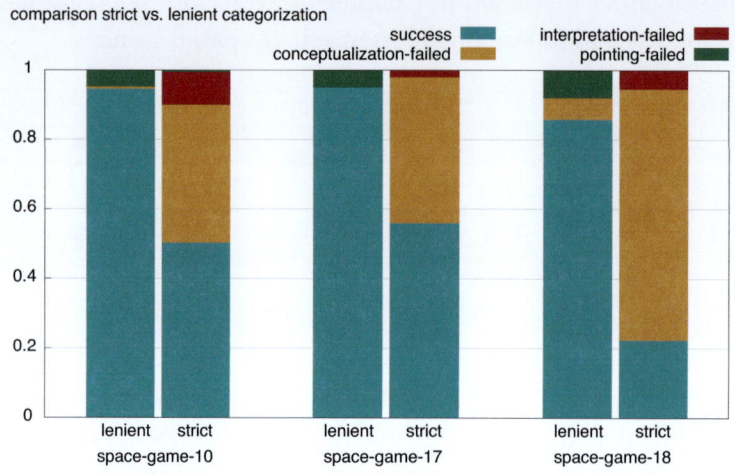

Figure 8.13: Results of comparing strict versus lenient categorization on different sets of spatial scenes

Failures to conceptualize in the case of strict category membership are caused by insufficient clustering of the input space. The problem is that categories are not dense enough to allow the speaker to conceptualize for the particular topic. Failures to interpret on the other hand are caused by perceptual deviation. Strikingly, there are no interpretation failures in the case of the lenient approach highlighting its power to deal with perceptual deviation. Maybe for the strict approach the problem could be eased. For instance one could increase the number of possible decompositions of the sensorimotor space by adding more categories which allows the speaker to more easily conceptualize. Figure 8.14 shows the effect of adding more categories to the inventory of strict categorization agents. It compares four conditions (over the different spatial scenes): "german", "double", "triple" and "quadruple". "German" refers to the set of categories introduced earlier, e.g. front, back, left, right and so forth. "Double" refers to a set of categories where the number of categories is doubled. So for instance, instead of two lateral categories left and right there are now four. The same holds for frontal and proximal categories. In the "triple" condition agents are equipped with three times as many categories and in the "quadruple" condition the number of categories is four times compared to the german condition.

In some cases most notably for data set space-game-18 more categories indeed helps triple the success in interaction. This is not all that surprising in the sense that there was a lot of room for improvement in the first place. For the other two sets of scenes success in interaction stays pretty much the same. And it seems that also for space-game-18 a certain limit of improvement is reached, as success actually drops again for quadrupled number of categories. The most interesting point is, however, that overall success in interaction stays roughly the same for most spatial scenes and failures of the speaker to conceptualize are replaced by the inability of hearers to interpret. This is most strikingly the case in condition space-game-17 where this type of error accounts for 20% of all interactions and half of the unsuccessful ones. In other words, the more categories there are available, the more impact perceptual deviation has on the strict set approach. The reason for this can be found in the interaction of categories that determines the decomposition of the space. The more categories there are, the smaller the area of applicability of categories becomes, and consequently the more likely it becomes that an object that is categorized as belonging to a certain category by the speaker will be categorized differently by the hearer. One might wonder what the effect of more categories is on the lenient categorization approach. Figure 8.15 shows that while there is some impact of more categories in the difficult scenes of data set space-game-18, overall there is no significant increase in success in interaction.

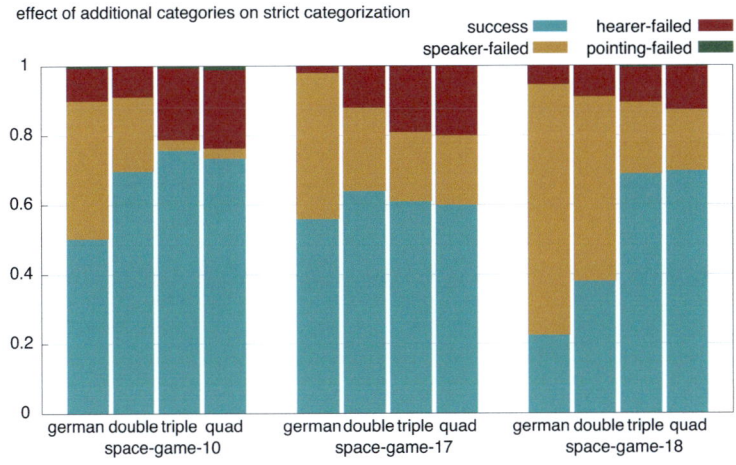

Figure 8.14: Results of comparing different sets of spatial categories and their effect on the strict categorization approach

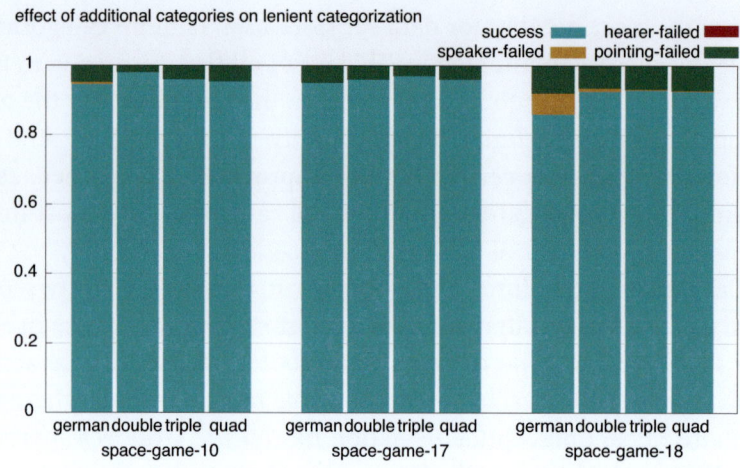

Figure 8.15: Results of comparing different sets of spatial categories and their effect on the lenient categorization approach.

8.4 Summary

We can conclude that the communicative intentions of an agent influence how spatial scenes are conceptualized, i.e. which spatial relation is chosen, which frame of reference, or which landmark. The most important factor is whether an agent wants to discriminate or describe an object. But, preferences for particular spatial relations, perspective or frames of reference are also important. This chapter showed that these factors are easily operationalized using IRL. Experimental results demonstrate that the system is powerful enough to enable robotic agents to reliably conceptualize spatial reality. The results of this chapter are further discussed in Pauw & Spranger (2010; 2012); Spranger & Pauw (2012).

9 A whole systems approach to processing

So far I have discussed processing of German locative phrases isolated for semantics and syntax. However, IRL and FCG are systems that have to work together to allow agents to talk. This chapter reflects on the integration of these two systems in a unified architecture. Consequently this chapter is technical in nature. It starts out by giving an overview of how processing is integrated (Section 9.1). Section 9.2 discusses the phenomenon of semantic ambiguity which requires a deep level of integration. The chapter concludes with results on the performance of the complete system (Section 9.3).

9.1 Integrating IRL and FCG

IRL and FCG are integrated via a mechanism which is called TASK ENGINE.[1] The task engine bundles the processing done by an agent and allows to track different hypotheses. For instance, in production a speaker might conceptualize different semantic structures and only later decide which of those he wants to use based on how well it can be verbalized. For this IRL and FCG is packaged into processes.

Figures 9.1 and 9.2 show the typical processing for the speaker and the hearer. Each of them runs different processes which bundle FCG and IRL for production and interpretation. The most important processes are

conceptualize This process takes as input the world model (context) computed by the vision system and a topic object. Using these input arguments, an ontology and a set of known chunks, the process uses the IRL search to produce one or several possible IRL-networks.

produce This process applies constructions in the direction of production. In other words, matching happens on the semantic side. Production takes as input an IRL-network and a set of constructions and produces one or more possible utterances using FCG's search process.

---

[1] All computational systems described in this book are integrated into a framework for running and evaluating experiments described in Steels & Loetzsch (2010).

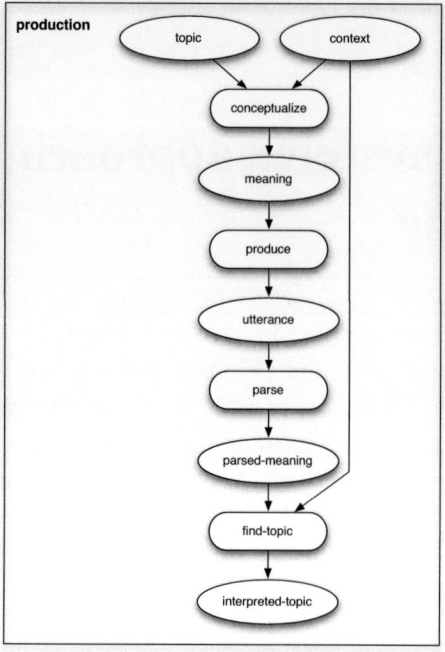

Figure 9.1: Processes running when a speaker produces an utterance. Ellipsis represent data structures, squashed rectangles represent processes.

parse Parsing is the process which takes a set of constructions as well as an utterance and computes one or more possible interpretations, i.e. IRL-networks.

find-topic This process uses IRL to compute a topic based on an IRL-network and the context (computed by the vision system).

All of these processes can produce one or many outcomes. The task engine branches on multiple results. For instance, when "conceptualize" has found different IRL-networks, the engine tracks their individual success in separate "produce" processes. The overall best result is determined by combining the discrimination score of the meaning and confidence of construction application. Moreover, as we can see in Figure 9.1, speakers also run processes vital for the hearer. Before passing an utterance to the hearer, the speaker parses and interprets the phrase he is about to use. The mechanism is called RE-ENTRANCE (Steels 2003). Applied to this process model, this means that agents can choose the best result based on the prediction how that phrase might be interpreted by the hearer.

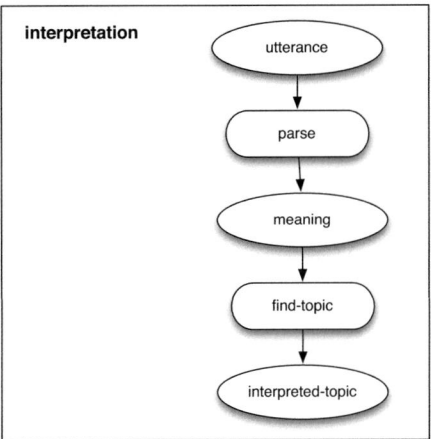

Figure 9.2: Processes running when a hearer interprets an utterance. Ellipsis represent data structures, squashed rectangles represent processes.

9.2 Handling semantic ambiguity

An example where the integration of the systems for syntactic processing and conceptualization can play out its power is semantic ambiguity. A phrase is semantically ambiguous if multiple semantic structures, i.e. IRL-networks, can be interpreted.

Many German locative phrases are semantically ambiguous. Let us consider the following two examples from German.

(1) der   Block   vor   der   linken   Kiste
    the.NOM block.NOM front.PREP the.DAT left.ADJ.DAT box.DAT.FEM

    'The block in front of the left box'

(2) der   Block   vor   der   linken   Kiste   von
    the.NOM block.NOM front.PREP the.DAT left.ADJ.DAT box.DAT from.PREP

    dir   aus
    your.DAT perspective

    'The block in front of the left box from your perspective'

(1) is semantically ambiguous with respect to how the landmark object, in this case the left box, is conceptualized. The phrase can have an intrinsic or relative reading. (2) does not have this problem. The perspective marker clearly signals a

relative reading of the phrase. Interestingly, this fact can only be established after parsing the complete phrase. To illustrate this dependency consider (2), which is not semantically ambiguous (with respect to intrinsic and relative readings) because it features a perspective marker in the end.

The first example is a clear instance of language as an inferential coding system (Sperber & Wilson 1986). Utterances merely hint at meaning rather than encoding complete information. In other words, the information communicated in utterances is incomplete and ambiguous. This puts considerable stress on hearers, as it requires them to integrate information from the context with the information available in the utterance to find the best possible interpretation of a phrase. The integration of IRL and FCG supports such active information integration and enables hearers to infer the communicative intention of speakers even when the information conveyed in the utterance is sparse, incomplete, and ambiguous.

This section first discusses the syntactic processing part (Section 9.2.1), before examine how syntactic processing and semantic processing interact (Section 9.2.2).

9.2.1 Syntactic processing

The main task of FCG in cases of semantic ambiguity is to correctly retrieve the possible interpretations of a phrase. For instance, if there is a relative and an intrinsic reading of a phrase then those two readings should be recovered in parsing – not more, but also not less.

This section shows how to handle phrases such as in (1) and (2) using a combination of these techniques:

1. logic variables, for representing uncertainty

2. percolation, for distributing information

3. the actual-potential design pattern, for constraining the application of constructions

4. sem-sem constructions, which are particular constructions that only apply on the semantic side of feature structures, for postponing decisions

When applied together, this set of techniques allows to represent the inherent ambiguity in certain German locative phrases in a concise way, while allowing constructions to collectively resolve the ambiguity where possible, or to otherwise interpret the phrase in all possible ways.

The semantic ambiguity discussed in this chapter focuses entirely on how a particular landmark is conceptualized. Consequently, such kind of ambiguity only surfaces in phrases involving overtly or covertly expressed landmarks. Examples of such phrases are prepositional and adverbial phrases, such as the following:

(3) der   Block   vorne
     the.NOM block.NOM front.ADV

     'The block in front'

(4) der   Block   links   von   der   Kiste
     the.NOM block.NOM left.ADV of.PREP the.DAT box.DAT

     'The block to the left of the box'

(5) der   Block   hinter   der   Kiste
     the.NOM block.NOM hinter.PREP the.DAT box.DAT

     'The block in back of the box'

(4) and (5) explicitly refer to the landmark object, whereas (3) implicitly refers to a landmark. In all examples, a projective term is used in relation with some landmark, denoting the particular spatial relationship of the object in question, in this case the block, to the landmark. Also in all examples, the landmark can be construed using an intrinsic or relative frame of reference. Hence, all of the examples have at least two possible interpretations.

Syntactic structure can provide additional information that allows for the disambiguation of the conceptualization underlying a particular utterance. This is the case when the phrase also features a perspective marker, such as in (6).

(6) der   Block   vor   der   Kiste   von   dir
     the.NOM block.NOM front.PREP the.DAT box.DAT from.PREP your.DAT

     aus
     from.PREP

     'The block in front of the box from your perspective'

The component *von dir aus* ('from your perspective') is a clear indicator that the landmark is construed from a certain perspective. Consequently, this phrase has a relative reading only. After all, interpreting a relative landmark always entails construing the scene from a certain perspective. This excludes intrinsic readings of the phrase, since construing a landmark using an intrinsic frame of reference is independent of the viewpoint of the scene.

The interaction with perspective marking makes the semantic ambiguity in German locative phrases an interesting problem because whether a phrase is semantically ambiguous can only be established upon integrating information from the complete phrase.

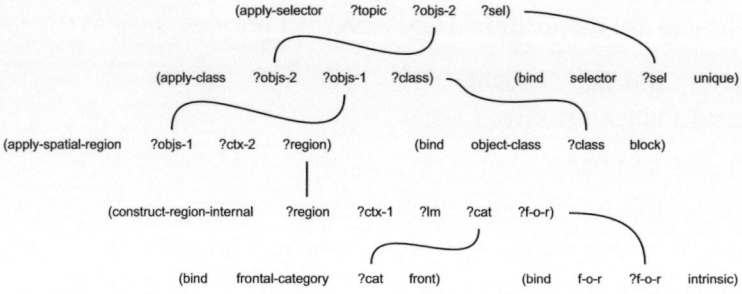

Figure 9.3: Semantic structure *der Block vorne* intrinsic reading

Figures 9.3 and 9.4 show the difference in semantic structure for the two interpretations of (3). The structures feature a number of operations, of which the most interesting for purposes of this section is the `construct-region-internal` operation. This operation has a number of input-output arguments that are all signified by variables starting with a ?:

`?ref-1691` is the region computed by this operation.

`?src-2910` is the input context.

`?reference-294` is the landmark.

`?cat-792` is the projective category that is used to construe the region.

`?f-o-r-294` is the frame of reference used to construct the region.

As a result, the operation has all necessary input and output arguments to compute a spatial region. In this case, it is an internal spatial region (i.e. a region that is inside the landmark), which takes into consideration the projective category, the landmark to which the category is applied, and the frame of reference. In this particular structure the frame of reference argument is linked to a bind statement explicitly introducing the intrinsic frame of reference into the structure. Because the phrase in (3) is ambiguous, there exists also another interpretation of the phrase involving a relative frame of reference. (compare Figure 9.4 which shows the relative interpretation with Figure 9.3 which shows the intrinsic interpretation).

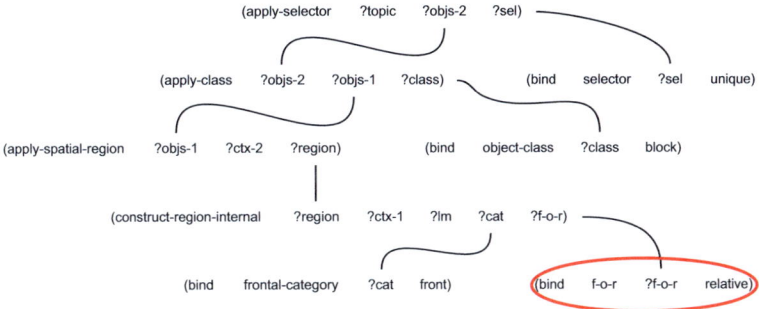

Figure 9.4: Semantic structure of *der Block vorne* with relative reading. The difference from an intrinsic reading is only in the bind statement referring to the frame of reference used in computation.

9.2.1.1 Representing ambiguity in the transient structure

The next question is how the semantic ambiguity and, in particular, the uncertainty about which interpretation is possible, can be represented in syntactic processing. For this, uncertainty has to be represented in the transient structure. Uncertainty is represented using a variable. Since the procedural IRL-networks have the same convention for variables, namely, that variables begin with a ?, parts of the semantic structure can be replaced using a variable. In order to allow FCG to contribute information to those parts in the semantic structure that are uncertain or ambiguous, the same variable is repeated in the construction. Below as an example is the functional construction for frontal adverbs:

(7)

```
(def-fun-cxn frontal-adverb
 (def-fun-skeleton frontal-adverb
  :meaning (== (construct-region-internal
               ?target ?source ?landmark ?category ?f-o-r)
                      (bind f-o-r ?f-o-r ?f-o-r-value))
  :args ((ref ?target)(src ?source)
          (cat ?category)(landmark ?landmark))
  :sem-function modifier
  :sem-class (region internal-region relative-region)
  :syn-function adverbial
  :syn-class adverb)
 (add-sem-cat frontal-adverb (f-o-r-value ?f-o-r-value)))
```

Parts of the semantic structure in Figures 9.3 and 9.4 are represented by adding them to the meaning of this construction. In particular, the operation and the frame of reference are part of the specification of the functional construction. Moreover, the actual frame of reference is left unspecified but is represented using the variable ?f-o-r-value instead, and it is this variable that is repeated as a semantic category attribute. Consequently, this specification expresses two things: firstly, when a frontal projective category is expressed using an adverb, its meaning is to construct a region, and, secondly, the frame of reference used to construct this region is unspecified. To summarize, the use of the same variable allows for the representation of the uncertainty in a unified way in the semantic structure as well as in the construction and, consequently, in the transient structure.

9.2.1.2 Constructions for processing semantic ambiguity

With the knowledge of how to represent semantic structure as well as the ambiguity in the semantic interpretation, I can now turn to the processing of potentially ambiguous utterances. I focus first on the ambiguous case only, that is, the case where no perspective marker is present in the phrase. Consequently, I am trying to solve the problem of letting FCG compute all possible interpretations of a phrase like the one in (3). The key property of the FCG search for an interpretation of such an utterance is that each branch in the search tree corresponds precisely to one possible interpretation. As a result, in order to represent the different interpretations of the phrase, the search tree must be split, yet it should only split into different branches at the very end of parsing. From a processing point of view such a late split is desirable, since branching the search at the end reduces computational complexity. From the point of view of modeling, it is necessary, because it is only when considering the larger semantic structure that the phrase can be determined to be ambiguous. In other words, to be sure about whether or not the phrase is really ambiguous, processing must be complete with no perspective marker observed.

To achieve these objectives, sem-sem constructions are used which are constructions that only work on the semantic side of the transient structure. Two of these constructions are needed, one for representing intrinsic readings and one for representing relative readings. These constructions apply at the very end of parsing, and their job is to set the frame of reference variable. Here is one of the two sem-sem constructions:

(8)

```
(def-sem-sem-cxn
 :meaning  (== (bind f-o-r ?target intrinsic))
 :sem-cat (==1 (f-o-r-value intrinsic)))
```

The construction directly applies to the part of the transient structure that represents the meaning of the frontal adverb. Since the f-o-r-value was set to the variable ?f-o-r-value, this part of the transient structure unifies with intrinsic and sets the attribute as well as the part of the bind statement in the meaning to the value intrinsic. A similar construction is used for applying a relative frame of reference. Figure 9.5 shows the split at the end of parsing the phrase *der block vorne*. These constructions are necessarily very general and apply equally to all other required cases, in particular to projective prepositions (i.e. frontal and lateral prepositions), but also to lateral adverbs.

Figure 9.5: Final part of the parsing search tree for the utterance *der block vorne*. sem-sem constructions apply at the very end and split the search tree, so that the two possible interpretations of the phrase are found.

The usage of logic variables allows for the representation of the uncertainty in interpretation directly in the transient structure. In interaction with semantic rules these variables are used in processing to provide the different semantic interpretations of ambiguous German locative phrases.

9.2.1.3 Handling perspective markers

Perspective markers pose a problem in terms of processing, since information about perspective marking is available on the phrasal level only. For instance, in (6), the part *vor der Kiste von dir aus* ('in front of the box from your perspective'), the perspective marker is the additional phrase *von dir aus*, which together with the prepositional phrase in the beginning makes up the complete phrase. As a consequence, the problem to be solved is to distribute the information about the used frame of reference so that a construction combining the two phrases can make the necessary semantic inference, namely, set the frame of reference. The information needs to spread all the way to the part of the semantic structure processing the region, that is, the functional unit representing the preposition or adverb. The answer to this problem is the use of percolation (Steels 2011a,b) for distributing the information, so that the information becomes available at the places necessary.

Before looking at percolation in more detail, consider (9), a simple example where a stand-alone adverb is perspective marked (i.e. an adverb that has no landmark phrase attached to it).

(9) der   Block   vorne   von   dir   aus
the.NOM block.NOM front.ADV from.PREP your.DAT from.PREP

'The block in the front of the box from your perspective'

Basically, a construction setting the frame of reference to relative is required. The prerequisite for which is that there is a region that has the potential to be interpreted as a relative region. Additionally, there needs to be a perspective marker that has the right syntactic relationship to the region. The construction in Figure 9.6 and (10) does exactly that.

(10)

```
(def-phrasal-cxn relative-region--perspective-marked
 (def-phrasal-skeleton
  relative-region--perspective-marked
 :phrase (?relative-region--perspective-marked
                :sem-function (modifier)
                :sem-class (region)
                :syn-function (adverbial)
                :cxn-form (== (meets ?relative-region-unit
                                ?perspective-marker-unit)))
  :constituents
  ((?relative-region-unit
    :sem-function-potential (modifier)
    :sem-class-potential (relative-region))
   (?perspective-marker-unit
    :sem-function-potential (modifier)
    :sem-class-potential (perspective-marker))))
  (def-set-cat ?relative-region-unit sem-cat
               f-o-r-value relative))
```

This construction captures all posed constraints. For this construction to apply there need to be two constituents. One constituent needs to have the sem-class potential relative-region, that is to say, it needs to be able to be conceived as

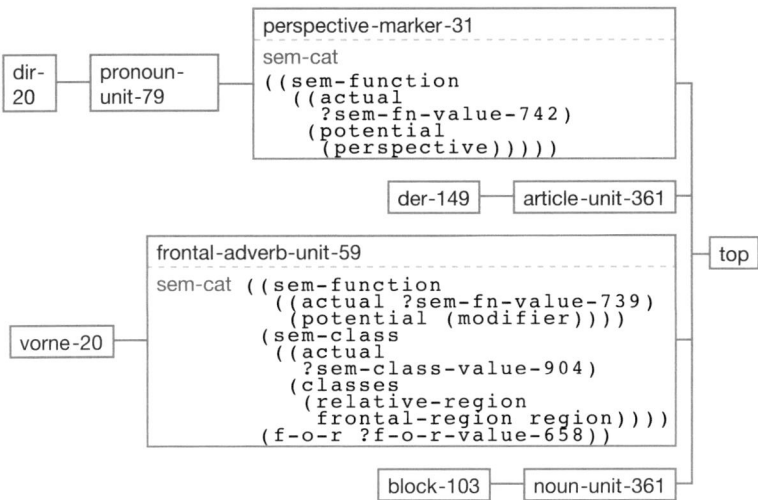

Figure 9.6: Transient structure before the application of the relative-region–perspective-marked construction (when parsing *der Block vorne von dir aus*). The f-o-r (frame of reference) sem-cat attribute of the frontal-adverb-unit-59 is set to a variable. Consequently, at this point in processing it is undetermined which frame of reference is used. For simplification, only the sem-cat features of relevant units are shown.

a relative region. The second constituent needs to be a perspective marker. If these conditions are met, the construction sets the frame of reference value of the region unit to relative. Now, in the case of the phrase *vorne von dir aus* ('in front from your perspective'), the region unit in parsing corresponds to the adverb unit, namely, to the unit setup by the adverb functional construction (see (7)). Figures 9.6 and 9.7 show the state of the transient structure before and after application of the construction.

The construction that handles the perspective marking of relative regions is very general. Its does not constrain the syntactic class of its constituents since it is used to handle not only cases of stand-alone adverbs but also landmark augmented adverbs and prepositional phrases. The problem that remains is how uncertainty about the frame of reference is spread, so that this construction can distribute its decision on the relative frame of reference to the place where this information is needed to compute the region, namely, the corresponding functional unit. The solution is to apply percolation through all intermediate processing steps. For instance, when parsing a frontal prepositional phrase, such as in *vor der Kiste von dir aus* ('in front of the box from your perspective'), the functional unit for *vor* first becomes a constituent of the frontal prepositional phrase *vor der Kiste*. Subsequently, the unit for the prepositional phrase becomes a constituent of the perspective-marked relative region phrase. Consequently, percolation is added to the angular-pp-phrase construction using an agreement macro (see Steels (2011a,b) for details).

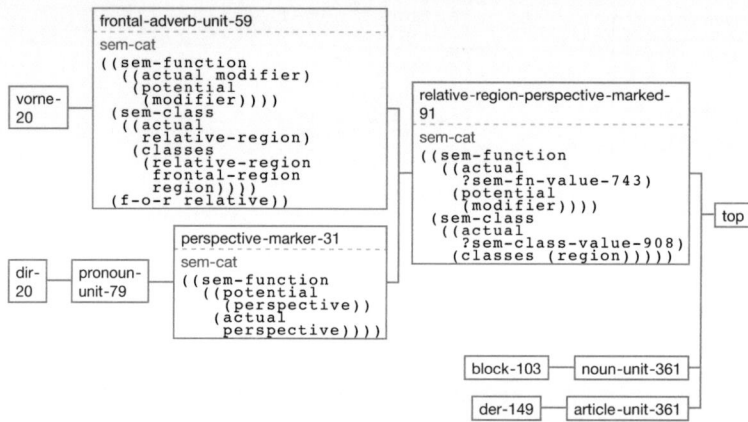

Figure 9.7: Transient structure after the application of the relative-region–perspective-marked construction (when parsing *der Block vorne von dir aus*). The f-o-r (frame of reference) sem-cat attribute of the frontal-adverb-unit-59 is set to relative and therefore determined.

(11)

```
(def-add-phrasal-agreement angular-pp-phrase
 (?relative-region-unit
  :sem-cat (f-o-r-value ?f-o-r-value)
 (?angular-pp-unit
  :sem-cat (f-o-r-value ?f-o-r-value)))
```

Similarly, this scheme has to be applied to landmark augmented adverbs in order for them to participate in these solutions.

Using a collection of techniques such as logic variables, percolation and a sem-sem of construction (that only operate on the semantic side), we are able to model the interaction of projective categories with perspective marking and their effects on semantic ambiguity pervasive in German locative phrases.

9.2.2 Semantic processing

The second part of handling semantic ambiguity is in interpretation. Let us consider the following phrase.

(12) der   Block   vor   der   Kiste
    the.NOM block.NOM front.PREP the.DAT box.DAT

    'The block in front of the box'

This phrase has an intrinsic and a relative reading. Consequently, FCG finds those two readings and passes them as potential solutions to IRL. The task engine splits in search which allows to trace each of the two interpretations separately (see Figure 9.8).

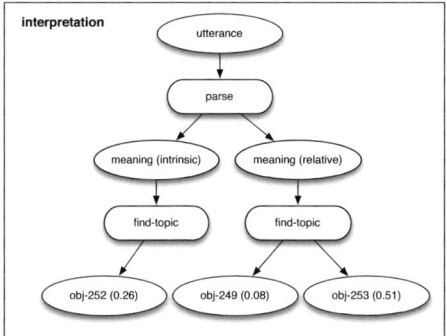

Figure 9.8: Interpretation of (12). In parsing, FCG finds two possible interpretations (relative and intrinsic). IRL is then called on each of these interpretations separately and recovers two possible conceptualizations for the relative reading. All three possible interpretations and their corresponding topics are scored. The hearer then decides that obj-253 is the best interpretation.

Suppose that a speaker uttered this phrase in the spatial scene shown in Figure 2.1 (which is repeated here in Figure 9.9) and he wants to refer to object obj-266 in his context (which is obj-253 in the hearer's context). In this scene there are at least three possible conceptualizations of the scene which are compatible with the information conveyed in the utterance. One is the intrinsic interpretation. The other two are variants of the relative interpretation. Relative conceptualizations of spatial scenes depend on perspective. The scene has two robots which both could in principle be used as perspective. IRL recovers all three conceptualizations of the scene. The hearer can then choose which of the interpretations is the best one (see Figure 9.10 for a depiction of the three possible interpretations and Figure 9.8 for an overview of processing). The final decision is based on the discrimination score of the three possible interpretations.

Figure 9.9: Example scene (same as in Figure 2.1).

In this particular configuration all three interpretations lead to different results. This is not always the case. There are three ways of dealing with semantic ambiguity.

- The speaker detects that the phrase would be ambiguous in re-entrance and chooses to avoid the problem by expressing himself differently.

- In some scenes even though a phrase might be highly ambiguous with many different interpretations, all of these interpretations refer to the same object. In this case disambiguation becomes unnecessary. An example where this happens are certain vertical relations for which intrinsic, absolute and relative interpretations often overlap (Carlson 1999).

- The speaker relies on the interpretation power of the hearer. This happened in the case study discussed in this section. For this particular scene the interaction was a success and the hearer correctly identified the topic.

Importantly, in all three cases agents rely on the power of IRL and FCG to deal with semantic ambiguity.

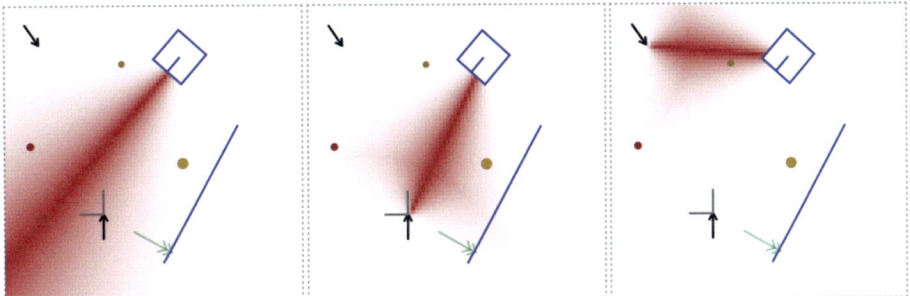

Figure 9.10: Possible interpretations of (12). From left to right (1) intrinsic interpretation, (2) relative from the perspective of the hearer, and (3) relative from the perspective of the speaker. All of these interpretations have different topics. The intrinsic representation evaluates to object obj-252, the relative interpretation from the hearer evaluates to obj-249, and the relative interpretation from the speaker to obj-253.

9.3 Discussion and results

We can now test the complete system and see how it performs on different spatial scenes. Figure 9.11 compares the average success of agents in varying environmental conditions. Agents play 20000 language games. After each of the games the success is measured. If the interaction was a success then a 1.0 is recorded, 0.0 otherwise. The German locative system is quite successful in the three conditions: "similar perspective", "no box landmark" and "many objects". In the first condition, the perspective of agents is similar and the number of objects is reasonable. The "no box landmark" condition is one where in every scene there are only the two robots available as landmarks. The third condition features varied perspective of the two robots on the scene. Most importantly, there are many objects in every scene in this condition . The system performs worst in the "many objects" condition, but overall copes well even with the complex "many objects" scenes.

These results suggest that the complete system works reliably and allows agents to talk about objects in their environment using German locative phrases and validates in some respect the reconstructed syntactic and semantic processing as well as the perception system. The results show the power of the whole systems approach. Success is high even in difficult scenes where humans would have trouble finding appropriate phrases.

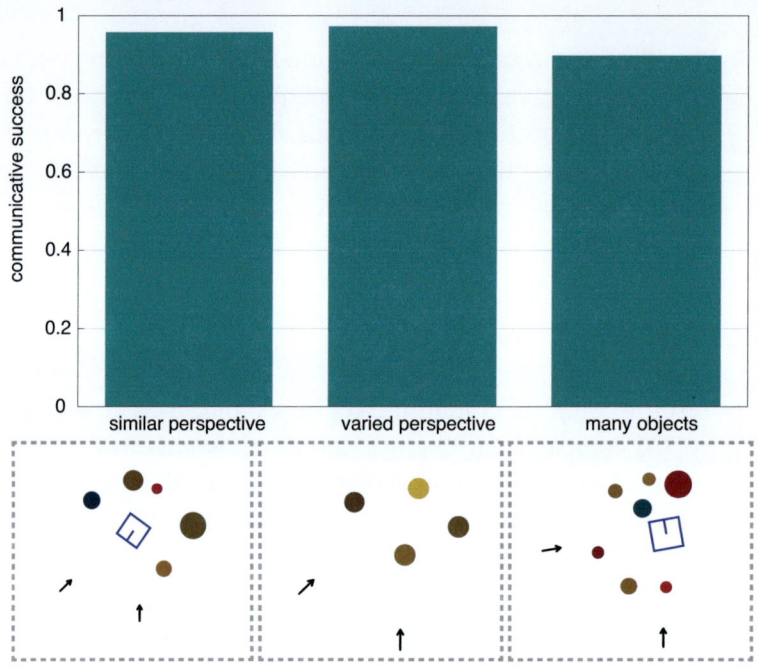

Figure 9.11: Average success of agents operating the German locative grammar and semantics in different spatial scenes.

Part III

Spatial language evolution

10 Evolution of basic spatial category systems

The first question that one can ask when approaching the general question for how spatial language evolved is how the basic building blocks of spatial language, in particular concepts and spatial relationships, arise and can become shared in populations of agents. This question is chiefly about the operators that organize the emergence and self-organization of spatial language systems. In a functional approach to language the semantic distinctions, i.e. the category system, as well as the syntactic distinctions, i.e. words and the syntactic structure, arise because they serve a particular function and contribute to fulfilling the communicative intentions of agents. Without doubt, the function of spatial language is to denote the spatial position of objects in spatial contexts. In order for agents to be able to reach their communicative goals they must be equipped with a set of learning operators and mechanisms that allow them to gradually become more and more successful in reaching their goals.

The learning mechanisms, their parameters and underlying categorization and conceptualization strategies are grouped into LANGUAGE STRATEGIES each of which is responsible for building a particular kind of language system. For instance, one can distinguish between the projective and proximal category system which each denote a specific set of words that have particular functions in syntax, e.g. in the grammatical structure of sentences. For instance, proximal relations are not expressed as adjectives, whereas projective relations can be expressed as adjectives. But in many ways their semantics also differ. While projective relations are denoting the position of objects using angles to some reference object (projective) and therefore are for instance relying on the frame of reference used, proximal relations denote the position of objects using distances. Language strategies are the operators that form language systems and I will explore in this section specific operators for building proximal, projective and absolute systems. But there are also language strategies which allow agents to build hybrid systems, and I will explore one strategy which forms projective and proximal systems at the same time. Lastly I consider mechanisms that allow different language strategies to co-exist.

In this chapter I focus entirely on lexical systems. I detail the cognitive architecture required for agents to learn and adapt their private representations with a specific focus on words and category distinctions as a prerequisite for studying grammatical development. I propose concrete learning mechanisms and their integration into the routine processing of spatial utterances. This chapter splits into two sections. In Section 10.1, I look at the necessary mechanisms that allow learners to pick up an existing language system from tutors that are operating a full language system. The insights presented in that section are a necessary precursor to Section 10.2, describing the formation of a language system.

Ideas and results presented in this chapter have been published in Spranger 2012b; 2013c.

10.1 Acquisition of lexical systems

Before we turn to the invention and formation of a language system, we will investigate mechanisms for the acquisition of lexical language. I call agents that initially have no spatial lexicon STUDENTS. Agents that know (parts of) the German locative lexicon are called TUTORS. In this section, I show how the right interaction setting, the right environment and the right cognitive machinery enable students to learn a complex lexical communication system from tutors.

10.1.1 Learning operators

The most important ingredient in the acquisition of a language system are the cognitive operations that allow agents to learn an established language from their peers. Besides the general capacity for parsing and production of language, conceptualization and interpretation, agents require learning operators that gradually change the internal representations of the learner agent so that he can become a successful participant in communicative encounters. A number of basic learning operations are needed for lexical systems. First, learners need ways to adapt their conceptual inventory which involves invention and shaping of spatial categories, and second, they need ways to adjust their linguistic repertoire, which involves the adoption of words and their association with concepts and categories conveyed by them.

So how does learning take place? Learning is deeply integrated into the cognitive architecture of agents. The activation of a particular learning operation depends on the state of the interaction, for instance, whether the interaction was successful, whether the speaker has already pointed to the topic, or on the particular state in linguistic processing as the learning operators draw on as much information as possible in order to constrain the learning situation. Agents constantly monitor the routine linguistic processing in production and interpretation and try to solve problems by applying adoption operators that invent a new category or adopt an unparsed string. But this is not enough. So-called alignment operators are updating the linguistic knowledge of an agent continuously after every interaction in order to gradually approximate the target system.

For now let us suppose learners are acquiring the German projective category system. Agents trying to acquire an existing language system foremost operate adoption mechanisms both on the semantic and syntactic level of processing. Upon encountering an unknown string in parsing, the learner detects a problem. For lexical category systems agents utter a single word and, hence, being unable to parse that word, the hearer gives up and the interaction necessarily fails. If that is the case, the speaker points to the object he intended to talk about which now leaves the hearer with enough information to adopt the word and associate it with some meaning. The actual learning process is divided into two parts. One is concerned with semantics and leads to the invention of a category. The second part is the association of the category with the single word in the utterance. Together they make up the adoption operation.

Let us suppose the tutor agent is equipped with the German projective lexical system and uttered the word *links* ('left') in context scene-3398065133 (see Figure 10.1 to follow this example). Furthermore, let us suppose the hearer, a student, has no knowledge of this word and, consequently, the interpretation process fails. The hearer then waits for the speaker to point to the topic. Upon observing the speaker point to the topic, the hearer *re-produces* for the now known topic. RE-PRODUCTION is a process by which agents try to fill in missing information in order to learn from the pieces of information available to them. Most importantly, the hearer *re-conceptualizes* a meaning for the topic, mirroring the speaker (see Figure 10.2). Because the agent does not yet have any spatial categories, re-conceptualize fails and no meaning is computed. To solve this problem the hearer invents a new category. The new category is directly based on the topic object. For projective categories, the direction vector of the new category is directly established from the direction the topic object lies in. When the hearer has invented the category he can conceptualize a meaning for the topic object and, subsequently, when trying to express it for himself in re-production, he fails, because this category is new and he has no construction covering it. At this moment, another repair strategy uses the conceptualized meaning and in particular the conceptualized category, as well as the fact that there was an

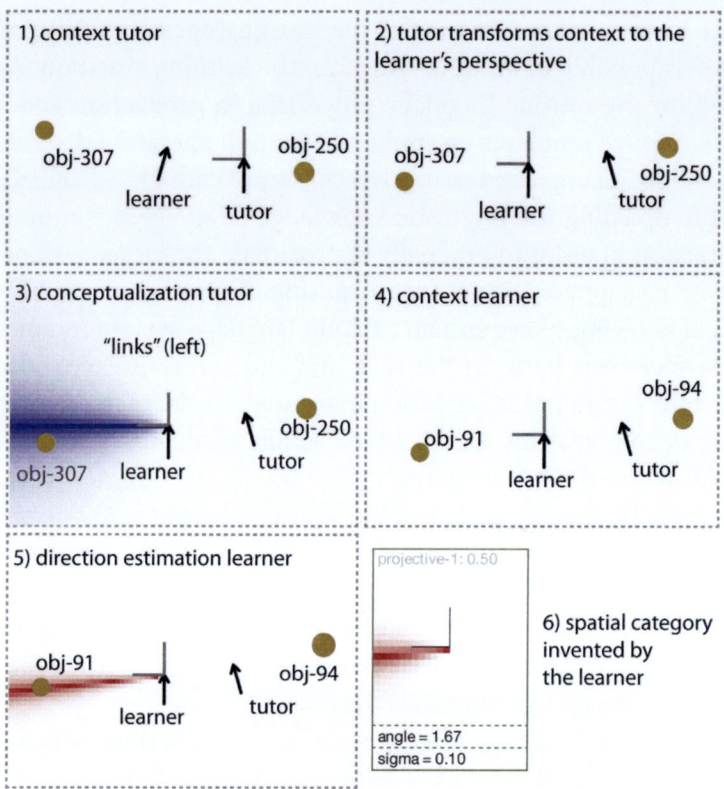

Figure 10.1: This figure details the adoption of an unknown string by a learner agent in interaction with a tutor agent. The tutor who is the speaker starts by conceptualizing for the topic object in his context (image 1). Here, obj-307 (obj-91 in the learner's context) is chosen as topic. In order to help the learner, the tutor conceptualizes a meaning for the topic from the perspective of the learner (image 2). For this particular topic and context the tutor finds the category left associated with the word *links* ('left') to be most discriminating (image 3). The speaker then utters the word to the learner, who himself has a particular view of the world (image 4). When this is the first interaction ever involving the word *links*, the learner does not know the word and the interaction fails. However, after the speaker pointed to the topic, the hearer can adopt the string and connect it to the newly invented projective category projective-1, which derives its angle value from the direction of the topic object (image 5). The initial σ is set to 0.1. This is a low value that focusses the category around the direction of the topic object (image 6).

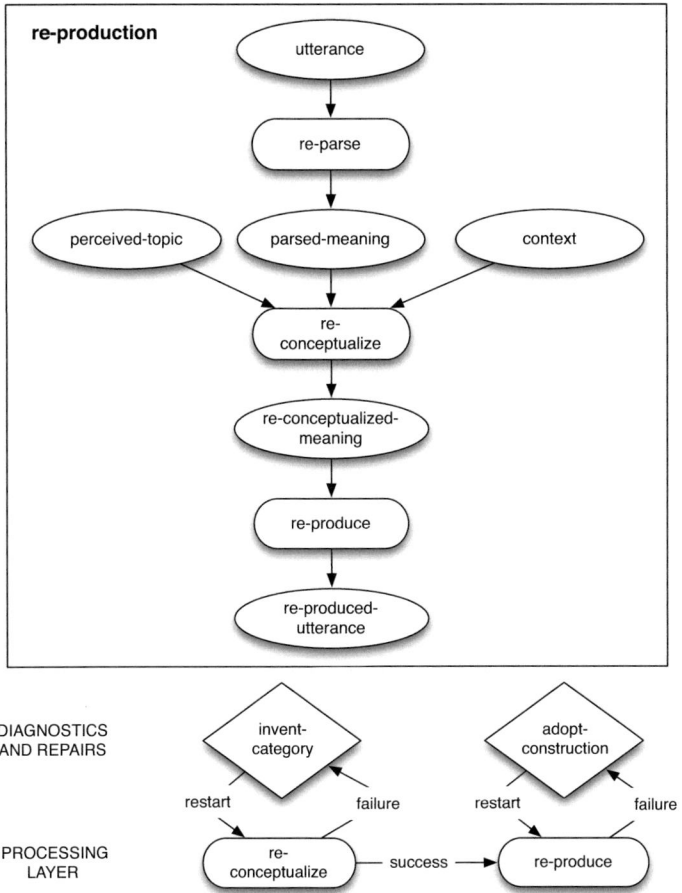

Figure 10.2: The top figure shows the processes that the hearer runs in re-production once it is clear that the interaction failed and the speaker pointed to the object (perceived-topic). The agent re-parses the utterance and re-conceptualizes based on the perceived-topic, the parsed-meaning and the context. Re-conceptualize is similar to both conceptualize (production) and find-topic (interpretation). It uses IRL to find semantic structure that is compatible with the semantic structure observed in the utterance and the topic. If re-conceptualize is unable to find a category distinction for discriminating the topic, this triggers the invent-category repair strategy (bottom figure) which fixes the problem by inventing a new category. Re-production continues by producing an utterance for the meaning (re-produce). If the meaning includes a new category this fails which triggers the adopt-construction repair.

unparsed string to create a new construction that links the category with the unparsed string (see Figure 10.3 for the new construction). After these two repairs operated, the learner ends up with one new category linked via the new construction to the word *links* ('left'). The new category is based on a single example of what the tutor agent equipped with the German projective system would call *links* ('left').

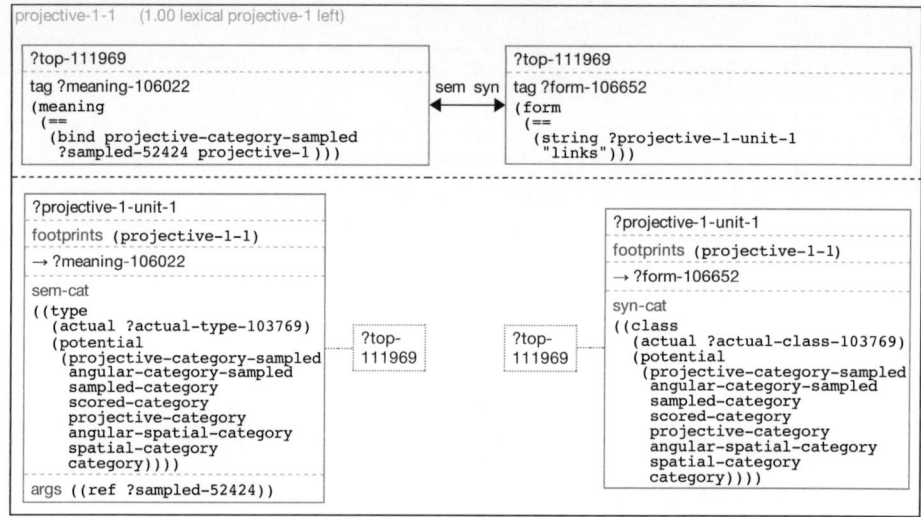

Figure 10.3: Construction invented by the repair `adopt-construction` which links the string *links* to the new category `projective-1`.

Adoption is necessarily based on a single example. Consequently, the category adopted by the hearer might be quite different or at least dissimilar to the category that the tutor used. Learners need a mechanisms that align the category representation of over many interactions with that of the target language system. Of course, the learner can never directly read out the category the tutor uses in communication, hence, the only possible source of data for learners are the samples of objects that the tutor names using the same word, that is to say, the topic objects in interactions in which one of the agents actually uses the concept associated with a particular string, for example, the word *links* ('left'). Category representations are updated in a continuous manner from interaction to interaction by adding samples and re-estimating the components of the representation. For projective categories, samples are used to re-estimate the prototypical direction by computing the mean direction vector of the samples using the following formula for averaging the angles of the samples S.

$$a_c = \left(\frac{1}{|S|} \sum_{s \in S} \sin a_s, \frac{1}{|S|} \sum_{s \in S} \cos a_s \right) \tag{10.1}$$

On top of that, the new σ value σ' which governs the shape of the similarity function is adapted using the following formula.

$$\sigma'_c = \sigma_c + \alpha_\sigma \cdot \left(\sigma_c - \sqrt{\frac{1}{|S| - 1} \sum_{s \in S} (a_c - a_s)^2} \right) \tag{10.2}$$

This formula describes how much the new σ_c of the category c is pushed in the direction of the angle standard deviation of the sample set by a factor of $\alpha_\sigma \in [0, \infty]$. Naturally, alignment and adoption operators have quite a number of parameters, for instance how many samples to consider, how eager to update the σ component using α_σ and so on and so forth. These parameters are typically quite robust and little to medium changes do not affect the overall performance of the system.

Alignment is not only important for re-estimating the category representation, but it also extends to all levels of semantic and syntactic processing. Every item in the inventory of an agent including every category and construction is scored. After each interaction scores of these items are updated by alignment operators based on the usage and communicative success. For lexical systems, the two important components are lexical constructions and categories. Student agents increase the score of successfully used constructions and categories and decrease the score if the item was used unsuccessfully. Constructions and categories with a score lower than or equal to 0 are removed from the inventory.

10.1.2 Experimental setup and measures

One can test the performance of the learning operators discussed above and their sufficiency for acquiring a language system by applying them in populations of two agents. One of the agents, the tutor agent, is equipped with a fully developed projective category system and corresponding lexical items. The second agent, the learner agent is equipped with the learning operators. Both agents are situated in the real world and are given the task to talk about objects in their environment in a spatial language game. The population continuously interacts over a number of interactions. Success, performance and development of the population are tracked with a variety of measures.

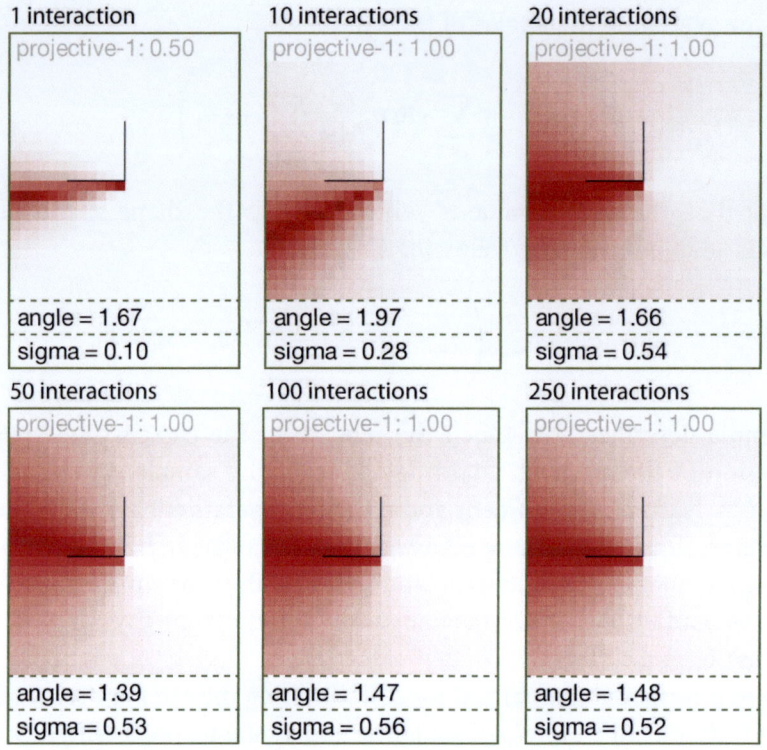

Figure 10.4: Development of the projective category whose initial adoption is depicted in Figure 10.1 over many interactions (after 1, 20, 50, 100 and 200 interactions). In the beginning the width of the category is narrow (small σ). Gradually its direction approaches the direction of the target category left and so does its σ (the target category's σ is 0.4).

Communicative Success Communicative success is the most important measure as it reflects the overall performance of the population. Every interaction is either a success or a failure. Success is counted as 1.0 and failure is counted as 0.0.

Number of Categories per Student This measure counts the number of categories known to student agents. Besides number of categories, number of constructions is an often used measure in acquisition experiments. But, since the number of categories is equal to the number of constructions, measuring the number of constructions is omitted for the acquisition experiments

Interpretation Similarity This measure tracks how similar the interpretation of each word known to the tutor is to that of the student. Technically this is measured by comparing the category the tutor links to a specific word to the category the student links to the same word. Since projective categories are described by a direction and a similarity function width parameter σ, two categories are most similar when both angle and σ are equal. The precise formula is based on the repertoire of words $W(a_{tut})$ known to the tutor a_{tut} and the similarity of the category $C(a_{tut}, w)$ the tutor associates with each word w to the category the learner a_{learn} associates with that word $C(a_{learn}, w)$

$$I(a_{tut}, a_{learn}) = \frac{1}{|W(a_{tut})|} \sum_{w \in W(a_{tut})} s\left(C(a_{learn}, w), C(a_{tut}, w)\right)$$

If the learner has no category associated with a particular word w, i.e., when $C(a_{tut}, w)$ does not find a category, the similarity is 0. If, however, the learner has some projective category associated with the word, then s is defined as follows.

$$s(c, c') = e^{-\frac{1}{2}(a_c - a'_c)^2 \frac{2}{\sigma_c + \sigma'_c}}$$

To be sure that this approach to acquisition works reliably, acquisition is not only tested in a single population, but multiple experiments are run in which learners have to acquire the lexical systems of the tutors. In every interaction between a tutor and a learner certain choices are random. Which agent is speaker? Which agent is hearer? Which object is topic? These are all choices that are made using a random number generator. Particular choices may or may not favor the acquisition of the lexical system by the learner. To account for such effects, 25 experiments are run in parallel, each starting with a student which initially knows no categories, no words and no constructions linking them. The progress of each such run is measured simultaneously, and, finally, all results are collected and the measures are averaged over the 25 runs.

10.1.3 Results

Interestingly enough, the basic mechanisms for adoption and alignment are sufficient to get a learner agent to acquire the German projective category system from a tutor. Figure 10.5 shows the results of 25 populations each consisting of one tutor and one student averaged over 250 successive interactions. Clearly,

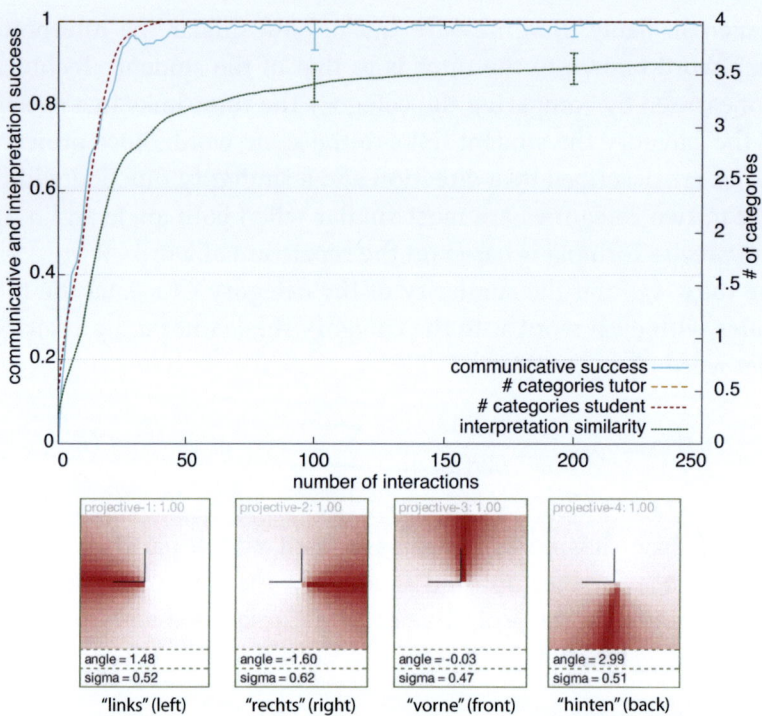

Figure 10.5: The top figure shows the dynamics of acquisition experiments over many interactions (25 runs averaged) in which a learner is trying to acquire the projective language system from a tutor. Agents quickly reach communicative success (the base line experiment of tutors communicating reaches 98% success for the same data set). After roughly 25 interactions, all categories and their corresponding strings have been adopted (the number of categories approaches 4). In the remaining interactions the alignment operator drives the interpretation similarity towards 1.0 (which is the highest value and signifies total overlap between the categories of the tutor and the learner). Interestingly, communicative success correlates with the number of categories of the student more than it does with interpretation similarity. This shows that agents do not need perfectly aligned categories to be able to communicate successfully. The bottom figure shows the categories acquired by a learner in one particular population of an acquisition experiment and to which strings they are linked. The resulting categories are very similar to the projective categories given to the tutor.

the learner agent is able to increase its communicative ability while adopting the lexical system of the tutor agent, which manifests in the increase in average communicative success over interactions which progressively approaches the value of 1. Two tutors interacting on the same data set interact successfully in 98% of the cases, which makes for a *baseline* communicative success of 1.0. So we can conclude that the learner easily acquires similar communicative abilities. These positive developments are on the one hand a result of successful adoption of words and categories, but on the other hand, they are due to the alignment operators that gradually push the categories of the learner agent to become more and more similar with those of the tutor which can be seen with the increase in interpretation similarity. Lastly, one can check the number of categories acquired which gradually approaches the number of categories in the target language system.

10.1.3.1 Acquisition of the proximal system

Similar learning operators are sufficient for learners to acquire the German proximal spatial category system. The only difference is that the learning operators are adapted to proximal categories. So, for instance, instead of using the direction of the topic object as a seed for a new category, its distance is used (Figure 10.6 details the process). Consequently, the alignment operators are also adjusted to use the average distances of samples and to update the σ of the categories using distances of sample objects.

$$d_c = \frac{1}{|S|} \sum_{s \in S} d_s \qquad (10.3)$$

$$\sigma'_c = \sigma_c + \alpha_\sigma \cdot \left(\sigma_c - \sqrt{\frac{1}{|S| - 1} \sum_{s \in S} (d_c - d_s)^2} \right) \qquad (10.4)$$

Furthermore, the adoption operator for constructions linking an invented proximal category to an observed string is the same as for projective category acquisition. We can test the performance of the learning operators using a population of agents where one agent, the tutor, is equipped with the German proximal system, and the other agent, the learner, starts without any knowledge of the system and is given proximal category adoption and alignment operators to acquire the system from the tutor. Figure 10.7 details results for proximal categories. The graph shows that the acquisition and alignment operators enable the learner to quickly pick up the two projective categories. Interpretation similarity also quickly rises;

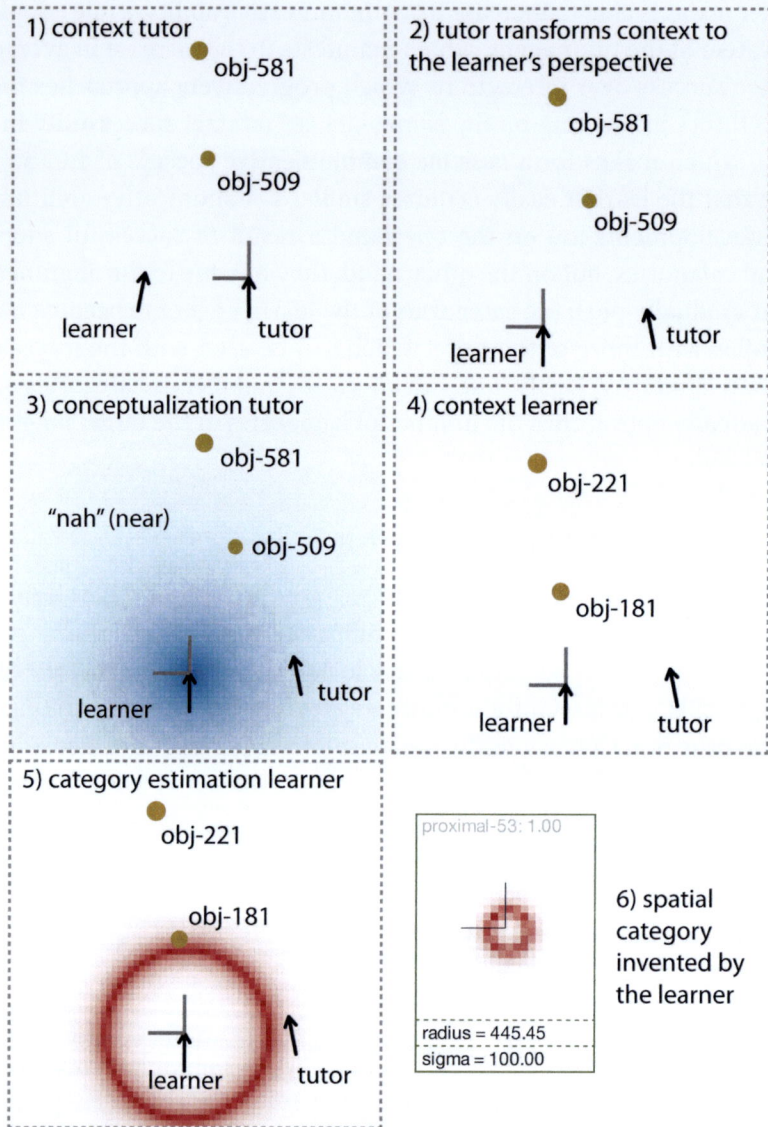

Figure 10.6: Acquisition of a single proximal category. The sequence of steps are the same as for projective categories. However, since the the tutor is equipped with proximal categories, he conceptualizes a proximal category for the topic object (obj-181 in his context). In contrast to the projective case, the learner uses the distance of the topic object (obj-181 in his context) to build the new category.

however, it stays low and does not approach 1.0 as in the case of projective categories. If one looks at the resulting categories of one particular run (bottom
Figure 10.7), one can easily see the reason for this. First, both the distance prototype of the proximal category associated to the word *nahe* ('near') as well as
the distance prototype associated with the word *fern* ('far') do not have the same
values as the corresponding tutor categories, which have been setup with 0.0 for
near and 2000.0 for far. Second, the σ values for these categories also do not overlap sufficiently (σ values in tutor categories are equal to 1000.0). The reason for
this is the distribution of objects in the spatial scenes used in the experiments. No
object is ever further away than about 1500.0 mm and no object is so close to any
of the robots as to approach a distance of 0.0. So the alignment operator has no
chance of picking up values even close to the ones set in the tutor categories. The
categories acquired by the learner, in other words, accurately reflect the actual
distribution of objects in the spatial scenes rather than the values picked for the
tutor. Nevertheless, learner and tutor are capable of communicating successfully
after the system stabilizes.

10.1.3.2 Acquisition of the absolute system

The last group of categories in the German language system discussed in this
book are absolute categories like `north` and `east` and so forth. Again, the learning
operators are adapted to be specialized on the acquisition of absolute categories,
which are very similar to projective categories in that they focus on the angular dimension (the same formulas apply). The only real difference to projective
categories is that absolute categories are applied slightly differently by taking
the global reference into account. Figure 10.8 details the acquisition of a single
absolute category and results of acquisition are shown in Figure 10.9. One can
conclude that acquisition of absolute categories is easily established using the
learning operators suggested.

10.1.3.3 Co-acquisition of lexical systems

In all the above experiments, learners were acquiring a single category type, e.g.,
either projective, proximal or absolute. This entails that learners upon hearing
a new term could be absolutely sure about the category type the speaker used
for conceptualizing reality. The problem with this approach is, of course, that
this is rarely ever the case in acquisition and the learner never knows what type
of category he is supposed to acquire based solely on the word he is observing.
So the challenge remains as to how learners can acquire a complete system of

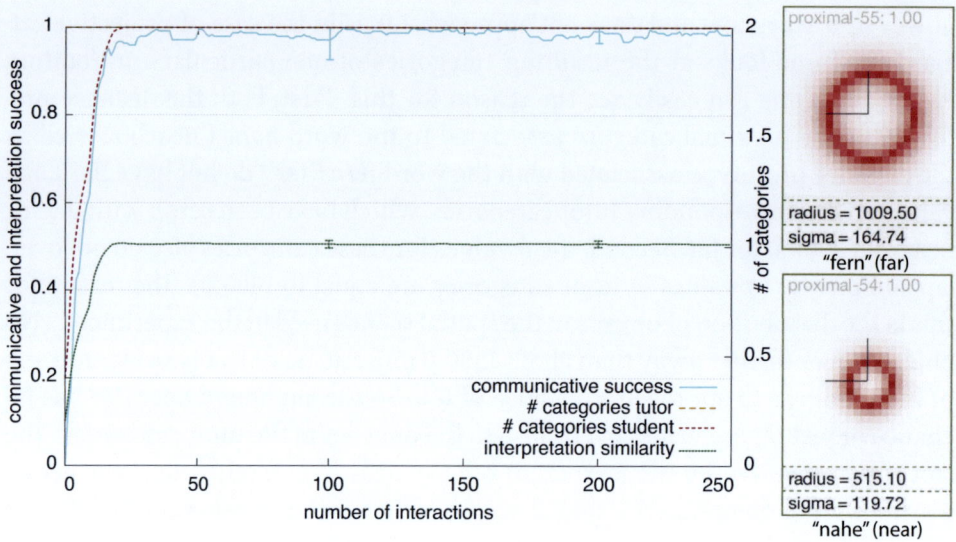

Figure 10.7: This figure shows the dynamics of acquisition experiments over many interactions (25 runs averaged, left image) in which the tutor possess a proximal language system. Agents quickly reach communicative success (the base-line experiment of tutors communicating reaches 98% success for the same data set). To the right, categories acquired by a learner in one particular run of such an acquisition experiment are shown.

spatial categories including proximal, projective and absolute categories at the same time.

One idea is to endow the learner with additional machinery. What if the learner has the ability to make a best guess on what type of category he should learn based on discriminative power (see Steels 1997 for similar ideas). In other words, the learner should choose the particular category type based on the current context, the topic object and, in particular, based on the discriminative power of each category type in the current situation. It turns out, that we can easily use this insight to enhance the system. Instead of inventing a single category, the learner invents three categories one for each category type and in re-conceptualization chooses the category which *maximizes discriminative power*. In other words he chooses the category with the highest discrimination score. It is this category which survives the competition with the other two and it will be associated with the observed string using a newly invented construction, while

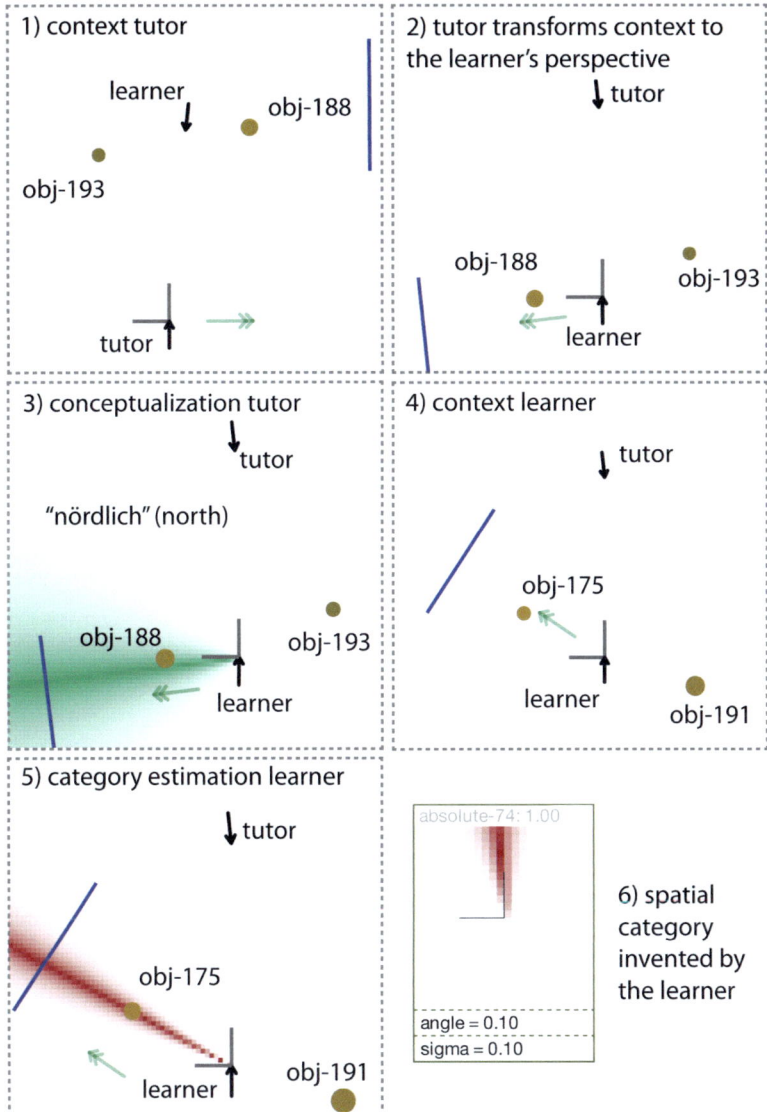

Figure 10.8: Acquisition of a single absolute category. The steps are the same as for projective and proximal categories, but the tutor conceptualizes using absolute categories which implies that he needs to take into account the direction to the global reference (green arrow). Consequently, the learner uses the direction to the topic object (here obj-188 in the tutor's context and obj-175 in the learner's context) given the global direction to build a new category.

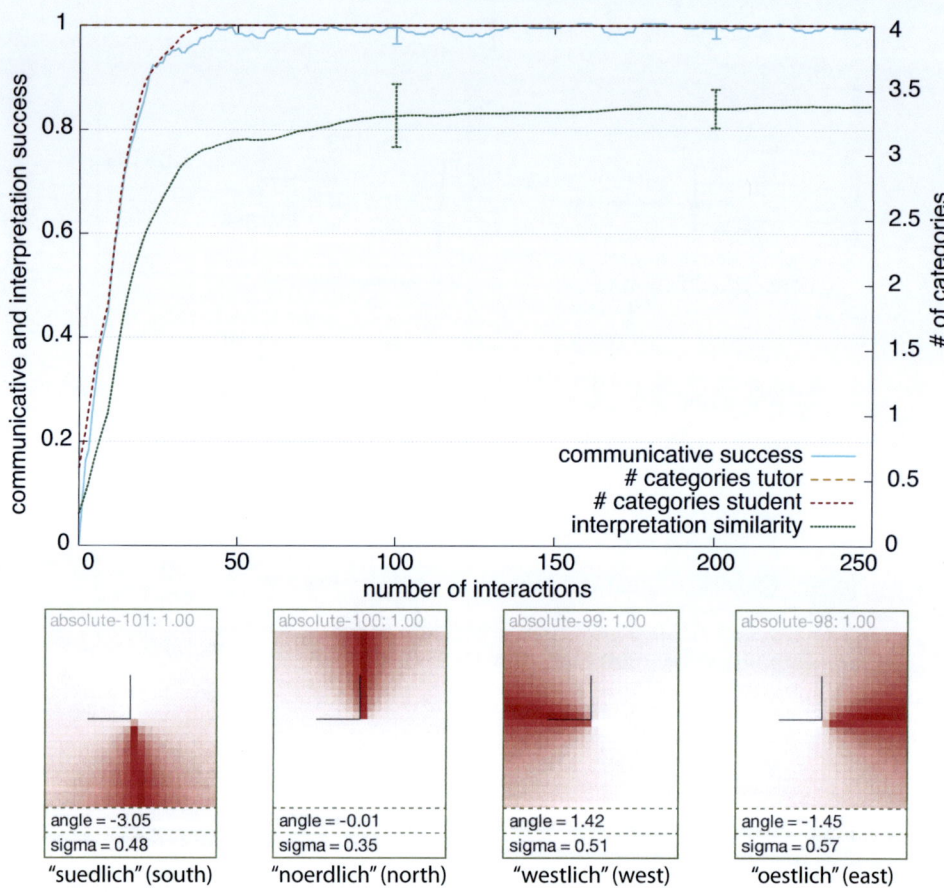

Figure 10.9: This figure shows the dynamics of absolute category acquisition experiments over many interactions (25 runs averaged, left image). Agents quickly reach communicative success (the base-line experiment of tutors communicating reaches 98% success for the same data set). The bottom figures show the categories acquired by a learner in one particular run of such an acquisition experiment. The interpretation similarity develops comparably to the projective case.

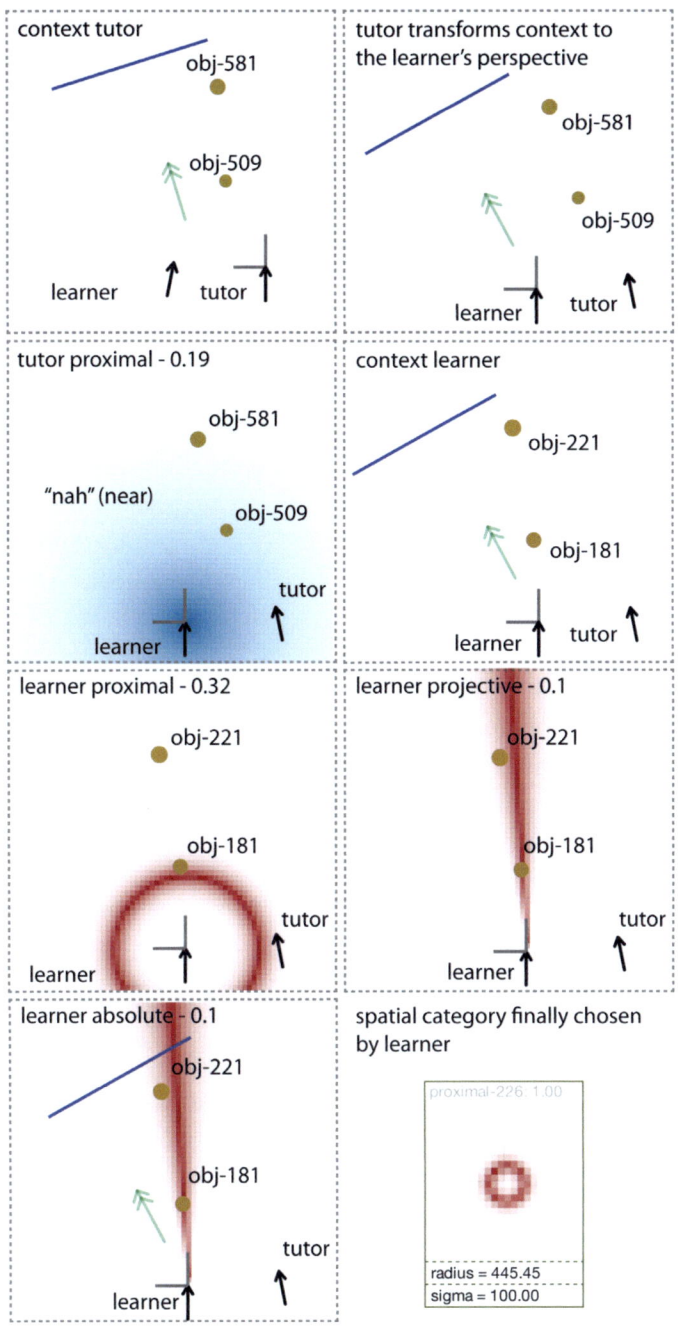

Figure 10.10: Inference in re-conceptualization

the losers will be removed. Figure 10.10 gives an example of the process (Figure 10.11 sketches the implementation). In the example of the figure the tutor used the projective category near to conceptualize for the topic obj-509 (in his context). The learner invents three different categories one proximal, one projective and one absolute and uses them to re-conceptualize for the topic (obj-175 in his context). The proximal category has the highest discrimination score 0.32 and is, consequently, chosen by him as the seed for the projective category linked to the word *nahe* ('near').

The use of discrimination, fundamentally, rests on exploiting conceptualization as an inference process. The best of the three different possible category types is chosen based on what is the most plausible category given that the tutor also choose the category based on the principle of maximizing discriminative power. Figure 10.12 shows results both for an acquisition experiment where the tutor is equipped with proximal and projective categories at the same time and for a population in which the tutor is equipped with absolute and proximal categories at the same time. In both cases the dynamics of acquisition are comparable to the single category type cases, although reaching the baseline success takes longer due to the increased number of categories. Learners quickly pick up the categories and are able to communicate successfully. Hence, the inference in conceptualization based on discrimination scores is successful.

However, in certain combinations of category types using the principle of maximizing discriminative power has limits. Figure 10.13 shows a case where the target language system given to the tutor has both projective and absolute categories. We can observe that the learner is unable to achieve similar communicative success as in all other cases of acquisition discussed in this chapter. Second, learners also cannot advance in establishing interpretation similarity. Third, the categories acquired by the learner are of the wrong type, as for example, *westlich* ('west') was acquired as a projective category rather than as an absolute one and *rechts* ('right') was adopted as absolute rather than projective category. Why is that? A key to the answer can be found in Figure 10.10. The problem is that in contexts where there is a global reference the learner upon hearing a new word has no means to decide on whether a projective or absolute category was used. In the example described in that figure, both the invented absolute and the invented projective category have the same discrimination score, because both exclusively rely on the angle to the topic object. Now, the angle to the topic object for both absolute and projective category may be different in numerical value for the invented absolute and projective categories, but their discriminative power is the same (0.11 in the case described by the figure). In other words, the discrimination

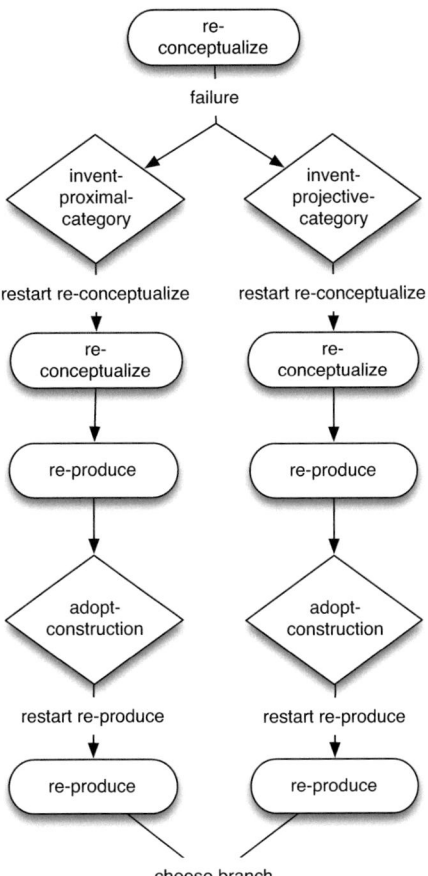

Figure 10.11: Schematic flow of control when `re-production` branches to track different possible inventions. If there is a failure in *re-conceptualize* and the agent is equipped with different strategies for solving this problem, the processing splits into two branches. Here, the `invent-proximal-category` learning operator (part of the proximal language strategy) and the `invent-projective-category` learning operator (part of the projective language strategy) both apply to fix the problem. Consequently, in each branch different categories are invented and different constructions that link each category to the utterance are adopted. At the end of processing the branch with the overall maximum score is chosen and the categories and constructions of that task are saved by the agent.

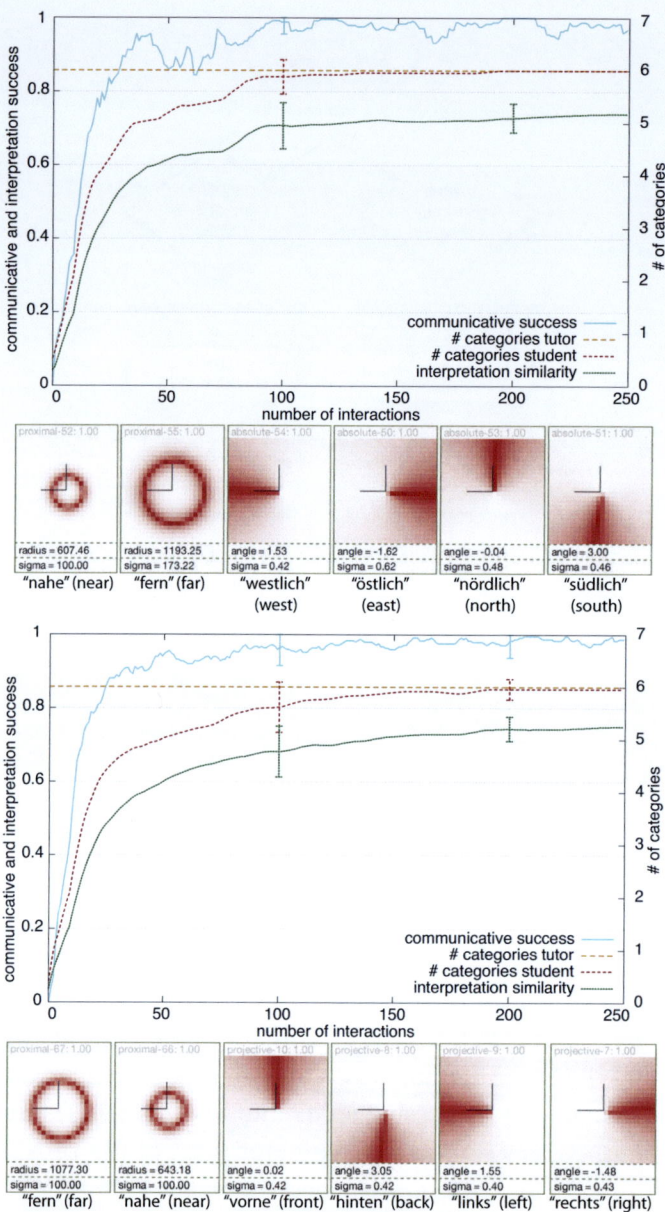

Figure 10.12: Results for two types of acquisition experiments using inference. One in which the tutor is equipped with proximal and projective categories (top) and one where the tutor is given proximal and absolute categories (bottom).

score does not distinguish between both the absolute and the projective systems in the same way as it does for the difference of both to the proximal category.

The reason why this problem appears in the particular constellation of this chapter is, of course, that both absolute and projective categories compete for the same angular dimension. If, for instance, the absolute categories would focus on a different angular dimension then the projective ones this problem would not occur. Consider the example of *über* ('above') and *unter* ('below'), which have a predominantly absolute reading, but they focus on a different direction than their horizontal counterparts. In this case the problem does not appear and discrimination could do its job. Similarly, if there would be a strong tendency or bias in the population to use a certain type of category if applicable, the problem can also be alleviated. For the case discussed in this section one can for instance add a bias to all agents to prefer to use absolute categories over other ones if a global reference licensing their application is available. Figure 10.14 shows the results of an experiment in which all agents are equipped with such a bias. The difference to the non-biased case in Figure 10.13 is obvious. Agents with bias can easily pick up the language system of their tutors. Biasing points to an additional layer of complexity which will be discussed in much more detail in the coming sections. The bias for absolute conceptualizations is implemented by boosting particular semantic structure used in conceptualization. Categories in conceptualization are always part of some semantic structure that applies them to the current context. These structures are necessarily different for different kinds of categories. A fact that I hinted at already in much more detail in Section 8. To introduce a bias, consequently, means to score semantic structure used for applying absolute categories to the current context higher than those for projective and proximal categories. Semantic structure, in particular, the operations used in conceptualization are themselves subject to acquisition and formation something which is discussed in more detail in later sections.

10.1.3.4 Hybrid systems

Another extent in which all previous acquisition experiments are equal is that in all of them learners are equipped with very particular mechanisms for each category type. A learner, for instance, in the case of a full language system encompassing absolute, projective and proximal categories is equipped with a separate learning mechanism for each category type. Let us for a moment put aside the problem of discriminating between projective and absolute categories and focus only on the case of proximal and projective categories. The assumption that there is a separate learning operator for each of these two in acquisition

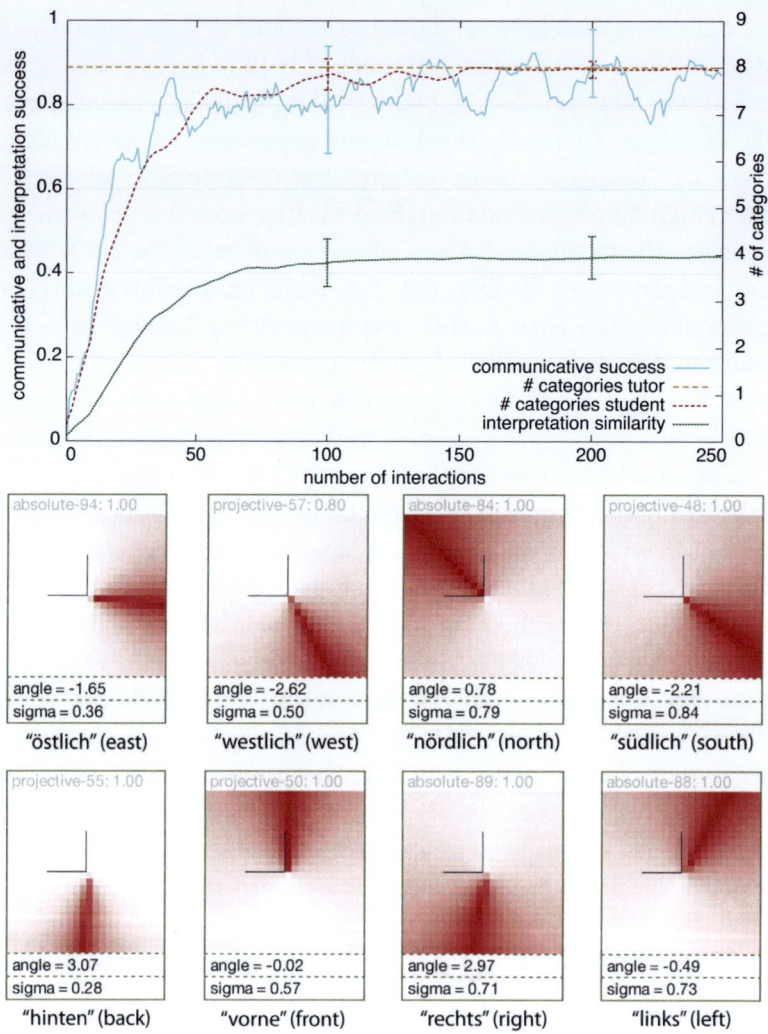

Figure 10.13: Results for an acquisition experiment in which learners face the German projective and absolute language system at the same time. Learners have no means of determining the strategy, and therefore have to guess the strategy behind each word. The system that learners acquire differs from the tutor systems quite substantially, the estimated categories have few similarities with their target, and they are also of the wrong type (e.g. *südlich* ('south') is learned as a projective category). Communicative success remains surprisingly high. However, a success rate of 80% is low in comparison with other acquisition experiments.

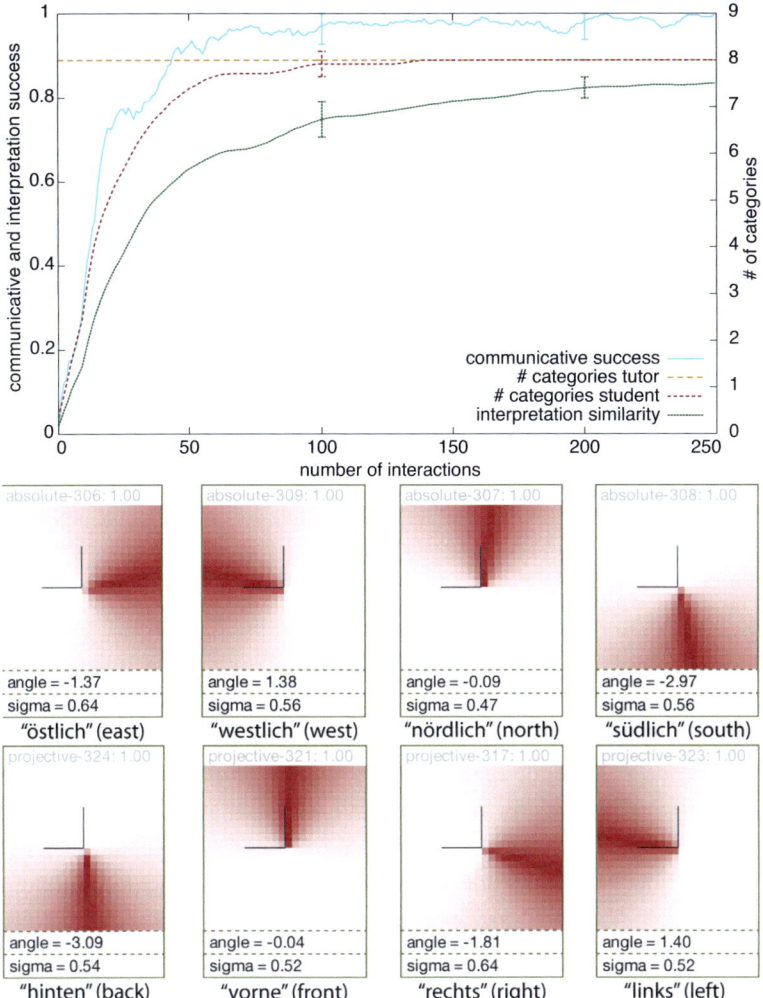

Figure 10.14: Results for an acquisition experiment where learners face both a projective and absolute system at the same time. In contrast to the results shown in Figure 10.13, agents are equipped with a strong preference for the absolute strategy. If the environment has absolute features agents prefer absolute conceptualizations of the spatial scene. Consequently, upon observing a new word in a context where absolute features are available, learners will adopt the word as part of an absolute language strategy. Based on the bias, learners successfully and correctly acquire the complete system.

is an assumption that can be questioned, based on the grounds that it presupposes the existence of learning operators for each particular input dimension,
namely distance and angle. In this section I propose a mechanism in which such
a bias for clear-cut channel distinctions is not given to a learner prior to acquiring the language system, but in which the channel focus of certain categories
is autonomously established by the learner. The mechanism consists, first, of a
representation that encompasses both distance and angle sensory channels and,
second, an alignment mechanism for both distance and angle channels in categories. The new category type is called PROXIMAL-ANGULAR and is essentially a
combination of the proximal and the angular category type. It consists of two
channel values, distance d and angle a, as well as corresponding sigma values
for each channel (σ_a and σ_d). The similarity sim of some object to a particular
proximal-angular category is computed as the product of angle and distance similarity.

$$\text{sim}(l, c) \quad := \quad \text{sim}_a(l, c) \cdot \text{sim}_d(l, c) \tag{10.5}$$

In the above formula sim_a is the similarity defined for angular categories (see
Equation 6.1) and sim_d is defined as the similarity for proximal categories (see
Equation 6.3).

The category representation, thus, does not really introduce something new
apart from the combination of two known representations. The similarity in
representation carries over to the invention operator which is a combination of
the invention operator for angular and proximal categories (see Figure 10.15 for
an example of the acquisition of a single proximal-angular category). When a
proximal-angular category is invented by the learner it does not cover just a particular channel. In fact, the invented category covers a small area both in angle
and distance around the topic object. How the category develops after it has
been invented is essentially a matter of the kind of objects which are successfully conceptualized and interpreted using the category. The alignment operator
after each interaction adds more samples to the category and recomputes the
distance d and the distance sigma σ_d exactly like for proximal categories (see
Equations 10.3 and 10.4) and the angle a and the angle sigma σ_a as for projective
categories (see Equations 10.1 and 10.2). Consequently, if more distance variation
is acceptable in the topic objects, the category's σ_d (the distance channel sigma)
can widen, in other words, the category is more discriminating in the angle direction. Vice versa, if topic objects are more angle varied then the category can
develop into a more distance discriminating category. Figure 10.16 shows how
the category whose adoption is shown Figure 10.15 exemplarily develops over
time.

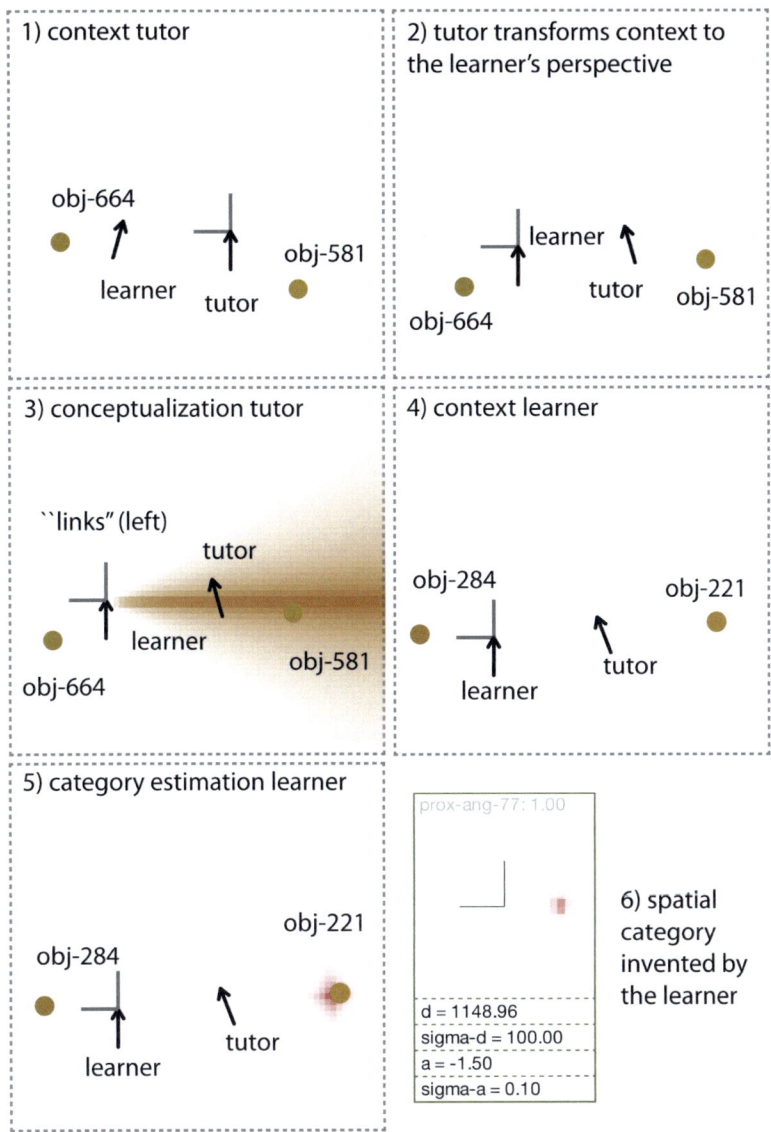

Figure 10.15: Acquisition of a single proximal-angular category. The steps are the same as for proximal, projective and absolute category adoption, except for the resulting category which is focussed around the topic object (obj-581 in the tutor's context and obj-221 in the learner's context) both in terms of angle and direction. Initial sigma values both for the angular and the distance dimension (σ_d and σ_a) are small.

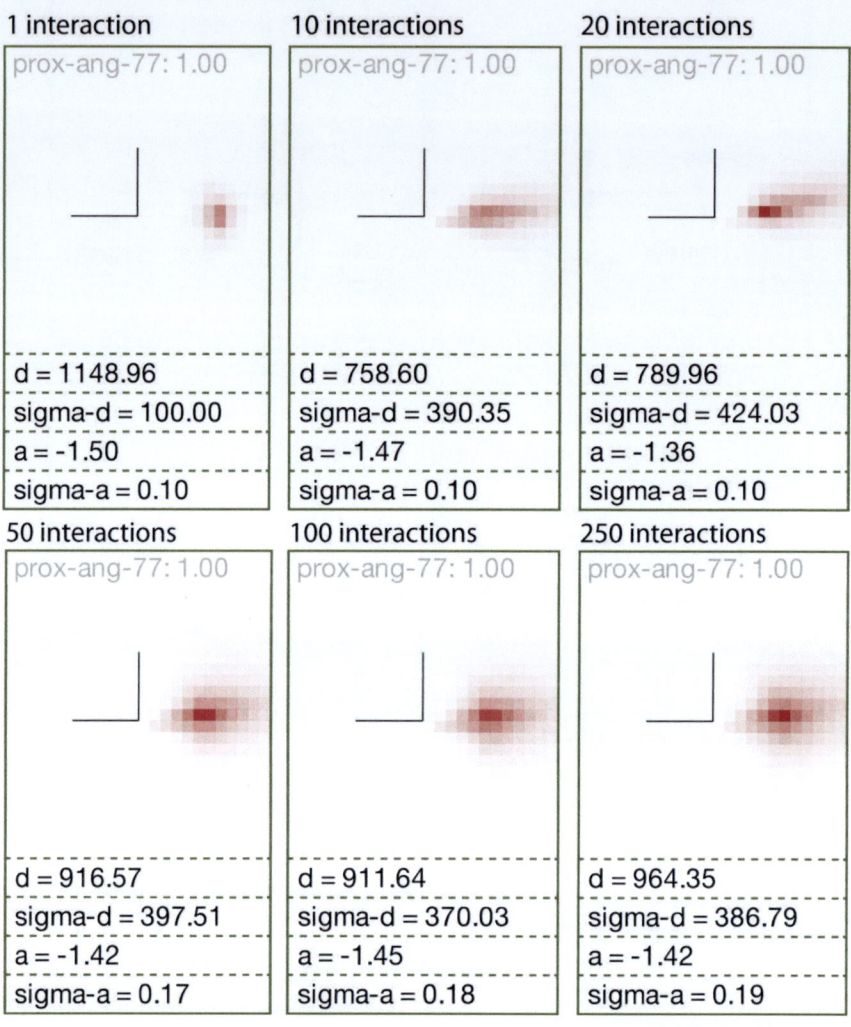

Figure 10.16: Development of a single proximal-angular category over time (see Figure 10.15 for the initial invention of that category). Over the course of many interactions this category which is linked to the word *links* ('left') develops into a category which resembles more and more the projective category left. The activation area is spread out in the distance dimension and more narrow in the angular dimension signified by a low σ_a value and a high σ_d value.

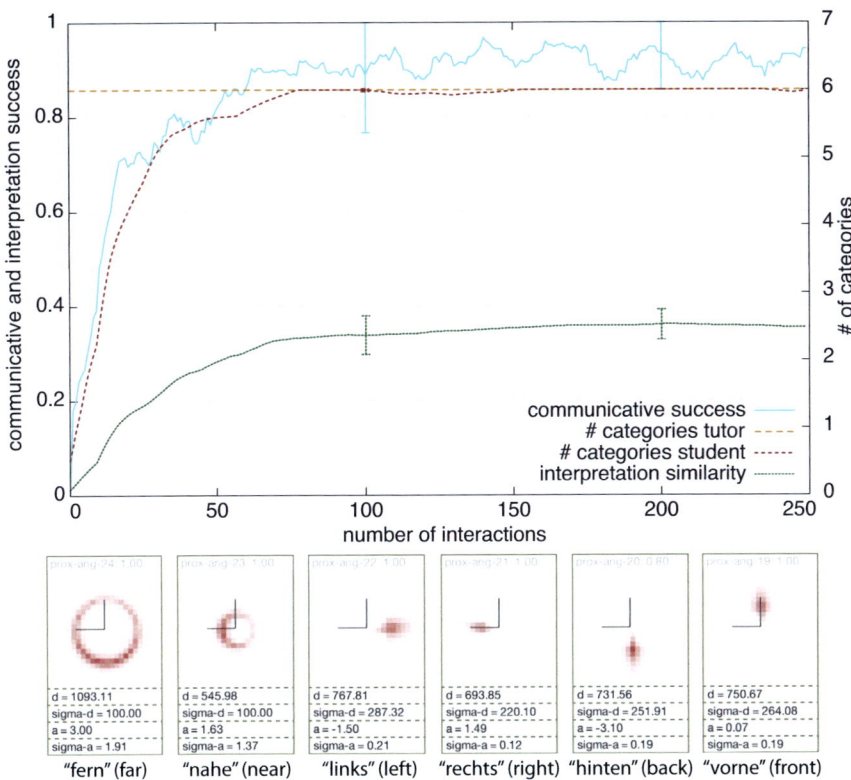

Figure 10.17: Results for proximal-angular acquisition experiments in which the tutor is given proximal and projective categories (25 runs averaged). Learners are equipped with proximal-angular category invention and alignment operations. Communicative success is more varied than in the case for single category acquisition. Nevertheless, agents manage to learn words and category mappings, but the shape of the categories, i.e., their preferred activation, mirrors the categories given to tutors. Overall, interpretation similarity stays rather low which is mostly due to the differences in distance and sigma distance of the acquired categories. The reason is the same as for proximal acquisition and lies in the distribution of object distances in the spatial scenes. The most important fact about interpretation similarity is that it stabilizes over time.

Figure 10.17 shows the results for acquisition experiments with proximal-angular categories. The tutor in these experiments is simultaneously equipped with the German proximal and projective system. The learner is given adoption and alignment operators for proximal-angular categories. Overall communicative success stays slightly lower than in comparable experiments (for instance, Figure 10.12 for acquisition of proximal and projective categories). However, the task is also slightly more difficult as agents have to acquire not only the mean values for distance *and* angle of a category, but also their distributional properties in the two sensory channels.

The way that the proximal-angular categories are implemented presupposes a particular way of applying the angular component. In the experiments discussed in this section the angular component was implemented to mirror projective categories. Technically speaking, one could have also chosen to use proximal-angular categories with an angular component that operates like an absolute category by taking into account the global features of the environment. Consequently, the problem of learning the absolute system at the same time as the projective system was left unexamined. In fact, the reasons for why this is even a problem apply just as drastically as they did before. Better answers will be given later sections.

10.1.4 Implementation details

In the above description I have glossed over some of the technical details. Specifically I have not explained how precisely the different conceptualization strategies are implemented. This section presents a simplified approach to spatial conceptualization which will gradually be extended in the next chapters to reach the full semantic complexity needed for spatial language. Figure 10.18 shows the IRL-network used to implement the projective and the proximal strategy. The cognitive operations `identify-object-proximal` and `identify-object-projective` implement the different categorization strategies. They are applied to an input set which for the learner is just the spatial context introduced by `get-context`. These operations are not only used by the tutor to apply German spatial relations, but they also serve the learner in invention.

Semantic Operation   IDENTIFY-OBJECT-PROXIMAL

---

description   Applies a proximal category to an input set and extracts the object with the highest discrimination score.

arguments	?identified-object (of type object)
	?source-set (of type entity-set)
	?category (of type proximal-category)

Semantic Operation IDENTIFY-OBJECT-PROJECTIVE

description	Applies a projective category to an input set and extracts the object with the highest discrimination score.
arguments	?identified-object (of type object)
	?source-set (of type entity-set)
	?category (of type projective-category)

10.2 Lexicon formation

From the acquisition of a lexical language system to the autonomous formation of a lexical language it is only a small step. In fact, in many ways the whole process of adopting a particular lexical item is already one of invention because learners invent categories based on the topic object and the current context followed by the invention of constructions that link some observed word to the invented category. Consequently much of the machinery for acquisition can be used for formation, the only difference being that the word to which a category is linked via a construction is not perceived by a learner but itself invented by agents. However, while there are some striking similarities, there are also some important differences. The most important of which is that formation is necessarily happening in a population of agents that is larger than two agents. This puts particular pressure on alignment operations as different words might pop up in a population for the same concept, but also since the categories themselves can diverge into different corners of the conceptual space within the population. All of this is caused by the fact that all interactions of agents are local involving always only two agents of the population. Any kind of agreement two agents reach, whether it is to use a certain word or to apply a certain category, consequently, requires adoption and alignment across the population.

When forming a language system, speakers, at least in the beginning, lack the proper categories to conceptualize reality and/or the proper linguistic means to express themselves. For instance, when an agent encounters an object that he cannot discriminate the categories known to him, the interaction fails. Now if no one in the population ever does anything about this problem, there will obviously be no communication. Hence, in contrast to acquisition where the learner being unable to conceptualize can wait until he picks up new semantic distinctions from the tutor, speakers in forming a language system are forced to resolve their problems by inventing distinctions themselves. The learning operators used in formation, however, are not that different from acquisition. Given some topic object, speakers are given the ability to invent a category comparable to the cases discussed in acquisition in Section 10.1. If there is a problem diagnosed in conceptualization, for instance, if the speaker cannot discriminate the topic object or he cannot discriminate it enough, i.e. the discrimination score of the best conceptualized meaning is too low, he can repair the problem by creating a new category based on the topic object. This solves his problem in conceptualization. If he then goes on to try and produce an utterance for the newly created category, he will face the problem that he has no means to express himself. The category was just invented and, hence, there are no constructions linked to the category yet. He resolves this problem by applying another repair strategy that of inventing a new word together with a lexical construction that links the new category with the new word. Given that the hearer is equipped with the same operators as learners in acquisition, he can pick up both the newly invented word, as well as invent a category that is very similar to the one of the speaker.

After such an interaction, two agents of the population have reached consensus about how to name a particular direction or distance, but this knowledge is still local to the two agents that have participated in the interaction. The newly invented string as well as the category now have to stand the test of time and they have to become adopted and shared in the population. The process of alignment on the population level is one in which the category can undergo change and adoption by agents in the population. It is particularly important to realize that in contrast to acquisition the target system is not fixed, in fact, it is unclear what the target system is and agents can freely develop the system and adapt it to their needs. The most important issue when adapting a language system is then, besides finding a suitable set of category distinctions and words to denote these distinctions, is to reach consensus on the population level. Alignment works on all levels of processing. The score of categories and constructions used in conceptualization or interpretation is updated based on the success of the interaction. The shape of categories used in production and interpretation is updated by adding another sample and re-estimating the particular distance or angle of the category (same as described in Section 10.1).

10.2.1 Experimental setup

I test the validity of this approach to formation by running experiments in which typically 10 agents start without any categories and constructions and gradually have to solve their communicative problems by invention and adoption of linguistic and semantic material. A set of measures tracks the progress of the population in establishing a communication system. The measures are the same as for acquisition (communicative success, number of categories and interpretation similarity), except that the average *number of constructions* in the population is also tracked, because the mapping between categories and constructions is not necessarily one to one due to synonymy. Also, the number of categories is not separately tracked for tutors and students but averaged across the population, because the distinction into tutor and learner agents does not exist in formation experiments. Every agent has the same capacity to invent and adopt constructions and categories. Consequently, the interpretation similarity measure is averaged over all agents and all words in the population.

Spatial language necessarily is always tight to a particular reference system which is to say every spatial relation is always applied with respect to some object. Even uttering single words like *links* ('left') entails an implicit reference system and the object discriminated by uttering this word depends at least on which of the two interlocutors is used as reference object. In acquisition this problem was solved by the tutor who always conceptualized from the learner, and, hence, the implicit reference system in every communication was the learner. In formation this problem occurs again. Agents can use themselves implicitly as reference points or they can use additional reference objects available to them in the spatial scene they are confronted with. A detailed discussion of these problems and their impact on lexical development is deferred to later sections. In order to focus only on lexical development, the problem is solved here by always using the box which is available in all spatial contexts used in this section as the reference object. Different categorization strategies are, thus, represented using different semantic structure which all involve the box in each context (see Figure 10.18 for details).

10.2.2 Results

I test the invention and adoption system separately for absolute, proximal and projective language strategies. Figures 10.19, 10.20 and 10.21 show both the communicative success averaged over 25 runs as well as examples of resulting language systems for projective, proximal and absolute systems each. The graphs

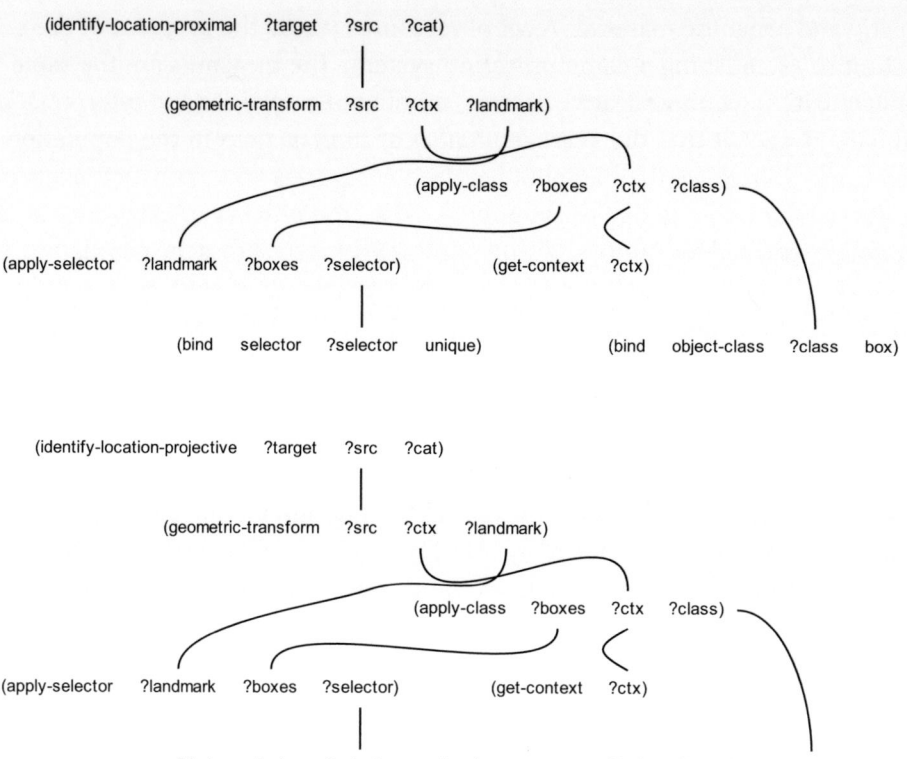

Figure 10.18: Semantic structure used by agents to conceptualize reality. The top
figure shows the IRL-network for the projective strategy, the bottom
figure for comparison shows the proximal categorization strategy.
Both differ in the categorization operation identify-object-projective
and identify-object-proximal. The rest of the network transforms the
complete context to the box landmark using the operation geometric-
transform.

convincingly demonstrate the power of the invention and alignment operators, in other words, they show that given the proposed operators agents can develop a language system and reach communicative success. Furthermore, these graphs show that the language system evolved by agents is not necessarily the same as the German language system. For instance, the categories of agents 1 to 3 in Figure 10.19 are quite different from the German front, back, left and right projective system which aligns its categories with the x and y axes of the coordinate system. In particular, three categories seem to be sufficient for the agents in these experiments to discriminate all objects in the spatial scenes successfully. So the main question given that we have established the success of the invention and alignment operators in formation is: what are the different factors influencing the shape of the language system developed?

Within the approach given in this book, there are two factors influencing the development of the category system which merit close consideration when it comes to explaining the outcome of formation experiments. First, the language strategy most importantly encompassing the conceptualization strategy as well as the learning and invention mechanisms including the set of parameters that come with them effect the forming language system. This is most obvious for the type of categories, e.g. absolute, projective or proximal, agents use for developing the language system because this entirely determined by the strategy. The second important factor are the particular spatial scenes and their properties that agents need to communicate in. The spatial scenes and the statistical distribution of objects are directly linked to the categories necessary for discriminating objects.

To shed some light on the two factors, I explore how the system reacts by manipulating each of the two parameters separately. In particular, one can study the systems emerging when the same strategy is applied in multiple runs to the same set of contexts, how different strategies perform on the same set of contexts and how the same strategy performs when applied to different sets of spatial scenes. In Figures 10.19 to 10.21 experiments are shown in which 25 times the same strategy is used to build either a projective, a proximal or an absolute language system. Each of these 25 runs across the different strategies are performed on the same set of spatial scenes (space-game-2 for the projective language system, space-game-3 for the proximal system and a combination of scenes from space-game-2 and space-game-9 for the absolute system). The only difference between different runs is which particular context was randomly chosen in each interaction as well as which agents from the population participate in each interaction. The graphs suggest given the same environmental conditions the system settles on the same number of spatial categories in different runs. A fact that is supported by measur-

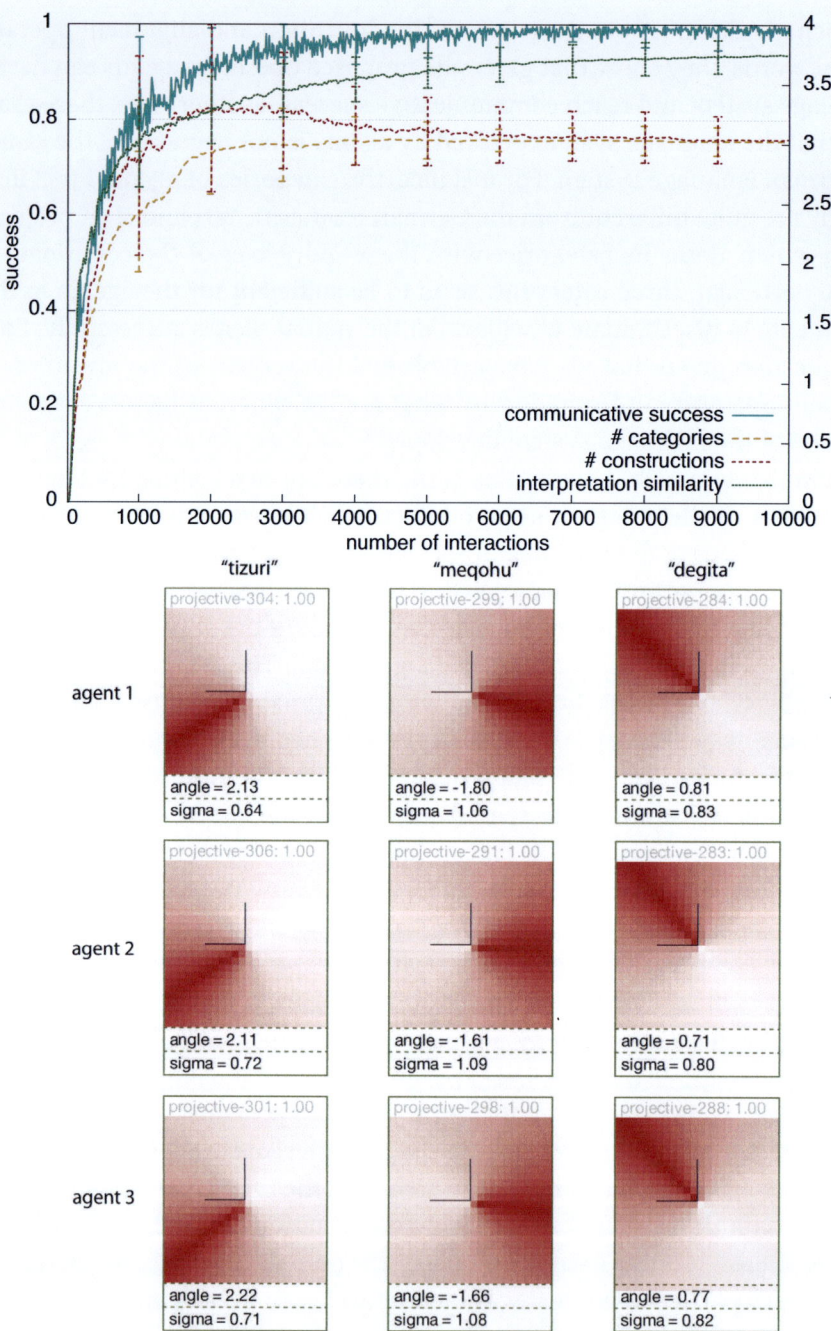

Figure 10.19: Results for a formation experiment in which agents form a projective category system (top). The bottom figures show the categories and words in the inventories of the first three agents.

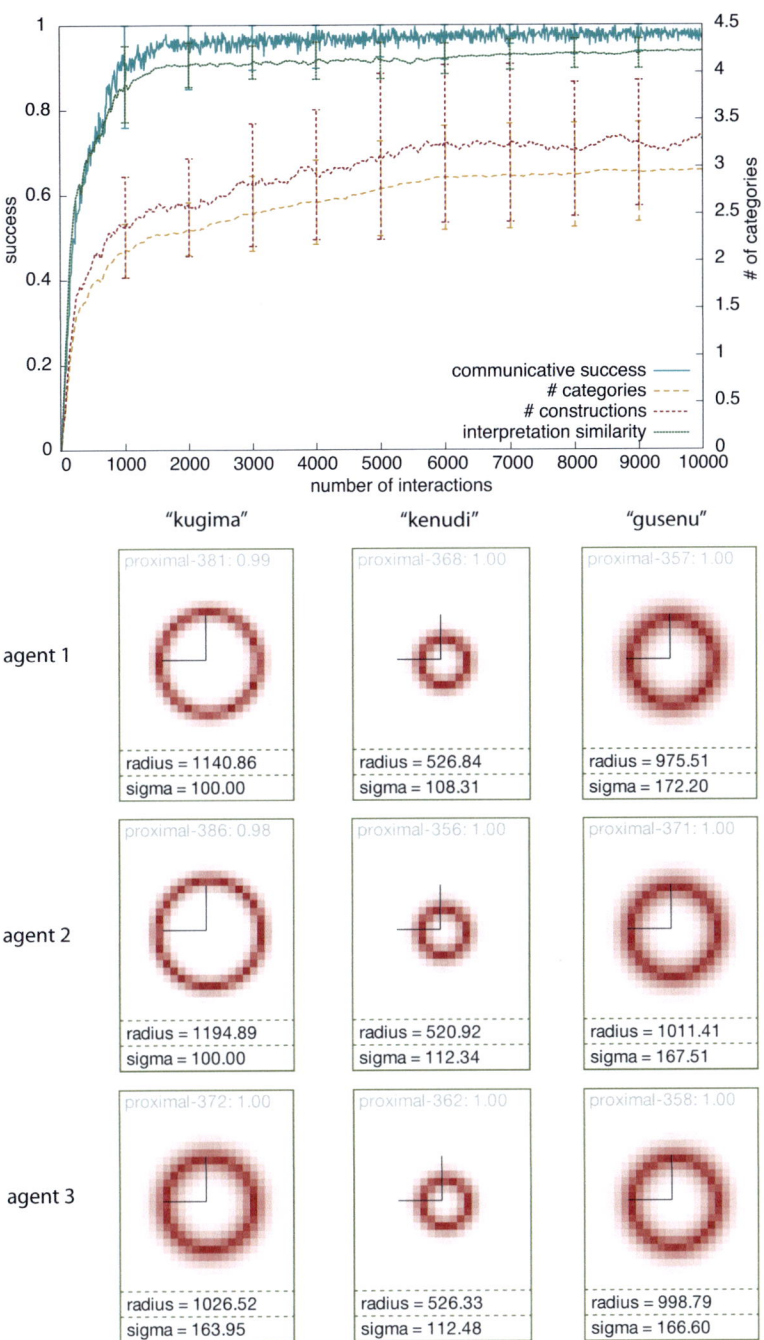

Figure 10.20: Results for a formation experiment in which agents form a proximal category system (top). The bottom figures show the categories and words in the inventories of the first three agents.

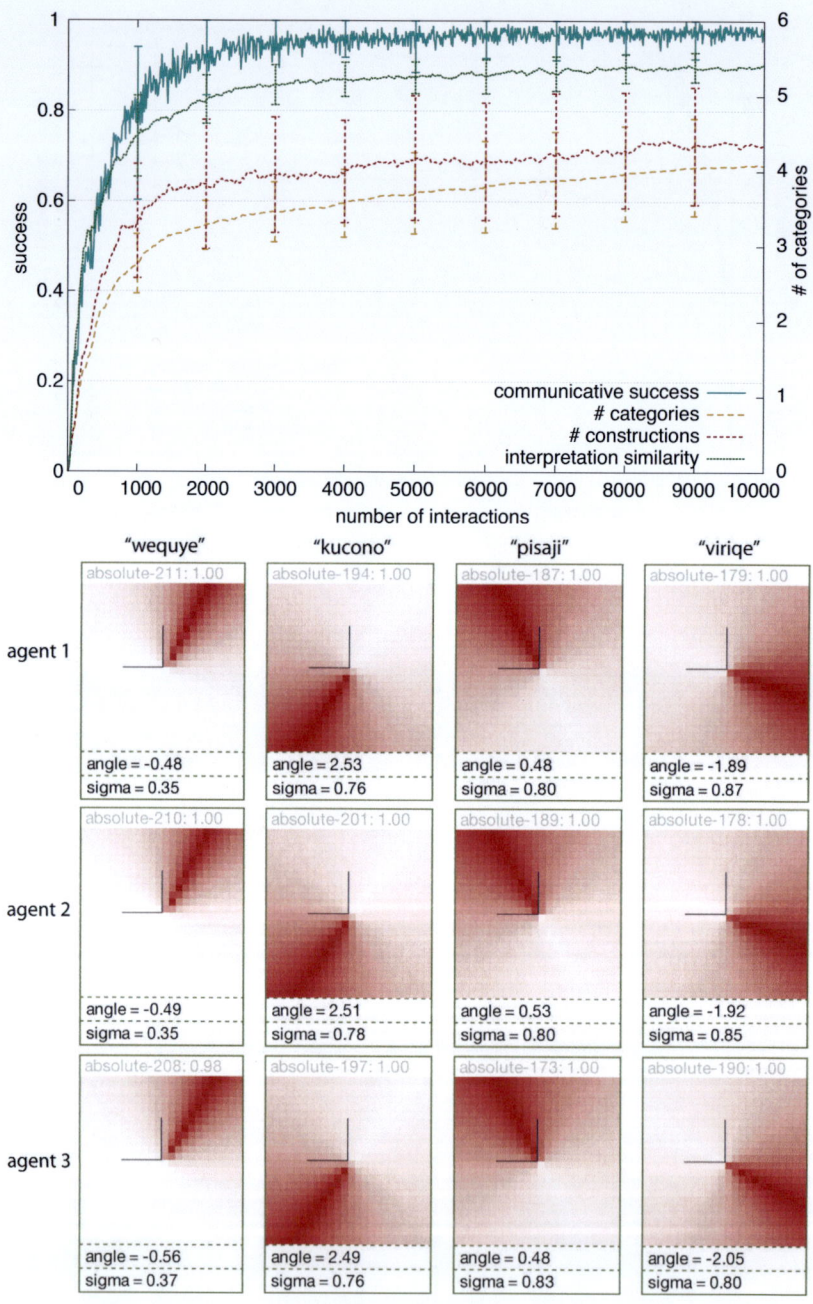

Figure 10.21: Results for a formation experiment in which agents form an absolute category system (top). The bottom figures show the categories and words in the inventories of the first three agents.

ing the similarity of categories across experiments in this case 0.749. Category similarity of populations is computed by maximizing the similarity of each agent of one population to each agent of the other population and averaging the results. So in that sense 0.749 is a rather high number which quantifies the amount of similarity in the category systems of different populations. We can conclude then that in the same environmental conditions the same strategy will develop very similar category distinctions. This, of course, only extends to the similarity of the categories themselves. The words floating in each population are different from other populations.

The second interesting question is: what are the differences in language systems that the same strategy builds when facing distinctly different environmental conditions? Let us look at the projective case. The results in Figure 10.19 were obtained on a set of spatial scenes in which each context consists of two objects which have a mean angular distance of 2.13, that is, the two objects in every context are on average a semicircle apart from each other. I compare the results of the projective language strategy on this data set to data sets in which the number of objects is varied and in which the mean angle distance between two objects is different. Figure 10.22 shows the impact of these two manipulations. From these graphs we can conclude that less angular distance between objects in spatial scenes require agents to make more distinctions which can be seen by the increase in categories emerging in the "smaller angle distance" condition. However, the real driving force behind invention of more distinctions seems to be related to the number of objects per context, for which the corresponding "more objects" condition shows a massive increase in emerging categories. In all three conditions, nevertheless, the system is able to stabilize on high average success proving the successful adaptation of the emerging language system to different environmental conditions.

A word of caution is in place here. There is no direct correlation between either number of objects nor average angle distance and the number of categories needed for discrimination. There are always border cases in which, for instance, a small average angle distance still leads to few distinctions. Consider environmental conditions in which in every context, two objects are at the same position a tiny angle distance apart from each other. In such a world agents will develop a projective category system consisting of two categories only, since this is sufficient for discrimination. In spite of such border cases, the general point is still valid. The less angle distance and the more objects in each context, the more likely it is that agents need to develop more category distinctions in order to be successful *and* the systems presented in this chapter allow agents to invent these necessary distinctions.

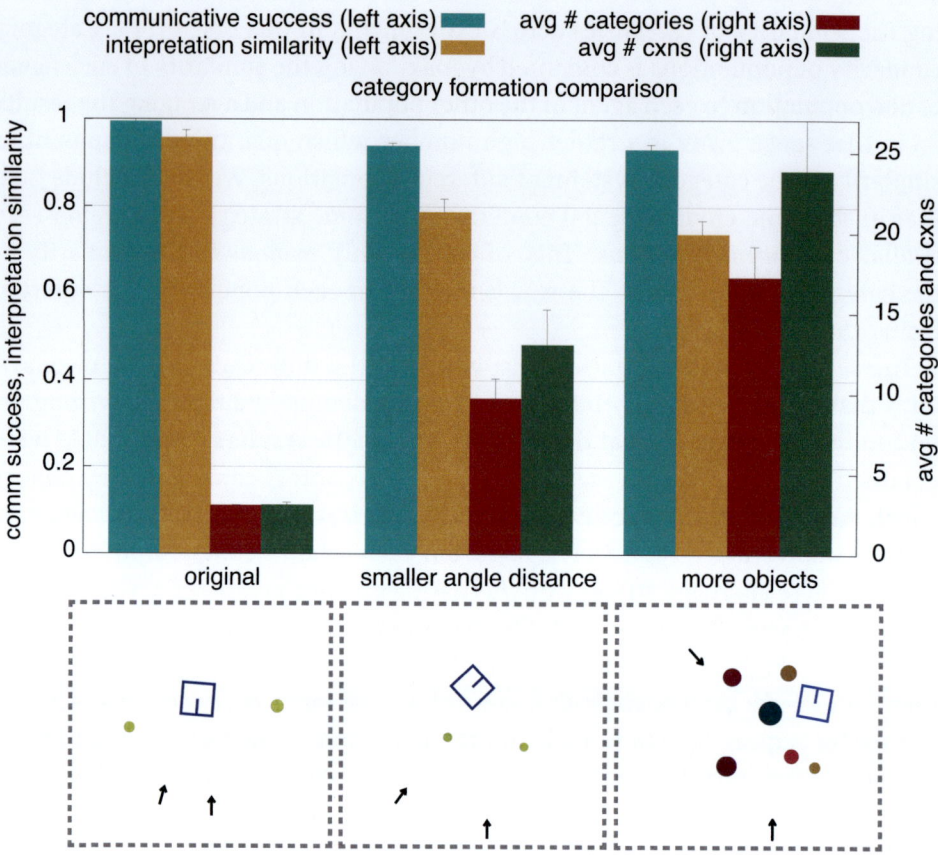

Figure 10.22: Comparison of the impact of different environmental conditions on the language system built by the projective language strategy. The "original" condition repeats the results from Figure 10.19. In the "smaller angle distance" condition agents are facing two objects in each context that have a smaller angle distance than in the "original" condition. The last condition is the more objects condition in which each context has on average 5.27 objects. This entails that also the average angle distance is lower than in the original condition (1.64 as opposed to 2.13). The difference is roughly speaking a semi-circle. Example scenes for each condition can be seen below. A clear increase in the number of categories for the two conditions "smaller angle distance" and "more objects" can be observed (right axis). The graphs are generated by averaging the results from 25 runs in each condition of 10000 interactions in which agents form a language system and 10000 interactions where the developed system is just tested without further invention and alignment.

Finally, one can study other influences on the dynamics of language evolution given the operators discussed in this section. One factor of interest is, for instance, the population size. Figure 10.23 shows the impact different population sizes have on the alignment and evolution of a projective language system. The figure shows that the systems discussed in this section are resilient to increases in population sizes and cope well with large populations of at least up to 100 agents (which is the maximum number of agents tested).

10.2.3 Interaction of strategies

The influence of environmental conditions on the unfolding language system can be studied separately with respect to each categorization strategy be it absolute, projective or proximal, but it can also be examined with respect to the interaction of these different strategies. In the previous section I discussed the simultaneous acquisition of two language systems a projective and a proximal one via semantic inference, a mechanism that allows agents to decide between different strategies based on discriminative power (the mechanism is described in Section 10.1). I extend this principle to formation of lexical systems by giving agents two categorization strategies, e.g., proximal and projective, at the same time and also equipping them with two invention strategies. Figure 10.24, for instance, shows agents developing proximal and projective categories at the same time. For such a coupled system environment factors are again the driving force behind the particular language system that is emerging. In environmental conditions where objects in each context are at large distance from each other, proximal distinctions should be more important and, thus, develop more strongly than, for instance, in environmental conditions where objects are situated with larger angle distance. Figure 10.25 shows that this is the case.

10.2.4 Hybrid systems

Lastly, one can consider a system were agents do not have different strategies focussing on a particular sensory channel, but where they have one strategy which allows them to develop the channel focus autonomously. This continues the strand of categorization introduced in Section 10.1. In order, to test this strategy in formation the system for acquisition is extended by invention operators that allow speakers to introduce spatial categories and lexical items for expressing them. Figure 10.26 shows that this strategy can also be successfully used to form a language system.

10.3 Summary

This chapter has shown how populations can (a) acquire, and (b) co-evolve an ontology and lexicon of spatial relations provided that they are equipped with a conceptualization strategy and invention, adoption and alignment operators. Moreover, this chapter studied the interaction of different language strategies particularly with respect to environmental conditions. We can conclude that the proposed operators allow agents to acquire and develop successful category systems under certain conditions.

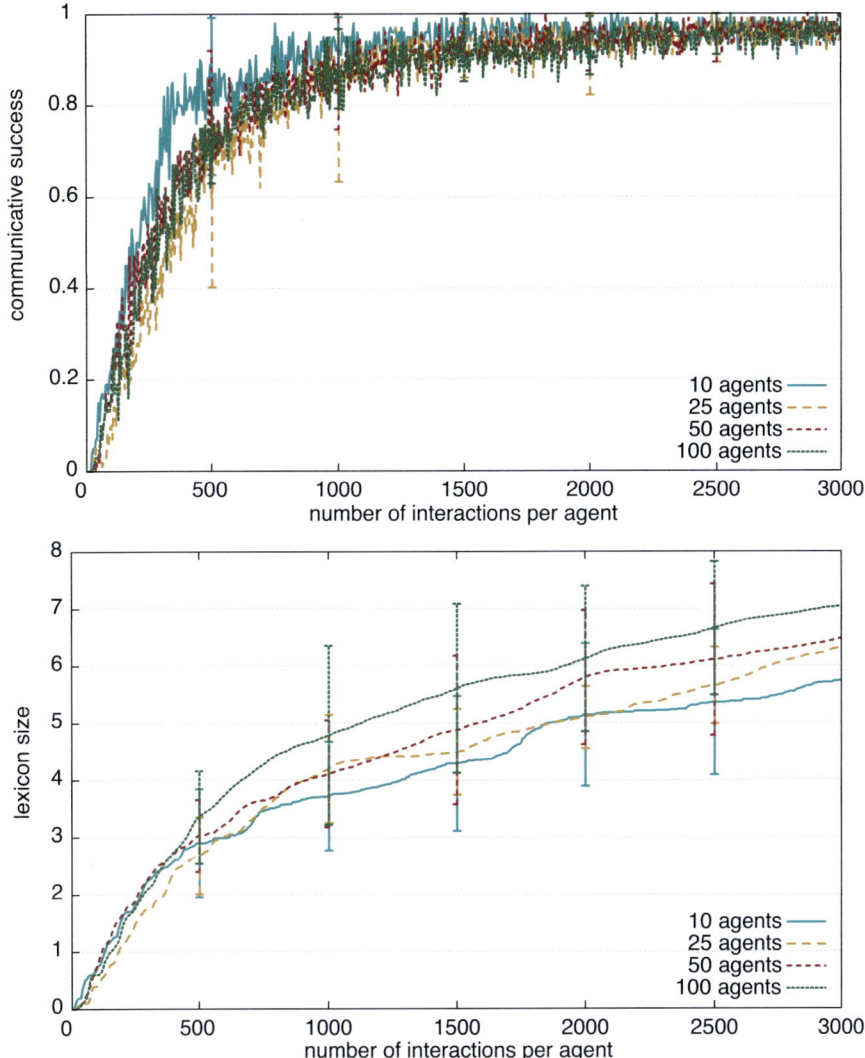

Figure 10.23: Impact of population sizes on category formation. On the x-axis is plotted number of interactions per agent. This is different from all other graphs discussed in this section. The figure shows that population size increases have a negligible effect on the dynamics of communicative success and the developing ontology of spatial relations.

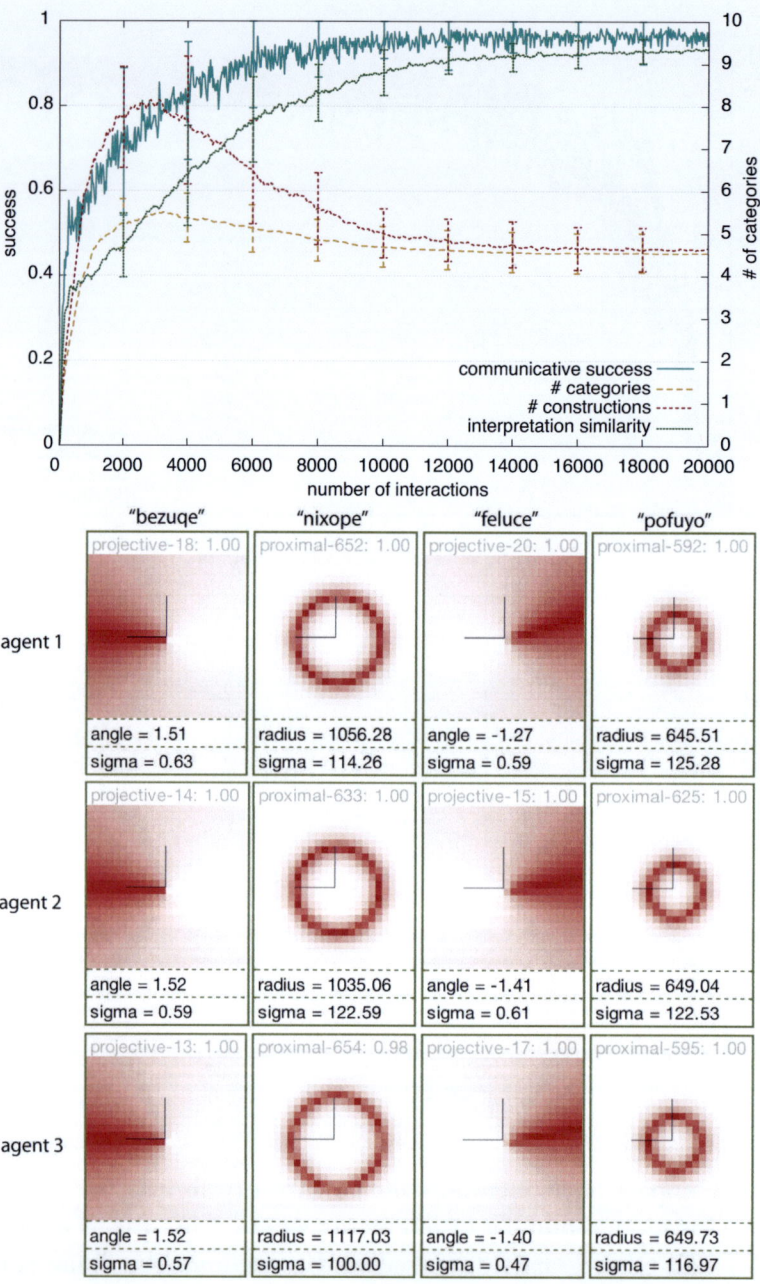

Figure 10.24: Results for a formation experiment in which agents are equipped simultaneously with a proximal and projective strategy. In invention, agents use the principle of maximizing discriminative power to choose between the two strategies.

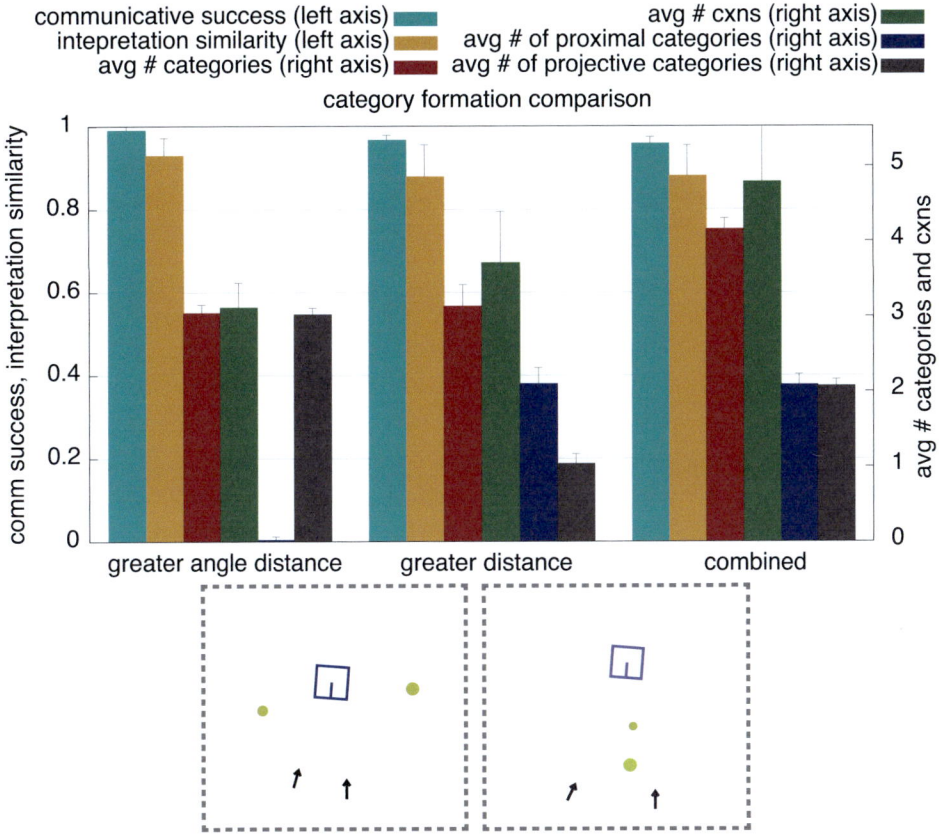

Figure 10.25: Comparison of the impact of different environmental conditions on the language system build by a combined projective and proximal language strategy. In environmental conditions where objects exhibit large angle distances (bottom left shows an example scene) agents prefer to rely on projective categories that allow to discriminate objects based on angle. In conditions where there is a bigger distance between objects (bottom right image) than angle distance agents chiefly rely on proximal categories. In the "combined" condition which has both scenes with large angle distance as well as scenes with large distances between objects a balanced language system consisting of proximal and projective categories is developed.

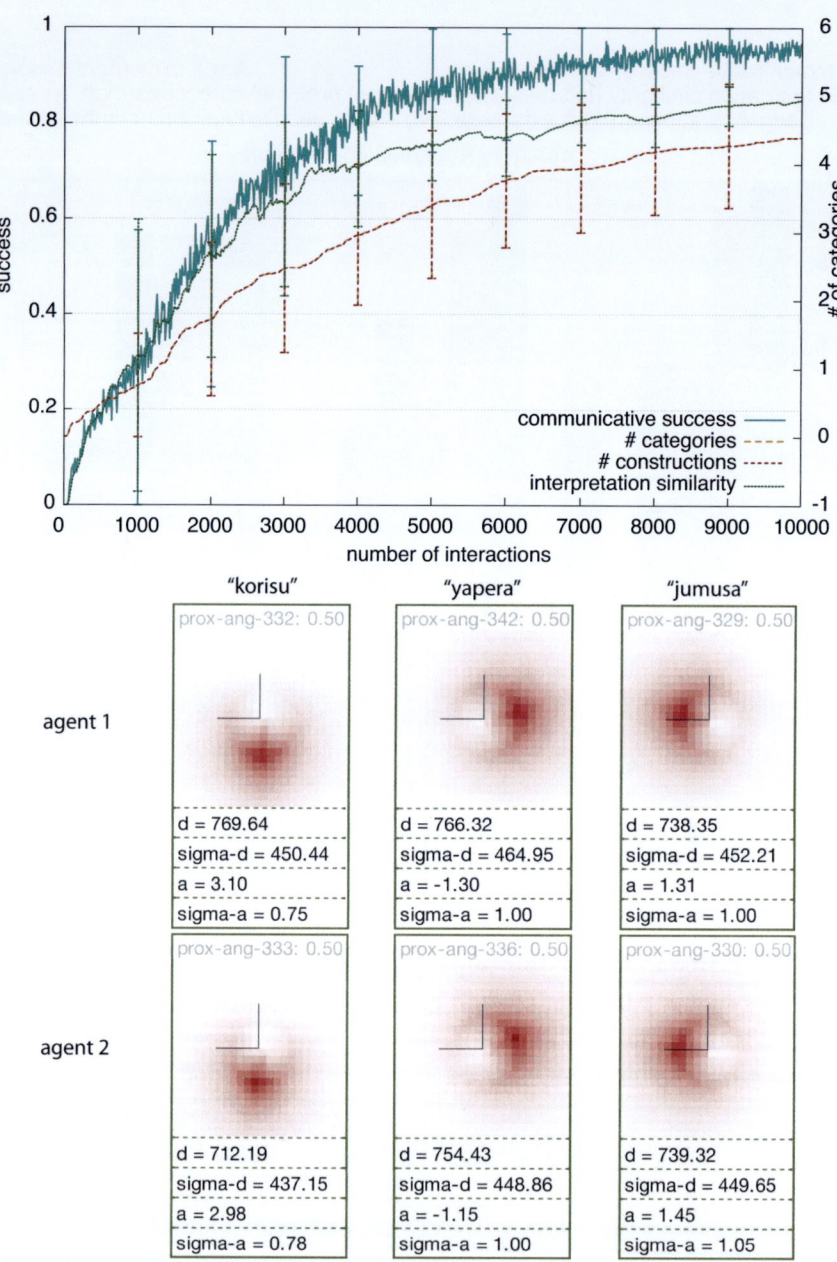

Figure 10.26: Results for a formation experiment in which agents are equipped with a hybrid strategy that does not distinguish between angle and distance channel but combines both channels in a single category representation.

11 Evolution of spatial conceptualization strategies

In this section I research the question how conceptualization strategies can form autonomously and align in a population of agents. The previous chapter studied one component of spatial conceptualization, namely categorization, in isolation. In this section I take a broader look at the prerequisites for building category systems. Every category system is part of a particular strategy of conceptualizing reality which encompasses a particular choice of reference objects but also frames of reference and perspective on the scene. Consequently, which spatial relation system emerges is governed most importantly by the strategies available to agents. In the languages of the world different strategies for the conceptualization of spatial reality have been attested. This is most strikingly the case for frames of reference. Some languages feature only absolute systems, an example being Tenejapan (Levinson 2003), while others have developed strong intrinsic and relative systems like German (Tenbrink 2007). But conceptualization strategies go further. Which objects can function as landmarks? How are spatial relations applied? What is the role of perspective reversal? These are all choices which are manifested in conceptualization strategies and shape the way a population conceptualizes reality. Consequently, the evolution of spatial language is intricately linked to the emergence and evolution of conceptualization strategies which together with learning and adaptation operators orchestrate the development of the language system. To understand the process of building conceptualization strategies this section details models of how agents invent strategies and how they become aligned in the population.

The important claim in this section is that conceptualization strategies are negotiated in a cultural process, similar to how the lexicon is negotiated, through local interactions by agents in a community. The negotiation process is fueled by the general cognitive capabilities of agents, in other words, the cognitive building blocks. Conceptualization strategies package the usage of certain types of spatial relations with landmarks and perspective. For instance, a conceptualization strategy might involve a set of spatial relations pertaining to a particular global landmark. Strategies are represented technically by chunks which are combinations of cognitive operations into particular semantic structures that allow agents to conceptualize reality. Which strategies are built and which strategies a population agrees on in the cultural process is subject to selective pressures that influences the preference for a particular strategy over others and drives the population to align on a particular way of construing reality. Factors influencing invention and alignment of strategies include primarily environmental conditions such as the spatial layout and the kind of objects agents face, but they can also include factors such as cognitive complexity of a particular strategy and expressivity of the language systems developed using that particular strategy. Furthermore, already established strategies and language systems upon invention of new strategies influence how and in which way new strategies develop. The idea is that a particular strategy survives when it is relevant to an agent because it is efficient and useful in discriminating objects and it contributes to the communicative success of an agent at least in a few spatial contexts. If a new strategy is potentially useful in certain spatial contexts but in case these spatial situations are already handled by another strategy then the new strategy has almost no chance of taking over the system unless it performs better with respect to other factors such as cognitive complexity.

In this chapter the focus is on one particular factor governing both invention and alignment of strategies: discriminative power. Discriminative power for strategies refers to the distinctive ability of a strategy to distinguish and single out objects in the environment. Each strategy known to an agent necessarily starts out in a single context. Which strategy is invented in a particular context is based on its discriminative power in comparison with other strategies available at that moment. New strategies are packaged into chunks and the success of the new strategies is tracked by updating the score of the corresponding chunk. So the invention, alignment and interaction of strategies is structurally organized very similar to categories. This chapter argues that discriminative power is an important factor driving the development of strategies, similar to how it drove the invention and alignment of spatial categories. In fact, the success of a strategy is intricately linked to the success of the the category system it builds. For instance, if an agent is building a language system with an absolute strategy this entails that the absolute relations built using the strategy and the strategy itself are subject to the same selective pressure. It is the success of this overall system the spatial relations together with the overall performance of the strategy that drives the organization of the linguistic and semantic repository of the agent.

Strategies are implemented using the chunking mechanism of IRL. A particular chunk represents a particular way of conceptualizing reality. Chunks are invented by assembling cognitive operations into ready-made semantic structure; they are scored and their scores are used to represent the success of the conceptualization strategy over many interactions. Invention operators orchestrate how chunks are built, and alignment operators update the score of chunks after interactions tracking the long-term success of a particular chunk. Spatial conceptualization strategies rely on spatial relations. Invention of spatial relations is tied to particular cognitive operations. For instance, if there is an absolute strategy developed, the cognitive operation doing the categorization has an associated invention operator that invents spatial categories if needed. These are the same operations as discussed in the last section. Important for the purpose of this chapter is that this connects the invented spatial relations to the strategies that incorporate the particular cognitive operation responsible for invention.

Before I turn to grammar and other linguistic means of expressing strategies, this section focusses entirely on alignment and invention of conceptualization strategies without explicit marking in language. In other words, the systems described in this section are purely expressed through the naming of spatial relations re-using all of the mechanisms of invention, adoption and alignment of spatial categories detailed in the previous section. I apply these insights on two components of spatial language separately. First, I study strategies for different reference objects, followed by a discussion of the interaction of different frame of reference strategies. Finally the chapter turns to invention of strategies.

The results presented in this chapter have been published in Spranger (2011; 2013b).

11.1 Alignment for landmark strategies

Landmarks are an integral part of spatial language because every spatial relation is implicitly or explicitly related to a reference object. Typically many different reference objects are present in the world and agents face choices as to which of the reference objects should be used in the particular communicative situation but also with respect to invention and development of language. Environmental conditions can be varied. In some environments a landmark such as a mountain might be visible in every communicative encounter between agents of a population which makes it a successful strategy to base the spatial language system on this landmark. In other environments landmarks might only be available locally and its usage, therefore, bound to a particular communicative encounter. One way of dealing with such choices is that agents agree on the usage of a particular conceptualization strategy that is bound to a particular reference object. This section explores how the use of certain reference objects might be aligned in a population of agents. I look at scenes which feature different landmarks, hence, exhibit a certain amount of choice, and I study under which circumstances agents are able to align on always using the same reference object across spatial scenes. Specifically, I compare allocentric strategies that are using objects such as boxes versus egocentric speaker and egocentric hearer strategies.

The key claim in this section is that conventionalizing a particular strategy of conceptualizing reality allows agents to be successful in communication. Technically, this claim is studied by setting up systems in which an alignment strategy is implemented that scores semantic structure, more specifically, chunks of semantic structure and updates the score of semantic structure based on success in communication. Chunks that were used in production and interpretation are rewarded if the interaction was successful and punished if the interaction was a failure. Moreover, chunks that were not used in the interaction are punished slightly which drives the alignment to find a single strategy most comprehensive strategy that works in many contexts. This, in essence, implements frequency based dynamics in which structure that is used successfully survives and structure that is never used or always used unsuccessfully is removed. Strictly speaking, however, structure is never removed, it just gets a score of zero which eliminates it from routine processing but leaves it available for recruitment should it become necessary.

The scoring of semantic structure has important consequences. First, the score of a chunk impacts the choices agents make in production and interpretation. The discrimination score of a chunk, i.e. its discriminatory power given the current context, is multiplied by its score. Consequently, a speaker might choose to use a less discriminating structure over another because it is more conventional, i.e. the score of the chunk is so high as to overrule the discriminative power of the competitive chunk. Second, the score of a chunk not only governs its usage in a particular spatial context, but also influences which categories will be invented. The world from the viewpoint of the speaker and the hearer might be different from the allocentric viewpoint and, consequently, the sensori distinctions, i.e. the categories required to be successful using an allocentric strategy can be different from those when the same set of scenes is construed from the viewpoint the hearer. The competition between the conceptualization strategies impacts, in other words, on the particular category system that will emerge. Because the chunks are under selective pressure, this creates a positive feedback loop in which categories might be invented using a particular conceptualization strategy such as allocentric, which in turn makes this strategy more successful in discrimination, which re-enforces the strategy and so on and so forth.

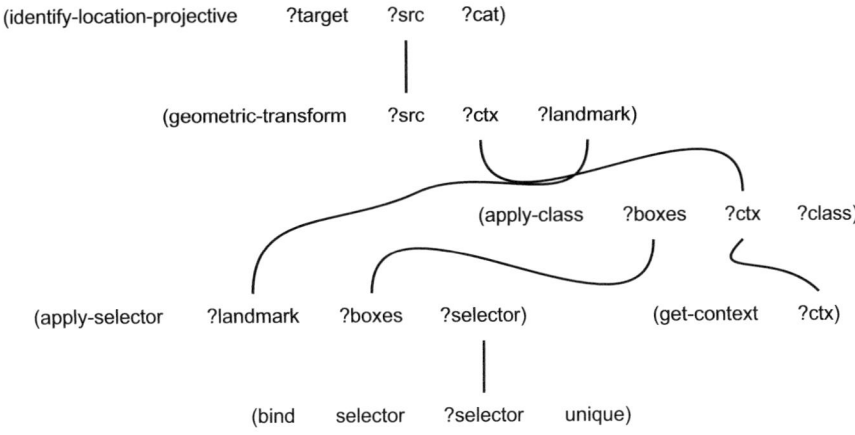

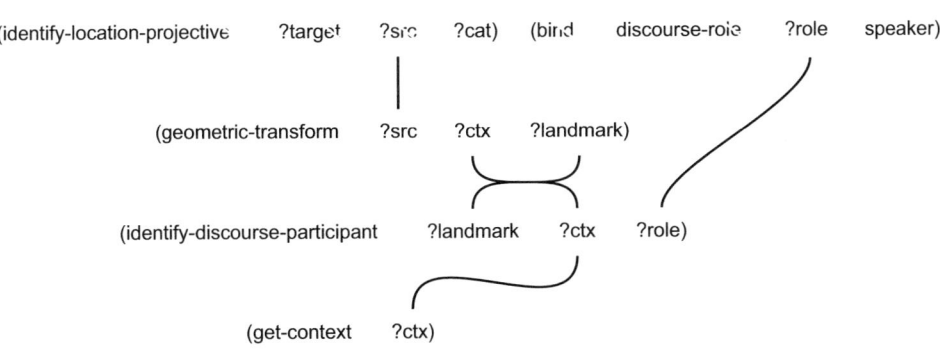

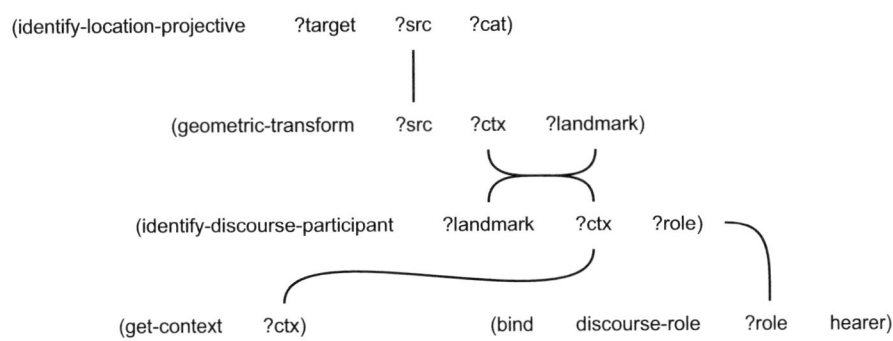

Figure 11.1: The three conceptualization strategies given to agents. Top: allocentric; middle: egocentric speaker and bottom: egocentric hearer.

11.1.1 Experimental setup and measures

I claim that chunk alignment is an effective mechanism that allows agents to conventionalize the choice for particular conceptualization strategy alongside forming a category system. The claim is tested by running experiments in which agents are given different conceptualization strategies: an allocentric strategy in which they can use a reference object available in each context, and two egocentric strategies one for using themselves and one for using the interlocutor as reference objects (see Figure 11.1 for the semantic structures agents are given) . At the same time as they are aligning their conceptualization strategy, agents develop a category system including names for category distinctions. The category systems and conceptualization strategies are tightly coupled. Every category is invented as part of a strategy and can only be used within the strategy it was created in. Success of a particular category in communication, therefore, directly impacts on the conceptualization strategy. Figures 11.2 and 11.3 show that the mechanism of chunk alignment works both in acquisition and in formation. Agents can successfully negotiate both categories and the conceptualization strategy at the same time.

The alignment of conceptualization strategies is measured using the CONCEPTUALIZATION STRATEGY SIMILARITY which is computed for a population of agents by averaging the agent conceptualization strategy similarity of every agent to every other agent. The agent conceptualization strategy similarity (acss) is computed by comparing the score of each strategy. Since strategies are never removed but merely reduced to a score of 0.0, one can compute a distance of scores between the chunks in each agent and envelope the result using an exponential decay function which results in the following formula.

$$\mathrm{acss}(a_1, a_2, S) := \exp\left(-1 \cdot \sum_{s \in S} |\mathrm{score}(s, a_1) - \mathrm{score}(s, a_2)|\right) \qquad (11.1)$$

In this formula a_1, a_2 are the agents whose similarity score is computed, S is the set of strategies given to agents and $\mathrm{score}(s, a_1)$ is the score agent a_1 gives to strategy s. The conceptualization strategy similarity (css) for the population P is defined as the average acss for every two agents. Since acss is symmetric, all combinations of two agents are considered. This measure is only one way to understand the dynamics of a particular chunk alignment experiment. Since all agents start out equipped with the same set of strategies this measure is equal to 1.0 in the beginning. However, when considered over many interactions, the measure provides important insights into how similar the development is. Particularly, large drops in similarity diagnose significant divergence in strategy use. Most information from css is drawn by analyzing its dynamics together with a second measure which tracks the average number of chunks in the population ignoring chunks with a score of 0. If the average number of chunks in a population of agents drops from 3 to 1 and css stays high, we can conclude that the population has agreed on a single conceptualization strategy (see Figure 11.3 for such developments).

11.1.2 Results

Figure 11.4 shows three different outcomes of the chunk alignment experiments on different data sets. All three graphs show the average score of the three different strategies over the first 1000 interactions of one particular experimental run. All strategies start with the same score 0.5 and for some time nothing happens, because agents have not started to invent categories yet. If the first category was invented using a particular strategy in a particular context, the strategy that was used to invent spreads in the population. Categories invented much later will be invented using the dominant strategy, which essentially has already been established when the second, third and fourth category spread in the population.

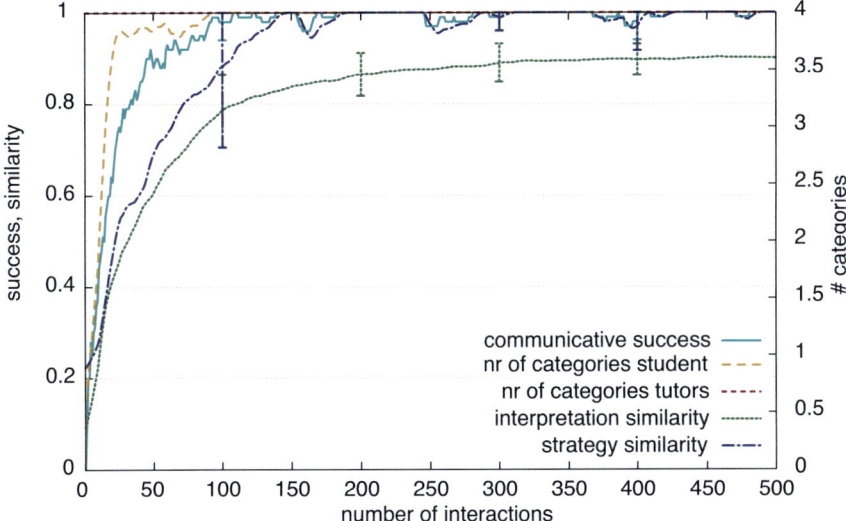

Figure 11.2: Acquisition experiment in which agents not only learn the category system from a tutor (projective in this case), but also the underlying conceptualization strategy of the tutor (allocentric).

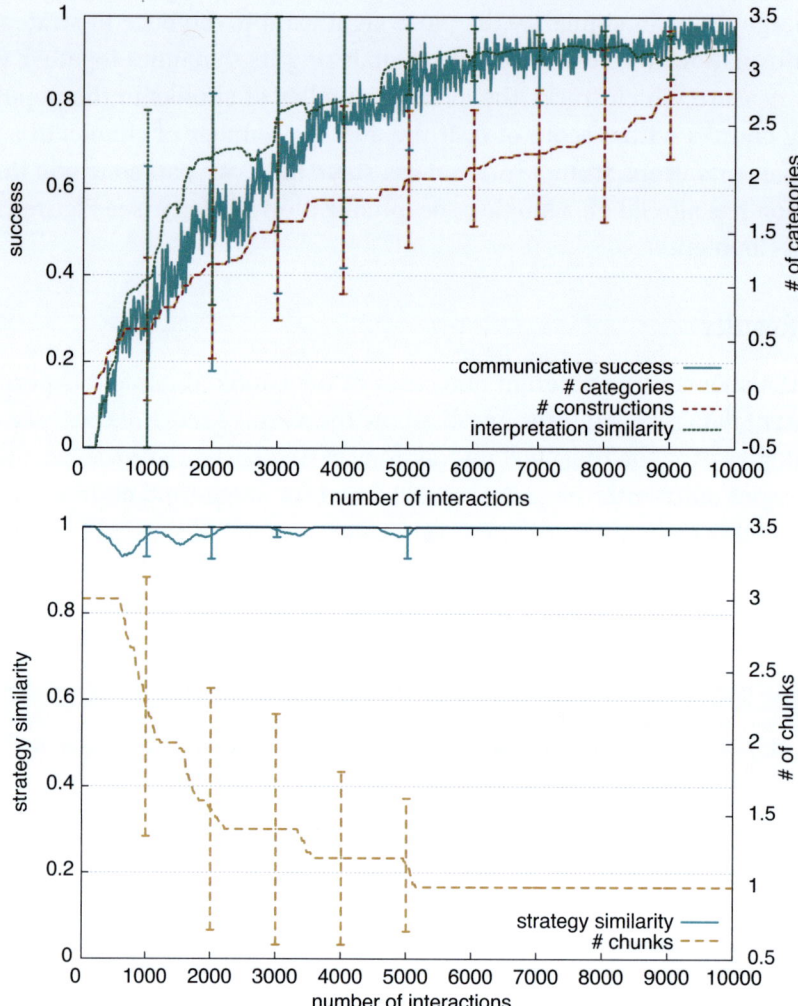

Figure 11.3: Experimental results for conceptual alignment. In these experiments
10 agents are negotiating conceptualization strategies while at the
same time agreeing on a system of spatial relations. The top shows
the development of categories and communicative success. The dynamics is quite similar to previous experiments using a dampened
invention approach to categorization. The bottom figure shows that
for this particular data set one specific strategy always unanimously
wins the competition. which can be seen both by the drop to a single
chunk and the corresponding high strategy similarity. Strategy similarity starts out high because all agents start with the three strategies,
but most importantly, it also stays high suggesting high similarity between the conceptualization strategies agents are using.

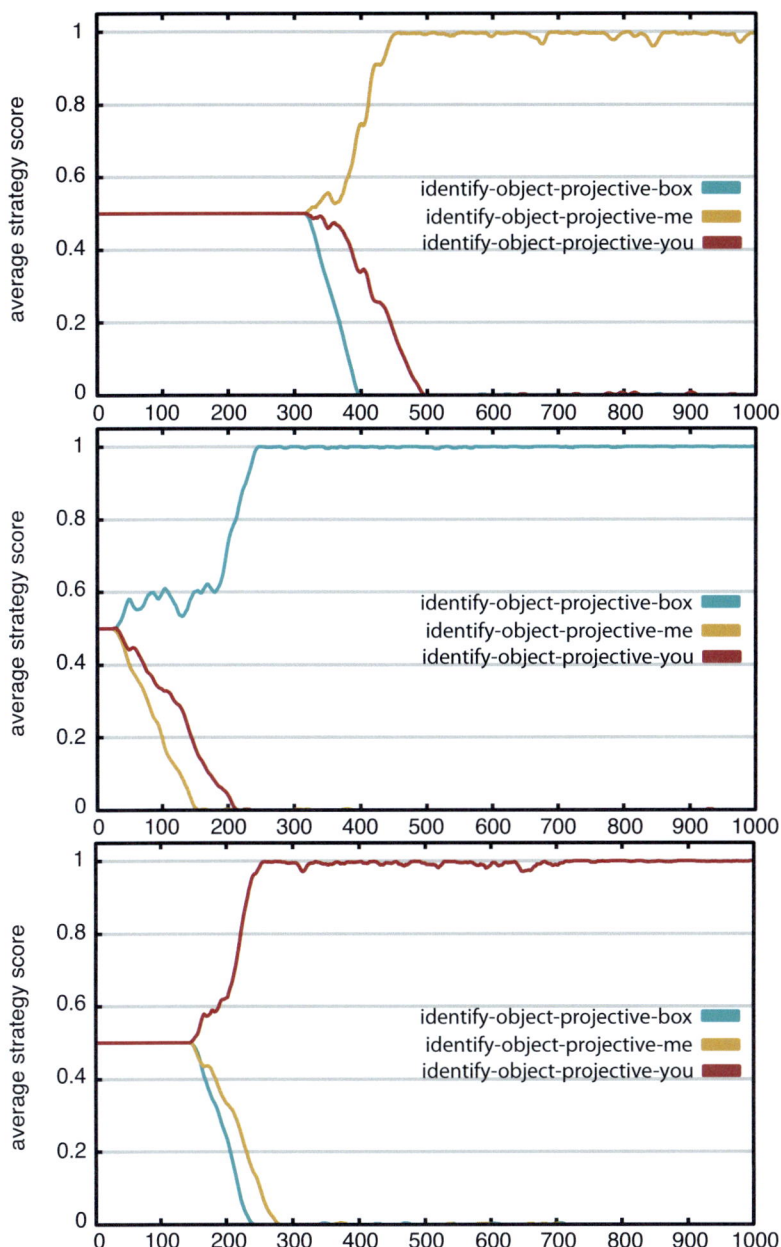

Figure 11.4: Different outcomes of the chunk alignment experiments on different data sets. All three graphs show the average score of the three different strategies over the first 1000 interactions of one particular experimental run. Top: the speaker egocentric strategy survives; middle: allocentric strategy wins and right: the hearer egocentric strategy wins.

The choices in alignment of strategies depend on the discriminative advantage of the strategy. This is a subtle effect which can easily lead to unaligned populations particularly because agents simultaneously develop categories which is a powerful and adaptive mechanism. The problem lies in adoption. If the hearer observes a new term, the only information given to him in order to decide which strategy to use for adoption is the current context and its particular spatial layout. Let us suppose the speaker thinks the conventional strategy in the population is allocentric and, consequently he uses an allocentric spatial category. If the context is indeed one that favors the allocentric strategy, there is no problem and the hearer will correctly adopt the category as allocentric. If, however, the context favors a conceptualization strategy from the viewpoint of the hearer and the hearer does not share the strong preference for the allocentric strategy with the speaker, he will adopt the term as part of a hearer strategy. Even though the category is essentially unaligned because different agents see it as part of different strategies, it might still be quite successful, particularly in context where there are few objects. If success of the category is above 50%, it is very hard for the alignment mechanisms to remove it, since success is rewarded much more than failure is punished to allow the system to get off the ground. In such cases, misalignment can appear while retaining success rates of above 50% in communication. In other words, agents might get stuck in local optima and without additional mechanisms might be unable to get out of such conditions.

11.2 Alignment for frame of reference strategies

The same mechanisms explaining alignment of reference object conceptualization strategies can be used to explain the alignment of other components of spatial language such as frames of reference, e.g. intrinsic and absolute conceptualization strategies. The claim is that agents can deal with the problem of aligning frames of reference by aligning chunks based on environmental conditions that favor one over the other. Particularly, I revisit the problem discussed in Sections 10.1 and 10.2 which argued that agents who are equipped at the same time with projective and absolute strategies are unable to develop category systems without clear preferences for one of the two strategies. Here, I turn to the question how such preferences can develop from scratch based on the long-term tracking of the success of each strategy. Just as for reference objects, I study environmental conditions and their impact on the success of strategies.

To understand the impact of environmental conditions, we have to understand the pre-requisites for the two strategies at hand. The absolute strategy requires the environment to exhibit absolute features such as a global landmark. The global landmark must be present in some contexts and it must help to discriminate objects in the context. That is to say, in environmental conditions where there are no absolute landmarks or the direction to the absolute landmark is not discriminating, agents do not develop an absolute system. For intrinsic systems the environment, most specifically the landmark objects that are used in conceptualization, have to have properties that allow to conceptualize a direction with respect to the reference object. So one can conclude that in environments were landmarks do not have an orientation or where the direction of objects in each context is not discriminating with respect to the orientation of landmark objects, no intrinsic system will develop. A word of caution is at place here, I will talk about the environment as having intrinsic or absolute features. This is in many ways loose talk, as it is never the environment that has such features but rather the environment is conceptualized by humans or robots as having such features and it is never the environment itself that has an absolute landmark or a landmark with intrinsic features. Now, a mountain range or any other feature of some environment may license or in some ways encourage agents to use the object as a global feature, but, certainly, the decision as to what counts as a global feature is still part of an active cognitive process. This process is simulated, here, by manipulating the spatial context to include an absolute landmark or a landmark that has an inherent orientation. Hence, I talk loosely about environmental conditions pertaining to absolute and intrinsic features, but readers have to keep in mind that this really is scaffolding much more complex processes.

The strategies an agent possesses always interact in local communicative interactions. Usage of a particular strategy in production, interpretation and invention of spatial relations is exclusively governed by the discriminative power of each strategy. In cases where the discriminative power of two strategies is equal, this leads to a problem in the sense that the agent cannot decide which strategy to use. This problem is especially pressing when agents have not started inventing spatial relations yet and need to decide which strategy to use. This sort of situation is precisely the problem occurring when intrinsic and absolute systems interact in conditions that license both. In order for agents to successfully develop a category system, the symmetry of equal discriminative power of intrinsic and absolute categories, must be broken. The mechanisms for alignment of conceptualization strategies can help break this symmetry by tracking the success of each strategy. Even if only in a few contexts there is a clear advantage for one of the strategies, the scoring of conceptualization strategies allows agents to track this advantage at which point the success can carry over to contexts that license no particular preference. For instance, if one context out of many features only an absolute landmark and no intrinsic features, agents use this context to start an absolute category system at the same time rewarding the absolute conceptualization strategy. This initial reward carries over to other contexts which feature both intrinsic and absolute features. The head start of the absolute strategy then leads to additional absolute spatial relations being developed which in turn make the absolute system more successful in communication rewarding both the individual absolute relations as well as the overall strategy. In this way the local discriminative power leads to consensus on the population level over time as to which strategy to use. The alignment on the population level can override the particular discriminative power of strategies in some specific context. That is to say, once there is an established strategy within the population, it gets chosen even in cases where another strategy would be more discriminating or equally discriminating.

11.2.1 Experimental setup

I test the power of chunk alignment using contexts which can be manipulated to feature absolute and intrinsic properties. More specifically, I manipulate the distribution of intrinsic and absolute properties in the environment. Figure 11.5 shows the dynamics of an experiment where agents start equipped with two strategies: an absolute and an intrinsic one. The environment is such that it favors absolute systems. In 50% of the scenes both intrinsic and absolute features are present. In the remaining 50% of the contexts only absolute features are present and no intrinsic ones. The environmental conditions have a strong effect on the development of the system in that all 25 populations agree on using an absolute strategy. What is important is that the contexts where only absolute features are present reward the absolute strategy and punish the intrinsic conceptualization strategy. Consequently, even in contexts where intrinsic and absolute features are present, the absolute strategy is preferred. The development of such a preference has important effects on the invention of categories. Because of the preference for the absolute strategy, invention of categories shifts to producing only absolute categories. The successful use of these categories enforces the absolute strategy and leads to further punishment of the intrinsic strategy. The effect is that only the absolute strategy survives.

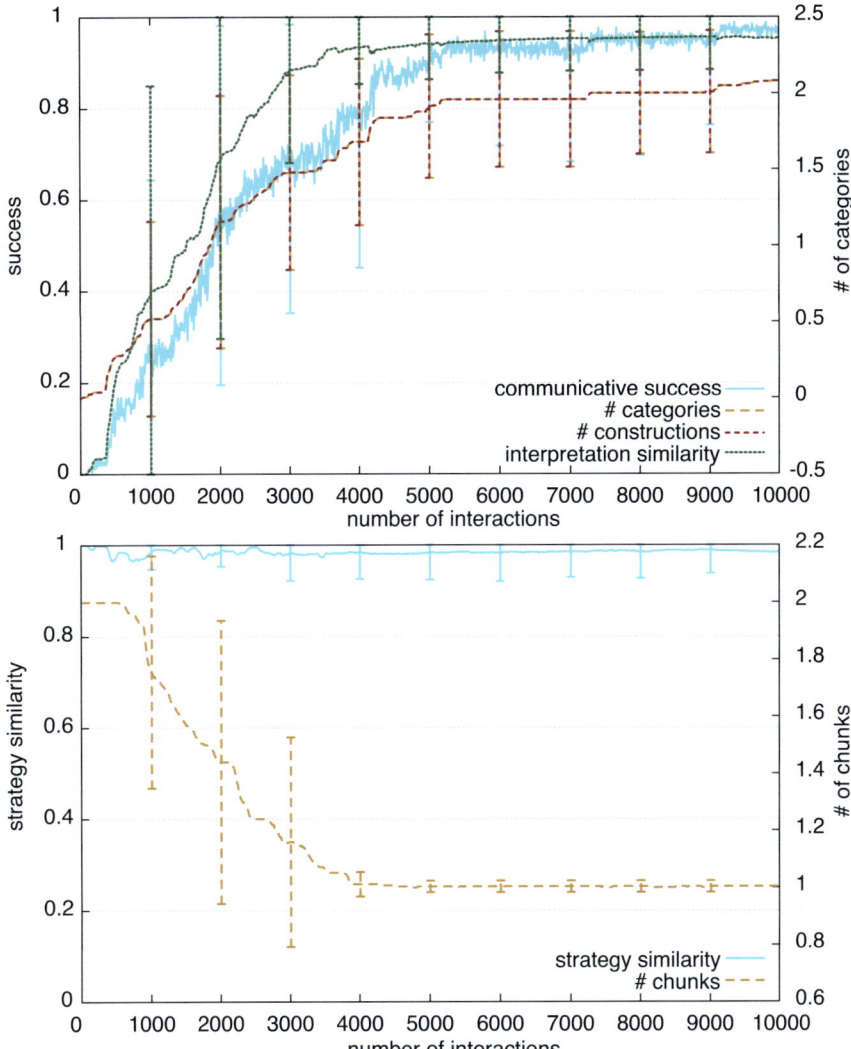

Figure 11.5: Dynamics of a category formation experiment in which 10 agents align the frame of reference used in conceptualization. The environment has a clear preference for the absolute frame of reference in that it is the only frame of reference available in certain context. In 50% of the contexts both intrinsic and absolute frame of reference are available, in the remaining 50% of the contexts only an absolute frame of reference is available. The strong preference of the environment drives agents to develop an absolute system which dominates across 25 runs of the same experiment. The graph shows that together with the category system agents align their conceptualization strategy.

11.2.2 Results

The influence of the distribution of features in the environment and its impact on the developing system are shown in Figures 11.6 and 11.7. Both figures show results for different experimental conditions. In all conditions 50% of the scenes feature both intrinsic and absolute properties. The conditions differ only in how the remaining 50% of scenes are divided. The following table overviews the conditions.

condition	both (%)	intrinsic only (%)	absolute only (%)
0.0	50	0	50
0.25	50	12.5	37.5
0.50	50	25	25
0.75	50	37.5	12.5
1.0	50	50	0

Conditions are named after the percentage of intrinsic only scenes in the 50% of scenes that feature either only intrinsic or only absolute properties. Figure 11.7 shows the average score of the absolute and intrinsic strategies (projective). In all three cases, 50% of the scenes feature both intrinsic and absolute properties. On the top results are shown for an environment that in the remaining 50% has only absolute features. The middle figure shows results where 25% have only absolute features and 25% only intrinsic features. The bottom figure shows results for 50% intrinsic features. Clearly, agents in all cases align strategies reflecting environmental conditions. If the environment clearly supports an absolute strategy, the absolute strategy wins. If there are clear advantages for having an intrinsic strategy (bottom), the intrinsic strategy takes over and suppresses the absolute strategy.

Figure 11.6 compares communicative success as well as resulting average scores of each strategy. Interestingly, the middle condition 0.5 exhibits a significant drop in communicative success to around 80%. The reason for this can be seen in Figure 11.7 (middle) which shows the dynamics of a single run of such an experiment. In this condition no strategy is particularly favored and to be reasonably successful both strategies are necessary. This leads to both strategies having high scores. In a particular moment of inventing a new category both agents might have slightly different preferences for strategies based on their respective recent history of interaction. One agent might have just used the intrinsic strategy successful, whereas the other has just the absolute strategy. In this situation, invention happens wrongly in the sense that one agent might invent an absolute category and the other adopt it as an intrinsic strategy. Such categories which have different types across the population are the cause of the drop in success. Overall, however, the system is able to self-organize under different conditions and successful communication systems emerge.

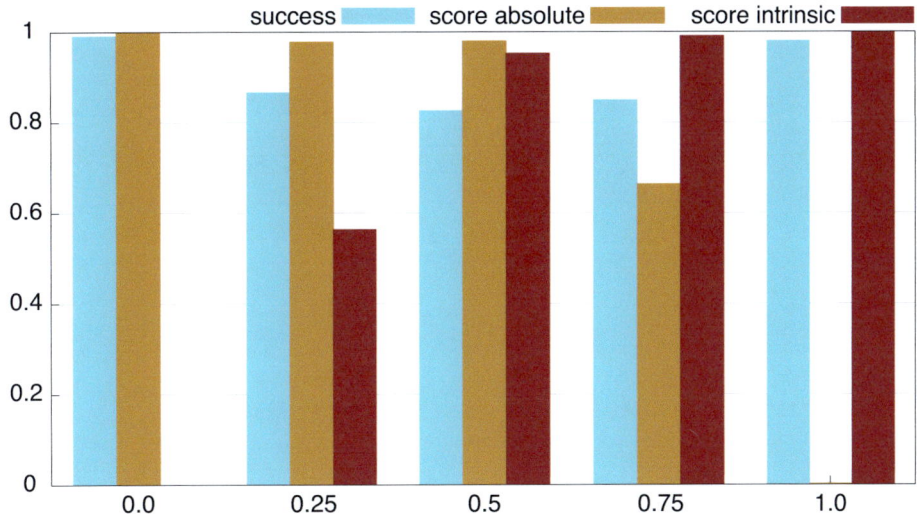

Figure 11.6: Results for experiments with different distributions of intrinsic and absolute features. Each condition was tested with 25 experiments of populations with 10 agents each. The figure shows the communicative success and the scores of the absolute and intrinsic strategy averaged over the multiple runs.

11.3 Invention of conceptualization strategies

The question of how conceptualization strategies can align in a population is important. However, another important ingredient is, of course, how conceptualization strategies come into existence in the first place. Invention is a necessary pre-requisite for the usage of conceptualization strategies and their alignment in a population. Invention of conceptualization strategies is based on the recruitment of basic cognitive operations which are assembled into chunks. Once a chunk is invented, it immediately extends the conceptualization capabilities of agents. Invention of a particular conceptualization strategy is always based on

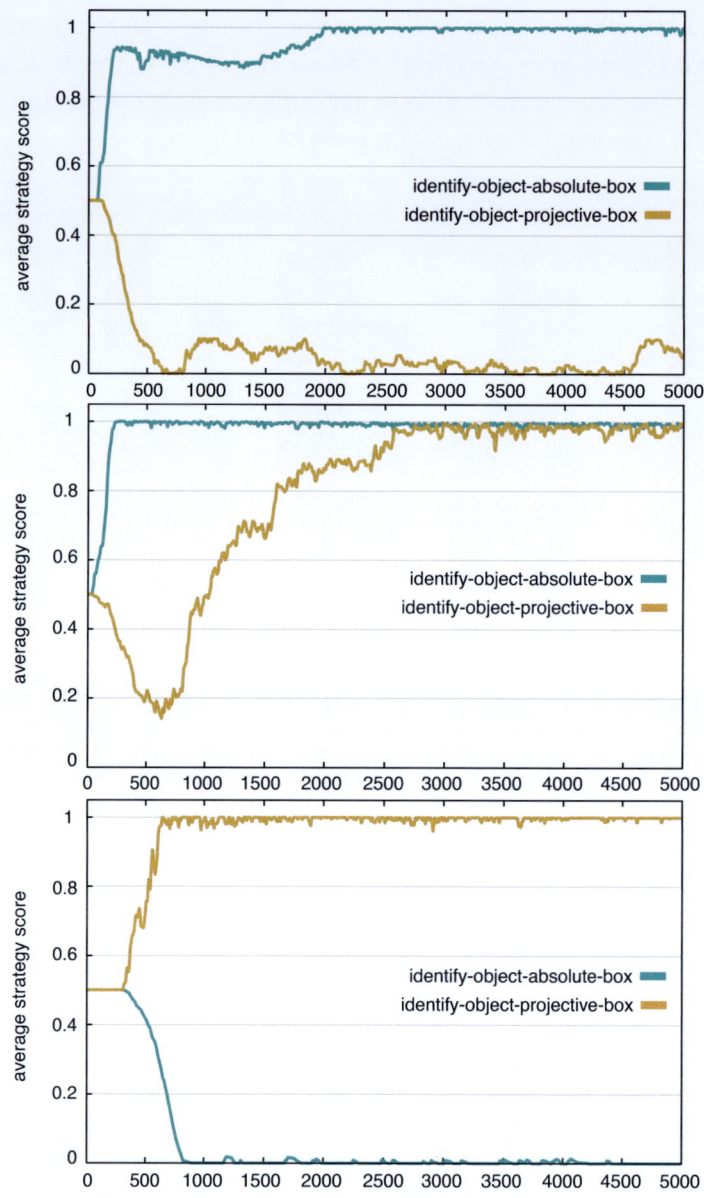

Figure 11.7: Dynamics of alignment for different environmental conditions. The graphs show the average score of the absolute and intrinsic strategy unfold over time. The top figure shows condition 0.0 (see Table 11.2.2, the middle figure shows condition 0.5, and the bottom figure shows condition 1.0.

Figure 11.8: When agents are unable to conceptualize, they search for new conceptualization strategies by assembling cognitive operations into new chunks. Every node is a particular semantic structure that is immediately tested using the current context and the current topic. Here, different possible new strategies (green nodes) were found. Other possible strategies did not work on the current context (blue nodes).

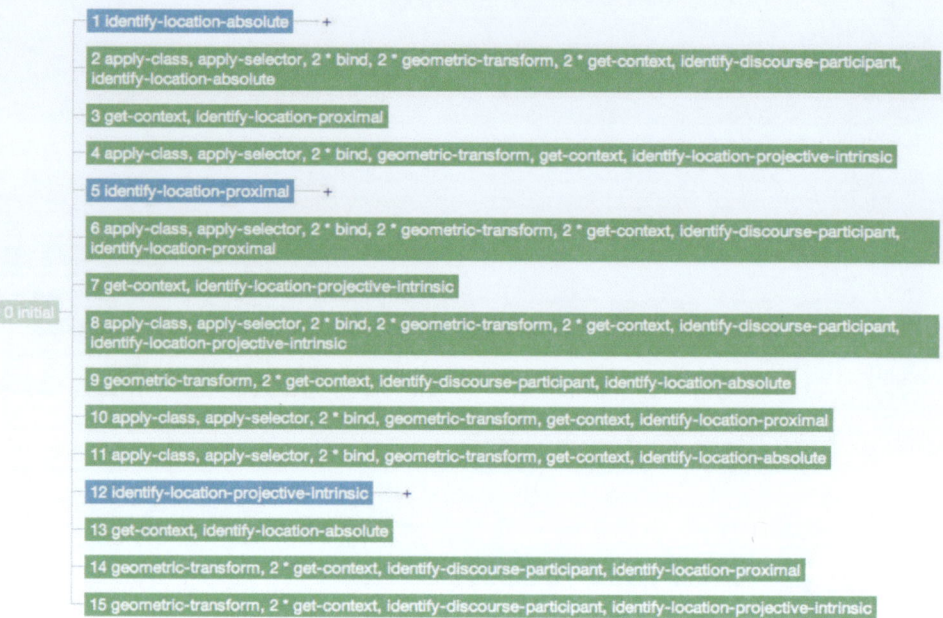

Figure 11.9: The new strategies assembled by the agent (Figure 11.8) are immediately stored in new chunks. This has the immediate effect of condensing the search process. The new strategies are now in competition with each other, as well as with strategies already invented by the agent earlier. Which of these new strategies survives depends on the context and topic that agents are processing at the moment of invention.

a specific communicative situation, a specific context and a specific topic. The starting point for invention is a problem in communication. The agent is unable to conceptualize a meaning for some topic or the meaning that he was able to conceptualize is not discriminative enough. To solve the problem, the agent starts an elaborate search process (see Figures 11.8 and 11.9) which combines basic cognitive operations and the set of conceptualization strategies already established by the agent into new strategies. This process leads to new strategies, which are tested on the current context based on the current communicative goal. The discriminative power of the new strategies decides if and which strategy is stored for future use.

Strategy invention is deeply integrated into the processing of agents. Agents unable to conceptualize or unable to conceptualize with a sufficient discrimination score diagnose a problem which is fixed by a repair that starts the search for new conceptualization strategies. The reason for this integration with other invention mechanisms such as category invention is that agents when inventing new strategies also immediately have to invent new categories with these strategies because the success of spatial strategies is tightly connected with the spatial categories that are part of the strategy. This sort of dual invention is especially important in the beginning of experiments, when agents have neither developed strategies nor categories. But there is a second reason for deep integration of strategy invention. When an agent already has developed a strategy, he might also solve a particular communicative problem by inventing new categories for these established strategies. Such decisions whether to use a new category with an existing strategy or a new strategy with an existing category, or even to use a newly invented strategy with a newly invented category are made based on the discriminative power of each of these different possibilities. So, for instance, if an existing strategy has a low score, the probability of inventing a new strategy increases, whereas if the current topic can be sufficiently discriminated using an existing strategy, no invention occurs.

Figure 11.10 shows the process of invention and alignment of conceptualization strategies in a population of agents. In the experiment generating such results agents have a large repository of basic cognitive operations from which they can draw new building blocks whenever there are problems in communication. They can choose different landmarks: the robot or the box and different category systems absolute and intrinsic projective as well as proximal. The agents manage to agree on one particular strategy while at the same time developing a category system and a lexicon from scratch. The process, however, does not show the same overall success as in the previously discussed experiments. The reason is that conceptual alignment is a difficult process which is complicated by the number of choices in strategies, population size (10 agents) and the variety of different contexts and discriminative situations which might all favor different strategies. In some contexts, proximal is the best strategy, some allow absolute and/or intrinsic categories to be invented. Nevertheless, agents do come to an agreement. Here, they agree on average on 1 conceptualization strategy.

11.4 Discussion

Invention and alignment of conceptualization strategies are powerful processes that together allow agents to develop successful communication systems in the

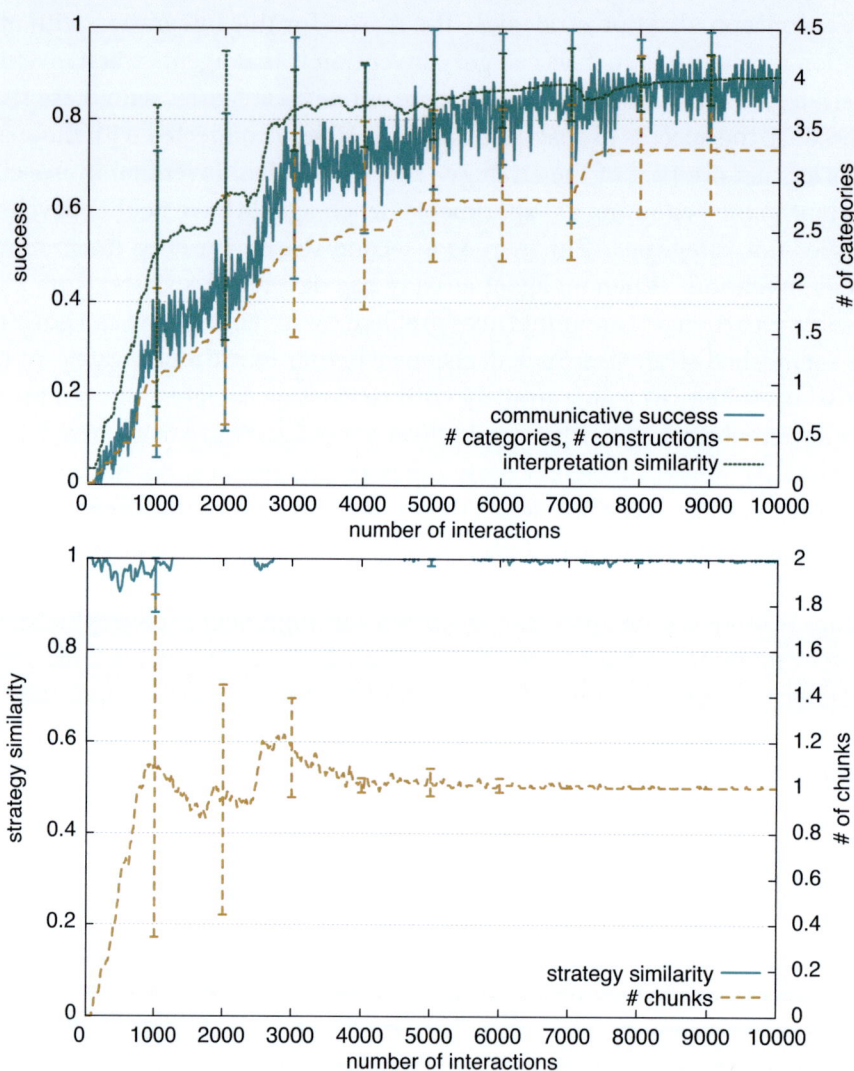

Figure 11.10: Results for strategy invention, alignment and category development. A population of 10 agents develops both conceptualization strategies as well as lexical systems for spatial strategies corresponding to these strategies.

face of varied environmental conditions. In turn, this allows agents to be more adaptive and ultimately more successful than the systems relying exclusively on categorization without taking into account reference objects, frames of reference and the different ways of conceptualizing space. The study of conceptualization strategies is necessarily an important cornerstone in every theory of linguistic selection that has meaning as an important part of the theory. The mechanisms proposed in this section are general enough that they can, in principle, be applied to many different components of language, spatial language being only one of them. For the particular theory of linguistic selection pursued in this book, this section provides substantial evidence in the form of concrete computational experiments. Language systems and in particular the conceptualization strategies underlying language systems, are the product of a cultural process based on the recruitment of cognitive operations and the environmental conditions the agents face.

This section shows that alignment of conceptualization strategies based on invention and selection can be successful if the environment exhibits strong incentives for developing certain conceptualization strategies rather than others. If this condition is met, discriminative power together with tracking the success of strategies, which is the organizing principle used in this chapter, can successfully orchestrate the self-organization of a complete lexical communication system including the conceptualization strategy that gives rise to the communication system. However, despite its success conceptual alignment has its limits, particularly in the approach presented here which relies exclusively on discrimination. For instance, from a theoretical standpoint the relative conceptualization strategy is the most dominant of the absolute, intrinsic and relative strategies. All these three strategies have in common that they rely on angular relationships between objects and reference objects. The relative system in comparison to the other two angle based strategies however does not require additional intrinsic or absolute features, hence, in theory it is applicable in every spatial scene that features some landmark. This leads to a complete takeover of the relative system in experiments where relative, intrinsic and absolute systems compete and where all scenes include a box landmark. Table 11.1 summarizes results in which certain spatial scenes have neither intrinsic nor absolute features.

The strong advantage of relative frames of reference over other frames of reference hints at why relative frames of reference might have emerged, but it cannot explain why certain languages seem to prefer other types of frames of reference over the relative one. Findings in natural language suggest, for example, that English speakers prefer the use of intrinsic frames of reference over relative frames

Table 11.1: Results for absolute, intrinsic and relative conceptualization strategy competition in different environmental conditions. This table shows communicative success and the final scores of the relative, intrinsic and absolute strategy (all allocentric) after 10000 interactions (10 agents, 25 runs averaged). Table 11.2 explains the different conditions.

condition	communicative success (%)	score relative strategy	score intrinsic strategy	score absolute strategy
0.25	100	1.0	0.0	0.0
0.50	100	1.0	0.0	0.0
0.75	100	1.0	0.0	0.0
1.0	100	1.0	0.0	0.0

of reference. The favored usage of intrinsic systems in English hints at the influence of important additional factors besides discrimination that govern the success of a particular strategy. One of such additional factors that was not studied in this section is cognitive complexity. For instance, relative systems are generally considered to be cognitively more demanding because they require tracking of perspective. It is relatively easy to add such constraints to the current system, but running such experiments essentially requires one to put a number on how much one thinks the cognitive complexity of the relative systems is different from other strategies. To avoid such ad hoc quantities I did not pursue this idea. Nevertheless, based on the experimental evidence described in this section, one can predict what will happen when factors additional to discriminative advantage are incorporated into the system. The mechanisms presented in this section function by packaging the successful conceptualization of a single context into strategies and tracking the success of these strategies over many interactions, amplifying patterns in environmental conditions and their effects over time and punishing rival strategies. Consequently, additional factors favoring a particular strategy lead to faster and more stable alignment in the population. So cognitive complexity, for instance, might be a factor that influences the alignment; in the best case, however, it leads to more robust alignment.

Despite its success, conceptual alignment as presented in this section is a process which requires the right conditions in order to flourish. Because agents not only develop strategies but also at the same time build category systems, the system is very powerful and even in cases where there is almost no strategy

Table 11.2: Statistical distribution of features in the environment for the different experimental conditions compared in Table 11.1.

condition	relative only (%)	intrinsic + relative (%)	absolute + relative (%)	absolute + intrinsic + relative (%)
0.25	25	30	7.5	37.5
0.50	50	20	5	25
0.75	75	10	2.5	12.5
1.0	100	0	0	0

alignment agents can reach medium levels of communicative success. The concurrent development of categories makes the system so powerful that in some cases alignment of strategies is prevented. Consequently, agents can be rather successful even though the strategies they use are not entirely the same. This brings us to another point: the role of exaptation. The underlying assumption in all of the experiments in this section is that strategies co-evolve with the categories and lexical systems from scratch. But often times new conceptualization strategies can re-use existing material including categories as well as lexical and grammatical constructions and extend them to work within the new conceptual space that a strategy spans. This has been attested in spatial language which often is thought to originate in language for body parts (see for example MacLaury 1989). For the results in this section this means that the harsh condition that agents start from virtually nothing can be relaxed. Applying this insight to exaptation one can predict that when systems become exapted and there are strong incentives for the population that direct invention of new strategies, this has positive effects on the success and on alignment in conceptualization. A more detailed account of this phenomenon is, however, deferred to later sections.

The results presented in this section are interesting because they show that agents can negotiate conceptualization strategies without marking them explicitly in language. Indirect feedback via the spatial relations and the lexical system associated with a particular spatial strategy are enough to allow the system to organize itself. However, an important factor of linguistic systems was deliberately avoided in the discussion so far: the role of syntax. Many of the problems which cannot be solved by discrimination alone can be solved by agents when they are able to mark and express their strategies in more complex ways than so far studied. The next sections picks up on this theme and gradually introduce additional invention and learning mechanisms particular to the mapping from conceptualization strategies to syntactic structure.

12 Multi-word lexical systems for expressing landmarks

Conceptual alignment is powerful but also has its limits. The most prominent of which is that conceptual alignment is based on the idea that the population agrees on using a single strategy. Now, even a superficial look at English and German reveals that, in fact, these languages support many different ways of conceptualizing space at the same time. The reason for allowing diverse strategies to flourish in a population is clearly related to the ability to discriminate and denote many objects in different spatial settings. German and English exhibit a rich system of different conceptualization strategies such as allocentric and egocentric, but they also allow the usage of different frames of reference, all of which enables agents to be successful in communication particularly when facing different spatial layouts and features of the particular environment. The grammar of the respective languages organizes the expression of these different strategies, but the expression of each strategy also relies heavily on lexical systems which go beyond simply expressing the names of spatial relations. In this section I consider the expression of compositional semantics using lexical items. This is the first step towards grammar and a necessary prerequisite for grammatical development.

In particular, this section details the step from single-word utterances encompassing only the lexical items of spatial categories to multi-word utterances which besides the spatial relation express semantic entities as part of the conceptualization strategy. A good example for these are reference objects which are typically themselves marked using lexical items such as in *links von dir* ('to the left of you') which explicitly marks the reference object as being the hearer via the pronoun *dir* ('you'). Earlier sections of this book already dealt with lexical systems and much of the discussion applies to extended lexical systems which incorporate lexical items for landmarks and the like. Essentially, one is left with generalizing the construction invention and adoption operators for spatial categories to include other semantic entities. This endows agents with the capacity for lexical marking of reference objects as part of conceptualization strategies. This single step to multi-word utterances alone, as is argued in this chapter, allows agents to be more adaptive and more successful in communication.

12.1 Invention and alignment operators

In order to study the behavior of systems that allow for more expressiveness using multi-word utterances, I adapt the operators that invent constructions for spatial categories and extend them to deal with semantic items that are not spatial categories. Technically, these operators enable speakers to invent constructions for bind statements in the conceptualized meaning they want to express. On the other hand, hearers can employ similar operators that adopt unknown strings by linking them to bind statements in interpreted meaning, specifically in re-conceptualized meaning. Figure 12.1 shows the meaning conceptualized for a particular context using an egocentric strategy. The meaning contains two bind statements, i.e. two semantic entities, for which the agent has invented two lexical constructions. One for the spatial category and one for the discourse role speaker. Consequently, the speaker utters two words for this particular meaning. In this case the meaning will be conveyed using the utterance *rexute calipo* with no word-order constraints applying. In fact, because there are no word order constraints, the strings are shuffled and the speaker is equally likely to utter any permutation of the two words. The hearer upon encountering such an utterance will use the power of re-conceptualization to find an appropriate interpretation of the utterance which sets up the learning context. Depending on how much he already knows, this might be an easy task. However, if he does not know any of the two words, he first has to invent a category based on the topic and the most likely conceptualization strategy given the current context. Let us suppose the hearer has already encountered the spatial category named by the word *rexute*. If he re-conceptualizes that the speaker most probably used an egocentric strategy, the interpreted meaning looks very similar to the meaning conceptualized by the speaker; the only difference being that he uses his spatial category. Because there is precisely one unknown word for the hearer and one bind statement in the interpreted meaning that is not linked to a word in the utterance, this presents a learning opportunity for the hearer and he can adopt the word *calipo* to mean the discourse role speaker.

There are two types of problems that lead to the invention of new markers. First, if production for a particular meaning fails altogether, i.e. no utterance can be produced, a specific diagnostic triggers and reports a problem. This problem immediately starts a dedicated repair strategy which scans the meaning, looks for bind statements and invents new words for all bind statements in the meaning. Preference is given for inventing words for spatial categories. The reason is that if an agent cannot express a spatial category used in conceptualization, this

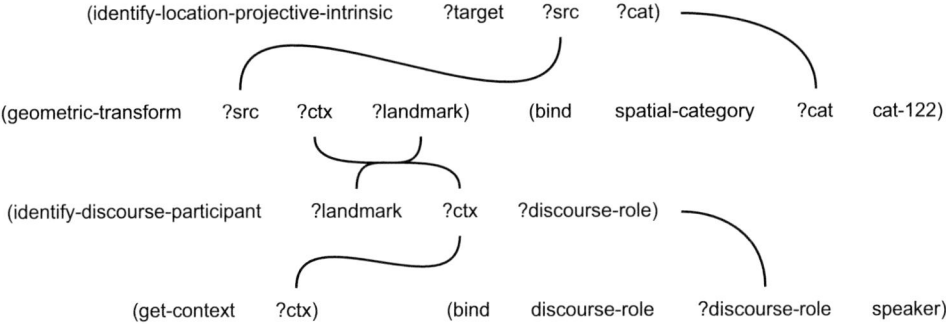

Figure 12.1: Semantic structure for an egocentric conceptualization.

category has just been invented by him. The invention of lexical constructions linking to other semantic entities is controlled by a parameter that adjusts how eager agents invent new linguistic items. The second situation that might lead to the invention of new markers is when agents notice in re-entrance that they might be misunderstood. This is typically the case if an agent is conceptualizing using a category that already has a name. In such cases production will use that name which leads to a single-word utterance consisting of the category name. If the agent re-enters, that is parses and interprets his own utterance before passing it to the hearer, he might find that the category name alone does not exclude other conceptualization strategies in interpretation. Let us suppose an agent has conceptualized the category cat-122 using an egocentric strategy. If he only utters the word associated with that category, other conceptualization strategies such as allocentric and egocentric hearer are possible and might lead to other interpretations. A special diagnostic identifies this condition and reports a problem. The repair strategy triggered by these problems will solves the problem by inventing a marker for the bind statement in the conceptualized meaning that the speaker could not recover when parsing his own utterance. The process of marking unexpressed meaning is important and will play a significant role in later sections. Figure 12.2 gives an overview of this process. The hearer uses the same learning operators for diagnosing and repairing the re-production process. But instead of inventing new strings, he re-uses unknown strings from the utterance passed to him by the speaker.

Lexical constructions denoting additional bind statements are subject to the same alignment control operations as all the other lexical constructions for spatial relations. However, there is a fundamental difference in the way semantic

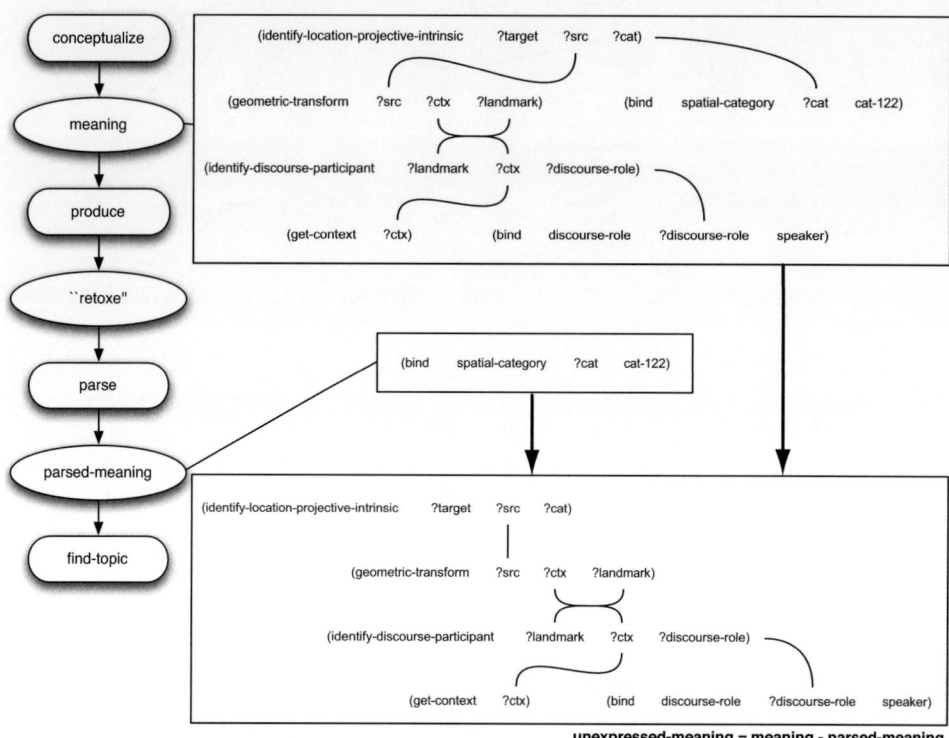

Figure 12.2: Example of a learning situation in which agents invent additional names for semantic entities in production. The left shows the processes run as part of production. Suppose the agent has conceptualized the meaning shown on top. He produces for this topic. Because he already has a construction to express the category cat-122, he would utter the word *retoxe*. Before passing the utterance to the hearer, he re-enters the utterance himself and interprets the parsed meaning. Having only expressed the category, he potentially interprets different target objects. He detects this problem and extracts the unexpressed meaning shown below which consists of the complete network without the category which was expressed in the utterance. A repair strategy can now scan the unexpressed meaning and potentially invent a lexical construction for the discourse role speaker which was not expressed. The same mechanism is re-used for the evolution of grammatical systems discussed in later sections.

entities like discourse roles and object classes are treated in this book from the way spatial categories are treated. The representations of spatial categories are shaped by agents and it is part of the argument how spatial categories are adapted. For object classes and discourse roles this does not hold. Rather, such entities are given to agents and their internal representation is fixed. For these items then the problem of language evolution reduces to mere naming problems, i.e. finding words for established concepts. The discussion of how these items, i.e. the agent internal concepts, can emerge and how they are shaped is not discussed here. For the emergence of naming systems, however, the same insights apply as for the lexical systems involving categories. Lexical constructions for naming such concepts are subject to continuous tracking of their respective success as well as punishment of competitors for the same concepts using lateral inhibition.

Lastly, a hearer encounter a situation where he is confronted with two unknown words in the utterance passed to him by the speaker. While the he might nevertheless be able to re-conceptualize some meaning involving two semantic entities, he faces a tough problem because in principle all possible linkings between the two semantic entities and the two words are possible. In such cases hearers give up and learn neither of them.

12.2 Experimental setup and results

I test the effectiveness of the learning operators on spatial scenes. The main factor manipulated is the objects eligible to be topics. The robots and the allocentric landmarks, in each scene are also sometimes topics of communicative interactions. So instead of just talking about the blocks in their environment agents now have to talk about themselves and the box landmark. The idea behind this is that scenes where the reference objects themselves are chosen as topic help agents develop a system for naming these objects. The growing lexical system for reference objects can then be re-used when inventing and adopting new spatial categories in conceptualization strategies featuring the reference objects. In other words, this allows the systems for marking reference objects and spatial categories to co-evolve.

Figure 12.3 shows that lexical learning operators extend well to semantic entities that are not spatial categories. Agents in the experiments summarized in the graph are equipped with allocentric and egocentric projective strategies (intrinsic). We can see that agents not only develop categories but also lexical items to name the three possible reference objects. We can see that agents reach success fast with synonyms arising for the different reference objects that are gradually

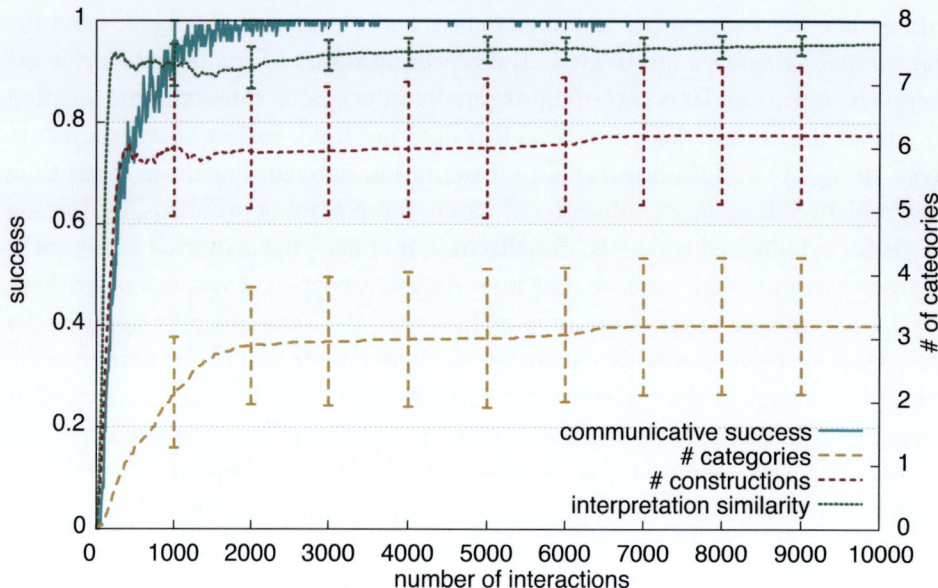

Figure 12.3: Results for an experiment were agents are equipped with three conceptualization strategies: allocentric, egocentric speaker and egocentric hearer. Additionally, agents are given invention and adoption mechanisms for lexical constructions to denote the landmarks themselves.

removed again from the population. The number of constructions stays consistently higher than the number of categories which refers to the lexical constructions that link to object classes and discourse roles. In total, agents need three additional constructions – one for each strategy.

One can contrast these results to some extent with alignment of conceptualization strategy results. Figure 12.4 compares the communicative success and shows that for all things being equal, allowing agents to mark the conceptualization strategy is overall more successful and reaches successful levels faster than relying on only on alignment of conceptualization strategies. Such comparisons, however, have to be read very carefully. First, the dynamics of alignment is subject to sets of parameters and sometimes small changes in these parameters have significant effects on overall communicative success, but also on the dynamics of development. Second, the experiment shows one particular run in a particular environment. Nevertheless, it seems reasonable to extrapolate these results. If agents have the capacity to be more expressive, this clearly helps them in being more precise in communication. In particular, the expression of reference objects eliminates the major source of errors in conceptualization alignment, namely the problem of guessing the strategy used. It is therefore plausible to assume that marking always outperforms strategy alignment in sufficiently complicated environmental conditions that necessitate the balancing of different strategies.

12.3 Discussion

One can conclude that lexical expressivity is enormously helpful and allows agents to develop communication systems more rapidly and more successfully. Additionally agents can be successful in different environments and spatial se-tups, because the different conceptualization strategies co-exist at the same time and there is no need for competition and alignment of strategies in the strict sense. Lexical marking, consequently, also leads to more adaptive systems if the environment changes later. All it takes, if new possible reference objects arise, is to invent new markers, whereas in conceptual alignment agents have to come up with new strategies altogether.

Lexical-only systems have an additional problem with respect to spatial language. Lexical marking cannot disambiguate semantic structure that encompasses the same semantic entities but different operations. For instance, the utterance *der linke block* ('the left block') has a different semantic structure than *links des blockes* ('to the left of the block'). Albeit both have the same lexical items, there is a clear difference in semantic function. In the case of the adjective noun phrase, *links* ('left') is used as a modifier modifying the set of blocks. In the case of the prepositional phrase *links* ('left') is related to a landmark denoted by the determined noun phrase *des blockes* ('the block').

More information can be found in Spranger 2012a; 2013a.

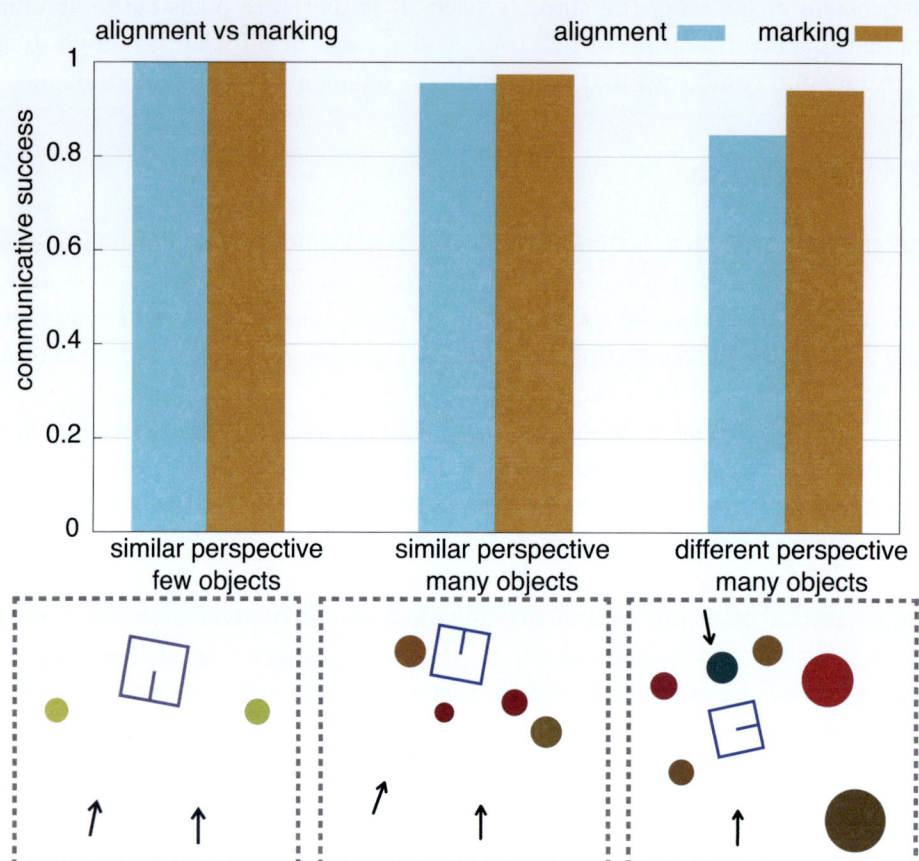

Figure 12.4: Comparison of alignment only versus lexical marking of strategies. The results are based on landmark selection and three strategies are available to agents: allocentric, speaker and hearer. In the "alignment" condition agents are given the three strategies plus mechanisms for strategy alignment. In the "marking" condition agents can develop a lexicon for disambiguating the strategy they are using in a particular language game. The two approaches are tested on different sets of spatial scenes. The more complex spatial scenes are, the larger is the advantage of marking the conceptualization strategy.

13 Function and evolution of locative spatial grammar

Purely lexical communication systems are limited because while they enable agents to express semantic entities, in a restricted sense they do not allow to encode how these semantic entities are supposed to be used, in particular, they do not encode how to process the spatial context. For instance, the following three utterances

(1) der   linke   Block
the.NOM left.ADJ.NOM block.NOM
'The left block',

(2) links   des   Blockes
left.PREP.GEN the.DET.GEN block.GEN
'to the left of the block',

and

(3) der   Block   links
the.DET.NOM block.NOM left.ADV
'the block to the left',

all consist of the same lexical material but their meaning structure is quite different. In (1) the spatial relation is used as modifier on the set of objects denoted by the noun, whereas in (2) the spatial category is applied to a landmark denoted by the noun. In (3) a determined noun phrase is followed by the category expressed as an adverb which denotes a region that is used to modify the set of blocks. In difference to (1), however, the spatial category is related to a covert landmark, not a group-based relative reference system. If an agent in a spatial language game is confronted with these utterances, he is supposed to process the context differently in each case. In some contexts the referent denoted by each of these two utterances might be the same, but this is not necessarily true for all spatial scenes. Clues for the different processing of these utterances are in the grammatical structure of each of them. In the first case, the word order and the morphology make it clear that the spatial category is used as an adjective within a determined adjective noun phrase. In the second case, it is the usage of the spatial category as preposition that encodes that the determined noun phrase tail of the phrase is denoting the landmark to which the spatial relation is applied. In (3), the lack of a following noun phrase reveals the use of the spatial category as adverb which entails inferences about the type of the region, e.g., the region can be internal or external and there must be a covert landmark. Consequently, these three examples show how the German grammatical system provides valuable indications as to how to interpret each of these utterances. In this chapter, I will be concerned with two claims following from this observation. First, grammar is necessary to avoid ambiguity and errors in interpretation. Second, given the communicative need to avoid such problems in communication, agents equipped with the right learning and invention operators can develop grammatical communication systems.[1]

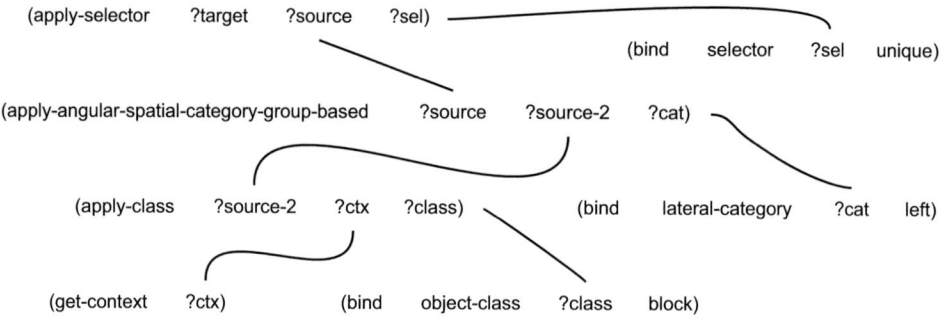

Figure 13.1: Semantic structure underlying (1) and (4). The semantic structure has three semantic entities which are linked in such a way that the set of blocks filtered by the primitive apply-class is further filtered by the spatial category left which is applied here to a group-based relative landmark. Finally, the selector unique is applied retrieving the best scoring element.

---

[1] Ideas and results presented in this chapter are published in (Spranger & Steels 2012) and (Spranger, Pauw & Loetzsch 2010).

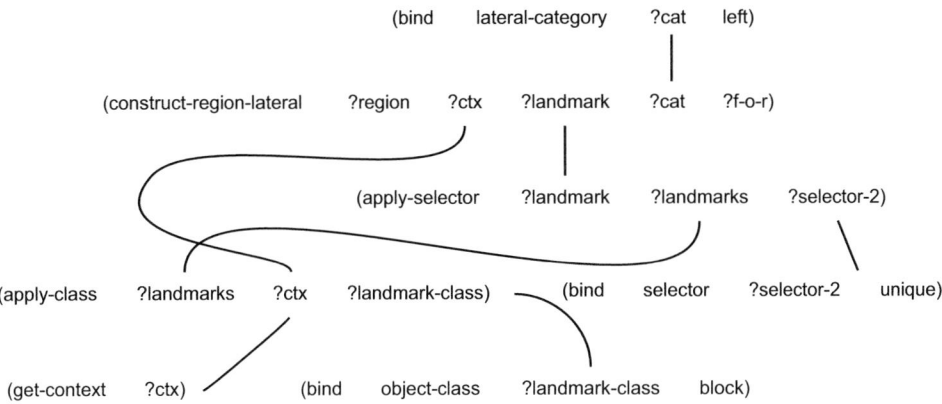

Figure 13.2: Semantic structure underlying (2) and (4). This semantic structure encodes how to construct a lateral region based on the spatial relation left using the landmark that is provided by the subpart of the structure singeling out an object from the context by applying the object class block and the selector unique.

13.1 The importance of grammar

The main hypothesis pursued in this section is that grammar is important because it conveys information as to how lexical items, e.g. spatial relations, interact in semantic structure and which role the lexical items play within the semantic structure. By providing this important information on how to process the context, grammar reduces the search space of possible interpretations of a phrase and thereby enhances the communicative success of the population. To see this, it is helpful to consider what is left if one were to "remove" the grammatical cues from (1) to (3). In principle, one ends up with a phrase like the following.

(4) link block der
     left block the

This phrase is non-grammatical because it lacks proper German morphology and word order among other things. Now this phrase can be interpreted in many different ways. Since semantics are represented using IRL, we will immediately make this point using IRL-networks to formalize what is meant by different semantics. Three plausible spatial semantic interpretations of (4) are shown in Figures 13.1, 13.2 and 13.3. The semantic structures shown in these figures formalize the intuitive notions formulated in the beginning of this chapter as to what the

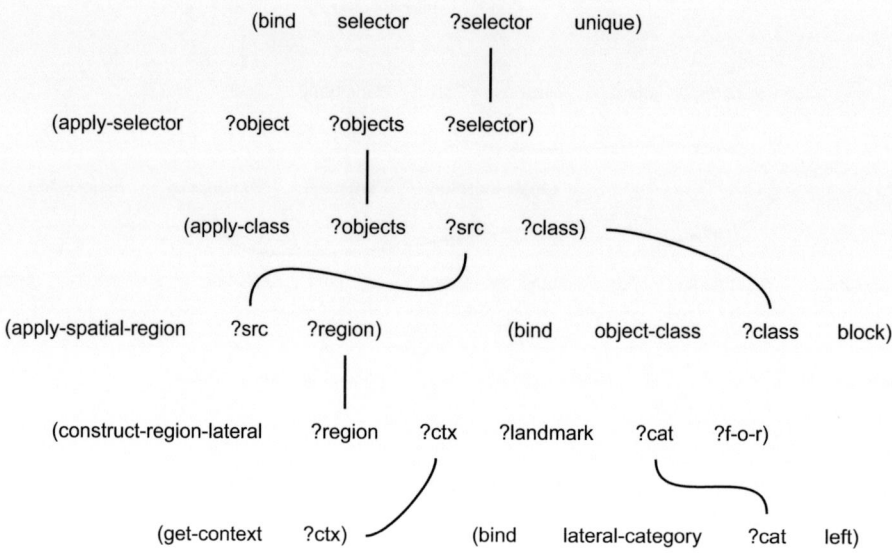

Figure 13.3: Semantic structure underlying (3) and 4. The spatial relation left is used here to construct a region based on an unspecified landmark. The region is used to filter the context, followed by the application of the object class block to further filter the objects, followed by the application of the selector unique.

difference is in the semantics of (1) to (3) which are all utterances built using the same lexical material as (4). Mort importantly, however, all three semantic structures are valid interpretations of (4) because Example 4 only constraints the space of possible interpretations by providing a set of semantic entities that need to be part of the semantic structure. The three semantic entities encoded in this utterance are part of all three semantic structures. To understand then what information grammar provides in the formal framework of IRL, one can examine the differences in interpretations. There are two important differences between these structures; the first is related to the cognitive operations involved. For instance, semantic structure 13.1 involves the operation apply-spatial-category-group-based which is not found in 13.2 or 13.3. The other important difference is in terms of how operations are linked. The difference between the structures in Figures 13.2 and 13.3 is not only which cognitive operations are part of each of them, but primarily one of how the cognitive operations are linked. In Figure 13.2, the landmark of the spatial region is given by the subnetwork consisting of `apply-selector` and `apply-class`, whereas in 13.3 this subnetwork is linked to the output of the operation `apply-spatial-region` so as to further refine the set of objects which are filtered using the spatial region. In the formal framework pursued in this book, grammar is related to which cognitive operations are part of the semantic structure of an utterance and how the semantic structure is internally linked.

Removing the grammatical cues from (1) to (3) increases the number of possible interpretations of these phrases. Consequently, grammar is related to semantic ambiguity which I defined as different possible semantic structures underlying the same utterance (see Section 9.2). The increase in possible interpretations of a phrase impacts in two ways. First, it can lead to failure in communication because the hearer interprets the phrase differently and the different interpretation leads to mistakes in establishing reference, i.e., the hearer interprets the phrase to refer to the wrong topic. Second, semantic ambiguity leads to additional effort in interpretation on the part of the hearer. If there are multiple interpretations, of a phrase, the hearer has to test all of them in order to find the correct interpretation.

13.1.1 Experimental results

Figure 13.4 shows what happens when all grammatical constructions are removed from the German locative system. Every utterance produced by an agent operating a lexical system conveys only the semantic entities, e.g. spatial relations, object classes, determiners and discourse roles without explicitly marking their relationships in the semantic structure. Figure 13.4 compares the performance on different sets of spatial scenes with varying features and degrees of complexity. To the left the condition is one in which many objects are distributed around an allocentric landmark. The middle condition is one in which scenes have no allocentric landmark. The condition shown to the right has both scenes with allocentric and without allocentric landmark but is generally more complex with respect to the number of objects and distribution of objects. Additionally, the position of the interlocutors is more varied. Clearly, the more complex spatial scenes are the more important non-ambiguous communication is. On the other hand, it is quite strikingly not the case that communication breaks down completely when agents are lacking grammatical devices in their language. Rather, agents are in general successful in communication. They are able to establish correct reference in well over 70% of cases and, for instance in the middle condition in almost 90% of the cases. The reasons for this is the powerful active interpretation capacity that agents are endowed with which allows them to find

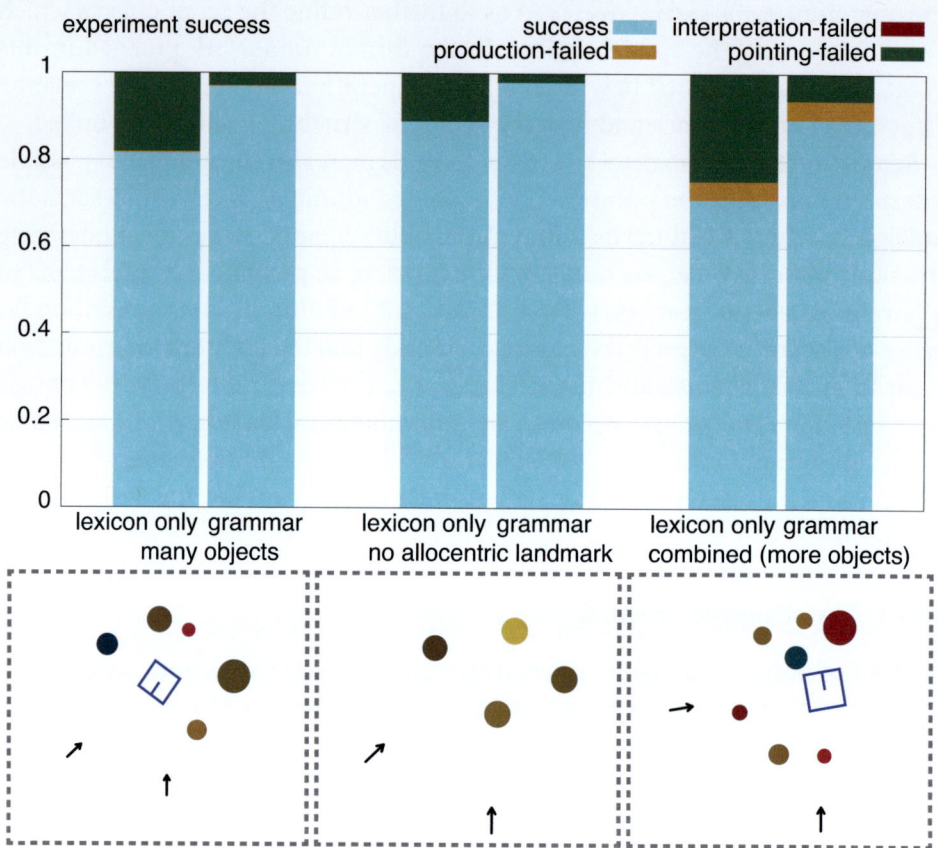

Figure 13.4: The figure compares the performance of agents equipped with a purely lexical system with a population in which all agents operate the German space grammar discussed in Section 7. There are three conditions "many objects", "no allocentric landmark" and "combined (more objects)". In the first condition, agents have similar perspectives on the scene and there are quite a few objects. In the middle condition, there is no box landmark. Agents can only use themselves as landmark or have to resort to group-based reference. The last condition is a combination of the two, but with scenes that have even more objects.

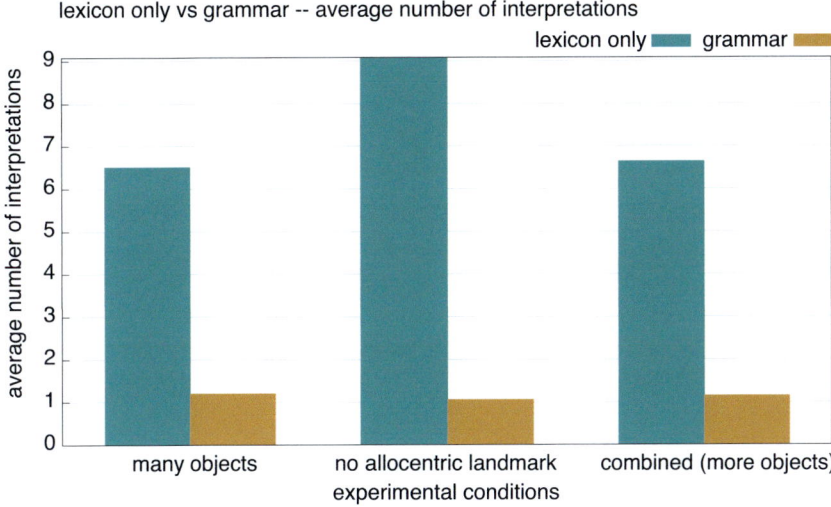

Figure 13.5: This figure compares the number of semantic structures tried in interpretation for German locative phrases processed with and without grammar.

the most probable object given the lexical material they observe in the utterance. But this success is also in part due to the overall limited nature of conceptualization strategies which for every scene is among the range of 10 but not infinitely large which allows agents to guess the meaning of purely lexical utterances.

Clearly, there is a communicative advantage for having grammatical constructions that allow agents to recover additional information not communicated by lexical items alone. Figure 13.5 shows the advantage of grammar in processing spatial utterances by comparing the number of interpretations hearers had to try in order to arrive at the best interpretation of the phrase. This number is significantly higher for lexical systems than it is for the German locative grammar discussed in this book. Essentially the results measure semantic ambiguity and show efficiency in interpreting utterances. The figure shows the average number of interpretations (10000 interactions). In the case of grammar, the average is just barely above 1.0. When agents are equipped with grammar, there is only one type of utterance that is really ambiguous in terms of processing. An example of such an utterance is *der Block links der Kiste* ('the block left of the box'), which can be interpreted in an intrinsic or relative way. For purely lexical systems the number of interpretations the hearer has to try for each phrase is high. On av-

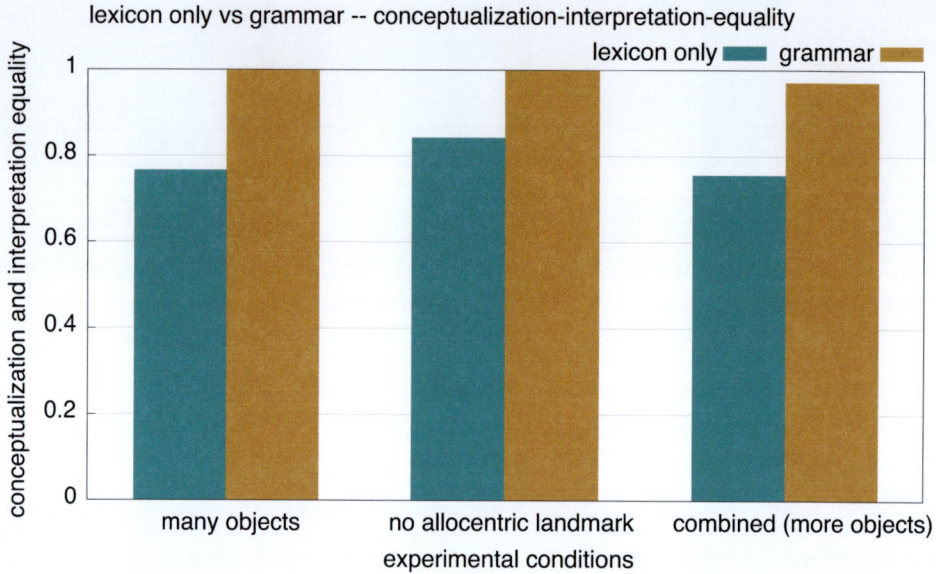

Figure 13.6: This figure shows how similar the semantic structure recovered by the hearer is to the conceptualization strategy of the speaker. The effect is compared for different sets of spatial scenes. If the semantic structures are equal, the interaction counts as 1.0, if not – as 0.0. The results show the average over 10000 interactions. In the case of grammatical systems, the speaker was able to recover the correct semantic structure in all games. For purely lexical systems this number drops to 80%. This number correlates to some respect with communicative success. But not in all spatial scenes is a drop in the number of scenes in which the hearer correctly interprets the phrase equal to to a drop in communicative success.

erage more than six interpretations have to be tried for every single utterance in all three conditions. The peak for the condition "no allocentric landmark" is due to the increased number of utterances consisting of three lexical items in this condition. Utterances involving three lexical items can be interpreted as determined adjective noun phrases, but also in many ways including covert spatial landmarks and even perspective. The middle condition licenses many three word utterances. Because of the lack of an allocentric landmark, speakers will often choose the adjectival strategy without being able to clearly express themselves and mark their strategy using grammar. Nevertheless, if we look back at the impact on communicative success, there is no direct correlation between number of interpretations of a phrase and communicative success. In the *no allocentric landmark* condition the drop in success is not as strong as the rise in number of interpretations per phrase. An explanation can be seen in Figure 13.6 which shows that while the number of interpretations increases, the rate with which hearers find the correct interpretation does not drop as strong for the condition.

13.1.2 Factors influencing the importance of grammar

If grammar has positive effects on processing and communicative success, one can ask the follow-up question: what are the factors determining how much impact grammar has. How much agents with grammar perform better in terms of communicative success is largely a function of the environment and the number of possible interpretations of each utterance. The more complex the environment and the larger the number of different possible interpretations of a phrase, the more problems occur in communication. If agents share similar viewpoints on the scene, if perceptual deviation is minimal and if there are only few objects in the scene, the effect of grammar is less strong than in cases where viewpoints are different, perceptual deviation is strong and the number of objects is high (a fact that is demonstrated in Figure 13.4). But these influences are quite subtle. For instance, the results shown in Figures 13.5 and 13.6 suggest that it is not only the number of interpretations that make a difference, but the ambiguity has to matter with respect to the environment. for instance, perspective is relevant to certain aspects of the German locative system, but it does not necessarily cause problems in communication. Many conceptualization strategies such as the absolute one are agnostic to perspective. One also has to be careful not to confuse the sensitivity of some conceptualization strategies with the impact of grammar. A strategy fully expressed in grammar can remain sensitive to perspective, e.g., determined spatial adjective noun phrases need to be interpreted with respect to some perspective. But the sensitivity remains if one expresses the underlying group-based reference conceptualization strategy lexically only.

The performance with respect to processing is governed by the number of possible different interpretations of a particular phrase. The higher the number of possible interpretations is the more conceptualization strategies need to be tested and processed. The number is essentially a function of how much re-use of lexical items occurs in the language or how much particular semantic entities such as spatial relations participate in different interpretations. For instance, in the German locative system, lateral and frontal projective spatial relations occur in relative and intrinsic conceptualization strategies. Absolute categories do not participate in intrinsic and relative conceptualization strategies but only in absolute ones. To remove the power of grammar to disambiguate, therefore, has less effect on absolute spatial relations. Consequently, if a semantic entity only participates in a single conceptualization strategy, removing parts of grammar related to that entity has little or no effect, whereas when the entity participates in many different conceptualization strategies this can have a big impact. Additionally, the increase in ambiguity is paired with features of the environment. If features of the environment are such that agents are not using a particularly ambiguous set of strategies, than ambiguity does not play a role in these conditions.

13.2 Emergence of grammatical markers

Following the argument for the impact of grammar on communicative success and processing, I can turn to the question: what are the necessary invention, adoption and alignment mechanisms so that agents can self-organize grammatical communication systems? I will attempt to answer this question by looking at a smaller set of conceptualization strategies than the full-blown German locative system and by reducing grammar deliberately to marking of conceptualization strategies. That is, I do not discuss how word order arises and may become shared or how the complex morphological system of German may be culturally negotiated. Rather, I look at grammatical systems that are marking the part of semantic structure related to processing of semantic entities. In this scheme, grammatical constructions map certain parts of semantic structure – namely cognitive operations and their links to strings, henceforth called markers. These constructions build up a shallow hierarchy. Their constituents are lexical items that provide semantic entities.

An important example of semantic ambiguity in German locative phrases is related to frames of reference. The lexical item *über* ('over') can be processed in all three frames of reference: absolute, intrinsic and relative. For studying the development of grammatical systems, agents are given four conceptualization

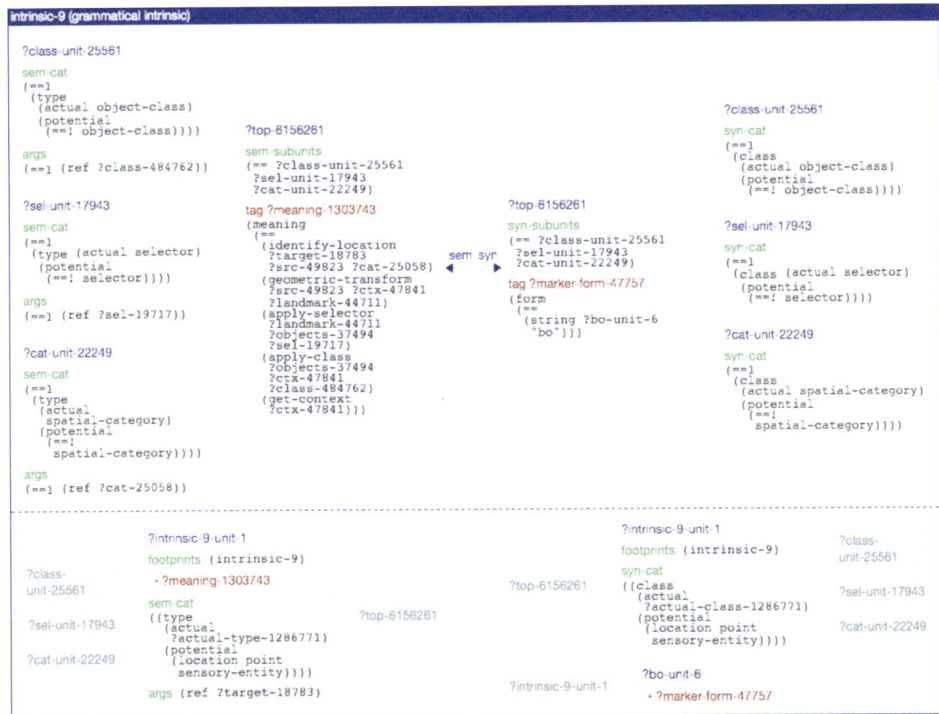

Figure 13.7: Grammatical construction for marking the intrinsic conceptualization strategy (see Figure 13.8). The construction has three lexical constituents: a spatial relation, a selector and an object class. In production, the intrinsic strategy is expressed using the three lexical constituents plus the marker *bo* that is introduced by this construction.
In parsing the construction fully recovers the intrinsic conceptualization strategies upon observing three compatible lexical items and
the marker *bo*. Notice that categories are the same on the syntactic
and semantic side which follows the design of lexical constructions.

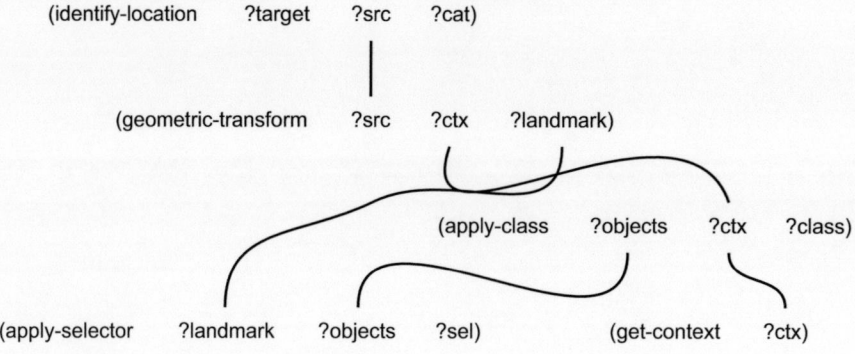

Figure 13.8: IRL-network of the intrinsic conceptualization strategy. A corresponding construction for expressing this strategy is shown in Figure 13.7.

strategies: intrinsic, absolute, relative from the perspective of the speaker and relative from the perspective of the hearer. Agents are equipped with four angular spatial relations, all of which are modeled after *vor* ('front'), *hinter* ('back'), *links* ('left') and *rechts* ('right') with the difference that they behave like *über* ('up') and partake in intrinsic, relative and absolute conceptualization strategies. Agents operating only lexical constructions will express themselves always in three word utterances. The utterances consist of the spatial relation as well as a determiner and a noun. All four strategies operate the same set spatial relations and all apply the frame of reference to an allocentric landmark which can be marked lexically. For any utterance the three words alone never distinguish between the four conceptualization strategies given to agents, but rather a hearer always has to try all four strategies, in order, to retrieve the most likely topic. The lexical agents can be contrasted with agents operating grammatical constructions. Grammatical constructions allow agents to communicate the conceptualization strategy they used by marking it. Figure 13.7 shows a grammatical construction that marks the intrinsic strategy (see Figure 13.8) with the marker *bo*. Consequently, an agent equipped with this construction, if he uses the intrinsic strategy in conceptualization, constructs an utterance involving a spatial term, the determiner, an object class term and the marker *bo*. Subsequently, in interpretation a hearer of this utterance parses a complete IRL-network and he is not required to additionally process the other conceptualization strategies to find the topic of the phrase. Figure 13.9 compares the performance of lexical agents that only operate lexical constructions with agents that grammatically mark the conceptualization strategy they are using. We can observe similar effects of grammar both on processing and communicative success as for the complete German locative system. Overall this justifies the simplified approach taken in this section.

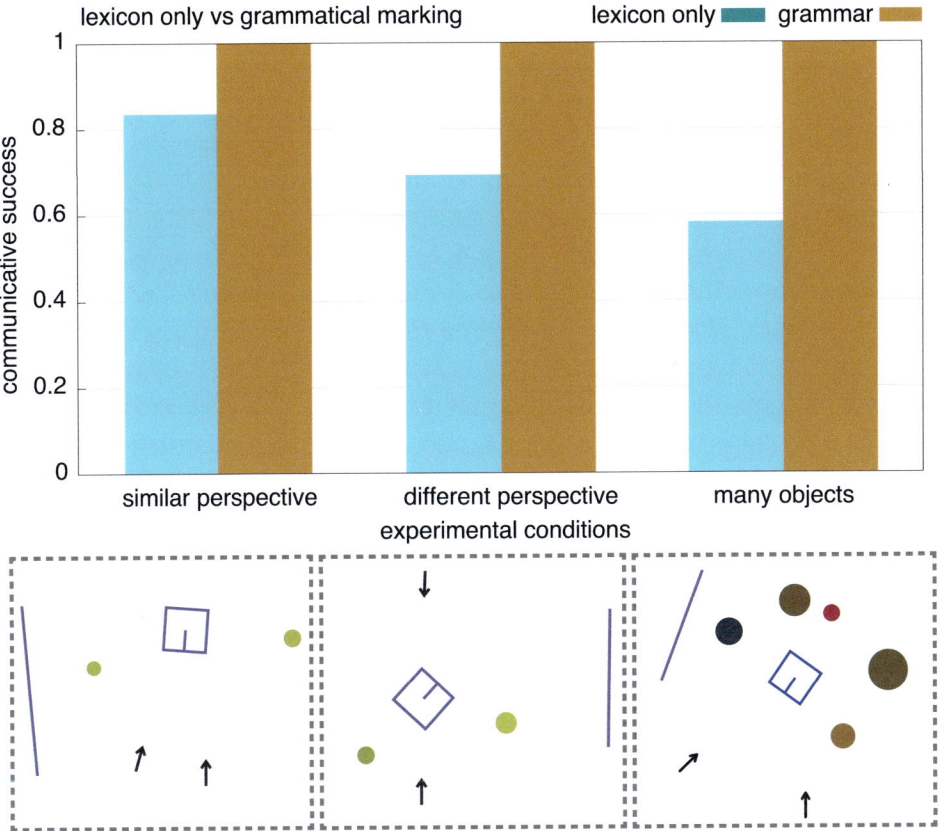

Figure 13.9: Comparison of purely lexical agents equipped with four angular conceptualization strategies. Half of the strategies are dependent on perspective, hence, the impact of changing the perspective of robots on the scene is a major impact. Another factor is the number of objects in each scene.

13.2.1 Invention and alignment operators

The results shown in this and the previous section undoubtedly demonstrate the advantage of a communication system that allows agents to mark the usage of the same semantic entities in different conceptualization strategies. The clear communicative advantages for grammar in spatial settings can fuel a process whereby agents are actively developing grammatical markers in order to communicate more successfully. To verify this claim I research which diagnostics and repair strategies are needed for agents to invent grammatical constructions, and which alignment operations are needed so that agents develop a successful and concise grammatical system that helps them solve their communicative problems.

Invention and adoption of grammatical markers is implemented using dedicated diagnostics and repairs. Agents monitor themselves, diagnose problems and potentially repair diagnosed problems in communication. When a speaker diagnoses that in production, particularly in re-entrance, the utterance he is about to produce has multiple different topics, he creates a problem called MULTIPLE-TARGET-ENTITIES. This problem is fixed by a dedicated repair strategy that invents a grammatical construction. The new construction maps the semantic structure used in conceptualization onto a grammatical marker. The speaker restarts production in the hope that the newly invented grammatical construction helps in disambiguating the conceptualization strategy he applied and, subsequently, reduces ambiguity in interpretation for the hearer. Upon hearing the new marker, the hearer diagnoses the problem uncovered-strings because he is exposed to the newly invented marker for the first time. The hearer in re-production invents a new grammatical construction mapping the observed unparsed string to the meaning he was able to re-conceptualize. At the end of the interaction both interacting agents have a grammatical construction that links the new marker to the conceptualization strategy both have used in production and re-production, respectively.

Besides invention and adoption, agents need alignment strategies. There are two goals for alignment strategies. First, the hearer might adopt the marker such that it links to a different conceptualization strategy then the one used by the speaker. In this case the alignment operators have to orchestrate that one of the wrong mappings dies out over time. The second goal is that if there are multiple markers floating in the population for the same conceptualization strategy, then the agents of the population should come to an agreement as to which marker to use for that particular strategy. Alignment for grammatical constructions is the same as for lexical constructions. Successfully used constructions are rewarded, unsuccessfully used constructions punished. Additionally, competitor constructions are punished; these are the constructions that could have been used in production but were not used because another construction covering the same semantic structure was applied and has a higher score. This of course implements lateral inhibition dynamics for grammatical constructions.

13.2.2 Experimental setup and results

The performance of the proposed invention, adoption and alignment operators is tested on different sets of spatial scenes. Agents are equipped with four spatial relations, one determiner and three object classes together with lexical constructions for expressing these items. In total agents are given eight lexical constructions for the four spatial relations, the determiner and the three object classes (robot, box and block). Moreover, agents are given the four conceptualization strategies discussed earlier. The task for agent is then to develop a system that allows them to increase their success from the lexicon-only baseline condition to 100% success. Figure 13.10 shows the dynamics of development for populations operating the invention and alignment operators as well as the lexical constructions and the semantic entities discussed. Agents are able to develop successful grammatical marking systems given the need to disambiguate semantic structure in all three environmental conditions considered. In all cases agents develop a grammatical marker system consisting of four markers marking the four conceptualization strategies. We can also see that essentially in all conditions markers are necessary for disambiguation. It is just the number of contexts that require disambiguation that drives development of the marker system. Clearly this number is low in the case of the "similar perspective" condition.

13.3 Discussion

The notion of grammar used in this section is weak in many respects. Syntax is a complex phenomenon. In German, for instance, one can find a myriad of different grammatical strategies such as gender and number agreement, morphology and a complicated case system for conveying important aspects of conceptualization strategies. Word classes, aspectual systems, verb particles – all these are patterns used to convey what the speaker has in mind. So the notion of grammar underlying the evolution experiments in this section is at best an abstraction that tries to preserve some structural properties, such as the relation of grammar to structural properties of semantic structure as well as the relation to cognitive operations, but in no way is meant to purport any general claims about grammatical evolution and grammaticalization. Nevertheless, this section shows why grammar is important on a fundamental level and how this purpose of grammar can be used for self-organization of such a system. The argument was backed up by experiments in which the grammar part is removed, reducing agents to use merely lexical systems. Subsequently agents grew back grammatical construc-

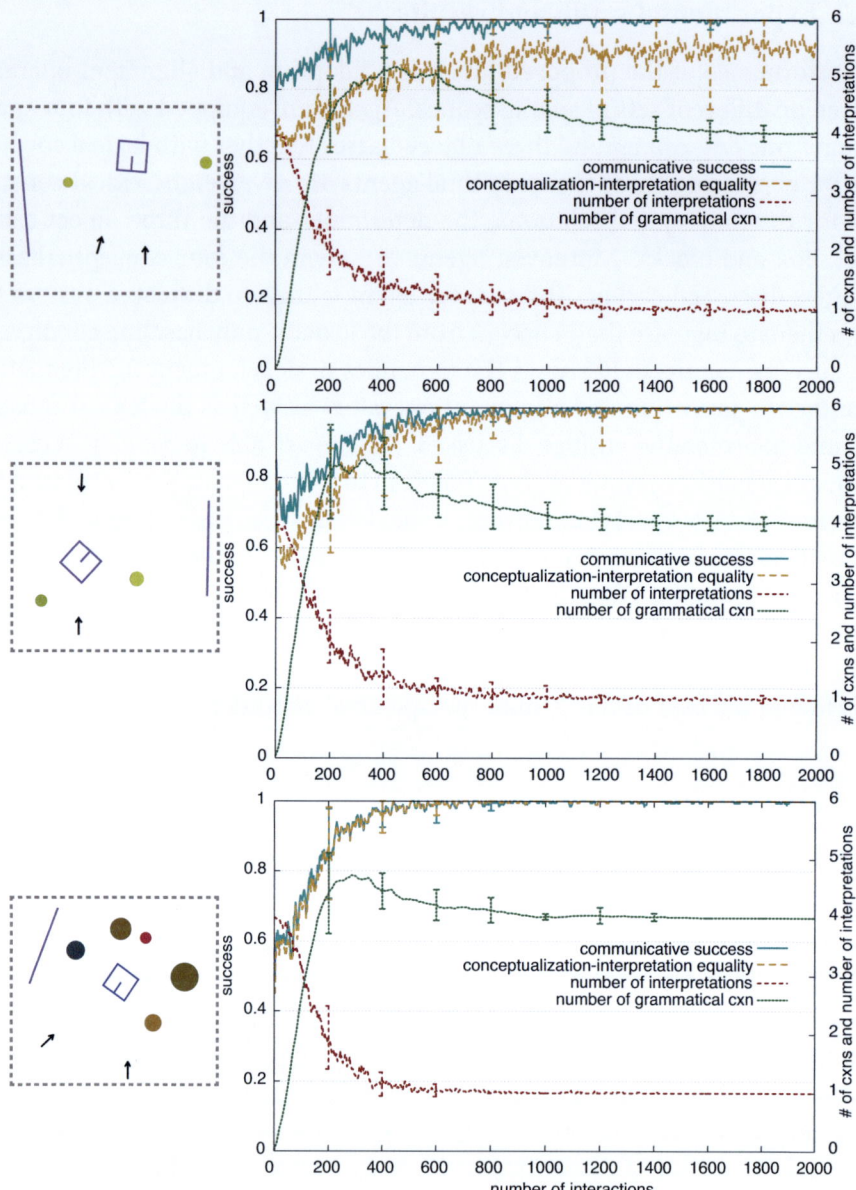

Figure 13.10: Development of grammatical markers over time. As the number of grammatical markers in the population increases, the number of interpretations per phrase drops. In all three conditions agents self-organize a grammatical communication system and are able to increase success from the baseline of purely lexical success to more or less 100%.

tions given the right set of invention and alignment operators. In principle, this sort of argument, therefore, shows less how a particular grammatical system evolves, but what the necessary conditions for the emergence of grammar are and how they can be exploited for agents to self-organize grammatical communication systems. This chapter, as a consequence, provides substantial evidence for the functional approach to language because it shows how the function of language for communication can be the driving factor in self-organization.

The results presented in this chapter have been published in Spranger, Pauw & Loetzsch (2010); Spranger & Steels (2012).

Part IV

Conclusion

14 Conclusion and future work

This book sets out to provide evidence for the theory of language evolution through linguistic selection using robotic experiments. It followed the hypothesis that spatial language evolution can be explained as a cultural process in which syntax and semantics co-evolve through selection, self-organization and recruitment (see Section 1.3).

This book achieved two main objectives (defined in Section 1.4).

- The first achievement is a detailed model of the computational mechanisms behind spatial language production and parsing, but also behind spatial conceptualization and the perception of spatial scenes. For this book a sufficiently complex part of German spatial language, namely, locative phrases was reconstructed and its success in communication tested.

- The second achievement of this book is to give evolutionary explanations for spatial language. Here, the book hypothesized a set of evolutionary stages and provided evidence for the theory of linguistic selection using computational models. The book demonstrates that the theory of linguistic selection can be applied to stages in the evolution of spatial language. Selection, self-organization and recruitment are shown to be vital parts of evolutionary explanations for (a) the formation of single-word spatial category systems, (2) the origins of spatial conceptualization strategies, (3) multi-word systems for marking landmarks, and (4) the evolution of grammar for marking semantic function.

This book shows how linguistic and conceptual evolution can be organized for different stages of complexity. What is certainly still missing is the evolutionary link between the different stages of complexity. The book does not show how agents develop from purely lexical systems into more and more grammatical systems in a unified experiment. Rather grammatical development was based upon fixed lexical systems. Consequently one interesting route of future work is to combine the stages on lexical development with the grammatical stage.

Besides a more holistic approach to evolution there are two important future avenues for research – textscexaptation and the evolution of syntactic and semantic categorization.

14.1 Exaptation

A complex of issues that was only touched in passing in this book is exaptation. Exaptation is a concept from biology (Gould & Lewontin 1979; Gould & Vrba 1982; Gould 1991) which explains the evolution of certain features in biological species through co-optation of structures originally developed for other purposes. A prime example for exaptation in biology are bird feathers which are believed to have originated as a system for thermoregulation of body temperature. Only much later did they develop into a complex flying mechanism (Ostrom 1974; Zhou 2004).

Such processes are ubiquitous also in language evolution. For instance, posture verbs in Dutch (or generally in Germanic languages) started out as a dedicated system for denoting human postures but since have developed into general verbs for denoting spatial configurations or even abstract meanings. So, for instance, speakers of Dutch find it perfectly natural to talk about clothes *lying* on the counter and oneself *sitting* in an economic crisis (Lemmens 2002; 2004; Spranger & Loetzsch 2009; Steels & Spranger 2009). Cognitive linguists tracing these phenomena hypothesize a trajectory in which the original terms for human postures become *metaphorically* extended to additional domains such as the spatial configuration of non-human objects, which triggers an extensions to abstract domains such as economic states of affairs (Lemmens 2004). Similar trajectories have been proposed for posture verbs in Bulgarian which seem to gradually develop into aspectual markers (Kuteva 1999). Most importantly though, the same phenomenon has been attested for spatial language, e.g. by MacLaury (1989), who claims that body part terms are gradually developing into locatives in the Zapotec language. A last example of such processes are metaphorical extensions from the domain of space to the domain of time (Boroditsky 2000; Tenbrink 2011). In many languages, time is conceptualized and talked about using prepositions and relations originating in the spatial domain. An example from English is the preposition *before*, which can be used to, e.g., talk about objects in space but also for the temporal arrangements of meetings.

There are quite a number of proposals for explaining such processes. Image Schema Theory (Johnson 1987), Conceptual Blending Theory (Fauconnier 1994), and Conceptual Metaphor Theory (Lakoff & Johnson 1980) have been proposed for explaining similar phenomena. From the viewpoint of evolutionary linguistics these individual trajectories of language change can be analyzed in terms of exaptation (Lass 1990; 1997). New conceptualization strategies emerge against the background of existing strategies and using mechanisms such as metaphorical extension exapt existing linguistic material for new purposes. Body part terms are re-used for locative expressions, posture verbs are exapted as aspectual markers. While initial experiments for these kinds of processes were carried out, a more concerted effort for tracing exaptive processes remains to be implemented. Such experiments can also close the gap from the abstract experiments reported in this book to attempts at explaining individual trajectories of language change such as the evolution of Zapotec locative phrases or even German locative phrases.

14.2 Evolution of semantic and syntactic categories

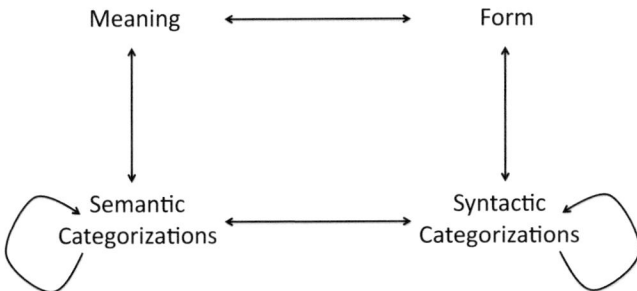

Figure 14.1: The grammar square (figure adapted from Steels 2011b). Lexical constructions directly link meaning and form, but grammatical construction go through an additional layer of semantic and syntactic categorization

A number of studies on grammatical development focus on another aspect of grammar which was not discussed in this book – syntactic and semantic categorization (Steels 2011a). One of the functions of grammatical constructions is to re-categorize meaning and syntactic form in different levels of abstraction and specificity. A well worked out example for such processes is argument structure (Steels 2002; Steels, van Trijp & Wellens 2007; van Trijp 2008). An example of a German phrase conveying the argument structure of a "give event" is the following

(1) Er   gibt ihr   ein Buch.
   He.NOM gives her.DAT a   book.ACC
   'He gives a book to her'

The phrase encodes that *he* is the one who gives a book, and *she* is the one who receives the book and *the book* is the item that is given. The participants of the event are semantically re-categorized into semantic roles such as agent or patient. Syntactically, categorizations such as case (e.g. nominative, dative and accusative) or gender (e.g. female, masculine, neuter) can be applied. The main purpose of semantic and syntactic re-categorization is to capture abstract semantic and grammatical mappings observed in natural language. The corresponding hypothesized constructions are consequently more abstract (Steels 2011a). For instance, an argument-linking construction does not depend on particular event participants such as giver and givee, but rather relies on abstract semantic roles such as agent and recipient.

In terms of evolution semantic and syntactic categorization are often connected. For instance, we know that case marking systems develop out of semantic roles (Blake 1994). A fact that has been traced using computational models of the evolutionary processes involved (van Trijp 2008). The line of research on case marking and semantic roles (Steels 2002; van Trijp 2008) stresses an important aspect of grammar that we can also see at work in German locative phrases. Syntactic and semantic categorizations were used throughout the German locative grammar in the form of semantic and syntactic functions and classes. These categorizations are important for organizing the grammar, since abstract constructions build on top of them. An example of such a construction in German is the postmodifier construction referring-expression–adverbial which handles different kinds postmodifiers such as adverbs and prepositional phrases (see Chapter 7).

In the experiments in this book, semantic categorization is either given by the experimenter or directly derived from the type system used in semantic processing of IRL. Semantic categorization was designed by the experimenter for the German locative grammar. Great care was taken to ensure that semantic classes, functions and types are given so that the grammar can function properly. For grammar evolution, semantic categorization immediately follows from the type system used to represent categories, spatial relations and object classes.

An interesting direction for future work would certainly be to study the evolution of syntactic and semantic categorization in spatial language. Semantic categories could start based on the type system implemented for spatial relations and could gradually become more abstract – the idea being that agents autonomously develop abstract constructions such as modeled for German locative phrases.

References

Arbib, Michael A. 2002. The Mirror System, Imitation, and the Evolution of Language. In Kerstin Dautenhahn & Chrystopher L. Nehaniv (eds.), *Imitation in Animals and Artifacts*, 229–280. The MIT Press.

Aurenhammer, Franz. 1991. Voronoi diagrams—a survey of a fundamental geometric data structure. *ACM Computing Surveys (CSUR)* 23(3). 345–405.

Bailey, David, Jerome Feldman & Srini Narayanan. 1997. Modeling embodied lexical development. In *Proceedings of the Nineteenth Annual Conference of the Cognitive Science Society: August 7-10, 1997, Stanford University*, 19. Lawrence Erlbaum Associates.

Barwise, Jon & Robin Cooper. 1981. Generalized quantifiers and natural language. *Linguistics and Philosophy* 4(2). 159–219.

Bateman, John A. 2010. Situating spatial language and the role of ontology: Issues and outlook. *Language and Linguistics Compass* 4(8). 639–664. DOI:10.1111/j.1749-818X.2010.00226.x

Bateman, John A., Thora Tenbrink & Scott Farrar. 2007. The role of conceptual and linguistic ontologies in interpreting spatial discourse. *Discourse Processes* 44(3). 175–212.

Bateman, John A., Joana Hois, Robert Ross & Thora Tenbrink. 2010. A linguistic ontology of space for natural language processing. *Artificial Intelligence* 174(14). 1027–1071. DOI:10.1016/j.artint.2010.05.008

Belpaeme, Tony & Joris Bleys. 2007. Language, perceptual categories and their interaction: Insights from computational modelling. In Caroline Lyon, Chrystopher L. Nehaniv & Angelo Cangelosi (eds.), *Emergence of communication and language*, 339–353. London, UK: Springer.

Bickerton, Derek. 1999. *Language and species*. Chicago University Press.

Billard, Aude & Kerstin Dautenhahn. 1998. Grounding communication in autonomous robots: An experimental study. *Robotics and Autonomous Systems* 24(1). 71–79.

Blake, Barry J. 1994. *Case* (Cambridge Textbooks in Linguistics). Cambridge University Press.

References

Bleys, Joris. 2010. *Language strategies for the domain of colour*. Brussels, Belgium: Vrije Universiteit Brussels (VUB) PhD thesis.

Bleys, Joris, Martin Loetzsch, Michael Spranger & Luc Steels. 2009. The grounded color naming game. In *Proceedings of the 18th IEEE International Symposium on Robot and Human Interactive Communication (Ro-man 2009)*.

Boroditsky, Lera. 2000. Metaphoric structuring: Understanding time through spatial metaphors. *Cognition* 75(1). 1–28.

Van den Broeck, Wouter. 2008. Constraint-based compositional semantics. In Andrew D. M. Smith, Kenny Smith & Ramon Ferrer i Chancho (eds.), *The evolution of language: Proceedings of the 7th International Conference (EVOLANG7)* (Evolang 7). Singapore: World Scientific.

Camazine, Scott, Jean-Louis Deneubourg, Nigel R. Franks, James Sneyd, Guy Theraula & Eric Bonabeau. 2003. *Self-organization in biological systems*. Princeton University Press.

Carlson, Laura A. 1999. Selecting a reference frame. *Spatial Cognition and Computation* 1(4). 365–379.

Carlson-Radvansky, Laura A. & Gabriel A. Radvansky. 1996. The influence of functional relations on spatial term selection. *Psychological Science* 7(1). 56–60.

Carpenter, Malinda, Katherine Nagell, Michael Tomasello, George Butterworth & Chris Moore. 1998. Social cognition, joint attention, and communicative competence from 9 to 15 months of age. *Monographs of the Society for Research in Child Development* 63(4).

Christiansen, Morten H., Rick A.C. Dale, Michelle R. Ellefson & Christopher M. Conway. 2001. The role of sequential learning in language evolution: Computational and experimental studies. In Angelo Cangelosi & Domenico Parisi (eds.), *Simulating the Evolution of Language*, 165–188. Springer.

Cohn, Anthony G. & Shyamanta M. Hazarika. 2001. Qualitative spatial representation and reasoning: An overview. *Fundamenta Informaticae* 46(1–2). 1–29.

Coradeschi, Silvia & Alessandro Saffiotti. 2003. An introduction to the anchoring problem. *Robotics and Autonomous Systems* 43(2–3). 85–96.

Coventry, Kenny R. & Simon Garrod (eds.). 2004. *Saying, seeing and acting. The psychological semantics of spatial prepositions* (Essays in Cognitive Psychology). Lawrence Erlbaum Associates.

Coventry, Kenny R., Mercè Prat-Sala & Lynn Richards. 2001. The interplay between geometry and function in the comprehension of over, under, above, and below. *Journal of Memory and Language* 44(3). 376–398. DOI:10.1006/jmla.2000.2742

Coventry, Kenny R., Angelo Cangelosi, Rohanna Rajapakse, Alison Bacon, Stephen Newstead, Dan Joyce & Lynn Richards. 2005. Spatial prepositions and vague quantifiers: implementing the functional geometric framework. In Christian Freksa, M. Knauff, B. Krieg-Brückner, B. Nebel & T. Barkowsky (eds.), *Spatial cognition IV. Reasoning, action, interaction*, vol. 3343 (Lecture Notes in Computer Science), 98–110. Springer.

Croft, William. 2001. *Radical construction grammar.* Oxford University Press.

Dale, Robert & Ehud Reiter. 1995. Computational interpretations of the Gricean maxims in the generation of referring expressions. *Cognitive Science: A Multidisciplinary Journal* 19(2). 233–263.

De Beule, Joachim & Luc Steels. 2005. Hierarchy in Fluid Construction Grammars. *KI 2005: Advances in Artificial Intelligence.* 1–15.

Dunbar, Robin. 1998. Theory of mind and the evolution of language. In James R. Hurford, Michael Studdert-Kennedy & Chris Knight (eds.), *Approaches to the evolution of language: Social and cognitive bases*, 92–110. Cambridge University Press.

Dunbar, Robin. 2003. The social brain: Mind, language, and society in evolutionary perspective. *Annual Review of Anthropology* 32. 163–181.

Ehrich, V. 1985. Zur Linguistik und Psycholinguistik der sekunären Raumdeixis. In H. Schweizer (ed.), *Sprache und Raum: Ein Arbeitsbuch für das Lehren von Forschung*, 130–161. Metzler.

Eschenbach, Carola. 1999. Geometric structures of frames of reference and natural language semantics. *Spatial Cognition and Computation* 1(4). 329–348.

Eschenbach, Carola. 2004. Contextual, functional, and geometric components in the semantics of projective terms. In Laura A. Carlson & E. van der Zee (eds.), *Functional features in language and space*, vol. 2 (Explorations in Language and Space), 71–93. Oxford University Press.

Eschenbach, Carola & Lars Kulik. 1997. An axiomatic approach to the spatial relations underlying left-right and in front of-behind. In *KI-97: Advances in Artificial Intelligence*, 207–218. Springer.

Evans, Nicholas & Stephen C. Levinson. 2009. The myth of language universals: Language diversity and its importance for cognitive science. *Behavioral and Brain Sciences* 32(5). 429–448. DOI:10.1017/S0140525X0999094X

Fauconnier, Gilles. 1994. *Mental spaces: Aspects of meaning construction in natural language.* Cambridge University Press.

References

Freksa, Christian. 1991. Qualitative spatial reasoning. In Martin Raubal, David M. Mark & Andrew U. Frank (eds.), *Cognitive and linguistic aspects of geographic space*, 361–372. Springer.

Freksa, Christian. 1999. Links vor – Prototyp oder Gebiet? In Gert Rickheit (ed.), *Richtungen im Raum*, 231–246. Westdeutscher Verlag.

Gapp, Klaus-Peter. 1994. Basic meanings of spatial relations: Computation and evaluation in 3D space. In *Proceedings of AAAI-94*, 1393–1398.

Gapp, Klaus-Peter. 1995. Angle, distance, shape, and their relationship to projective relations. In *Proceedings of the 17th Annual Conference of the Cognitive Science Society*, 112–117.

Garrod, Simon & Gwyneth. Doherty. 1994. Conversation, co-ordination and convention: An empirical investigation of how groups establish linguistic conventions. *Cognition* 53(3). 181–215.

Gerasymova, Kateryna & Michael Spranger. 2010. Acquisition of grammar in autonomous artificial systems. In Helder Coelho, Rudi Studer & Michael Wooldridge (eds.), *Proceedings of the 19th European Conference on Artificial Intelligence (ECAI-2010)*, 923–928. IOS Press.

Gerasymova, Kateryna & Michael Spranger. 2012. An experiment in temporal language learning. In Luc Steels & Manfred Hild (eds.), *Language grounding in robots*, 237–254. Springer.

Goldberg, Adele E. 1995. *Constructions: A construction grammar approach to argument structure*. Chicago University Press.

Gould, Stephen J. 1991. Exaptation: A crucial tool for an evolutionary psychology. *Journal of Social Issues* 47(3). 43–65.

Gould, Stephen J. & Richard C. Lewontin. 1979. The spandrels of San Marco and the Panglossian paradigm: A critique of the adaptationist programme. *Proceedings of the Royal Society of London. Series B, Biological Sciences* 205(1161). 581–598.

Gould, Stephen J. & Elisabeth S. Vrba. 1982. Exaptation – A missing term in the science of form. *Paleobiology*. 4–15.

Grabowski, Joachim & Petra Weiss. 1996. The prepositional inventory of languages: A factor that affects comprehension of spatial prepositions. *Language Sciences* 18(1-2): *Contrastive semantics and pragmatics, Volume I: Meanings and representations*. 19–35. DOI:10.1016/0388-0001(96)00005-8

Haddock, Nicholas J. 1989. Computational models of incremental semantic interpretation. *Language and Cognitive Processes* 4(3). 337–368.

Hall, Mark M. & Christopher B. Jones. 2008. Quantifying spatial prepositions: An experimental study. In *Proceedings of the 16th ACM SIGSPATIAL*

international conference on advances in geographic information systems, 1–4.
ACM.

Hermann, Theo & Werner Deutsch. 1976. *Psychologie der Objektbenennung*.
Hans Huber Verlag.

Herskovits, Annette. 1986. *Language and spatial cognition* (Studies in Natural
Language Processing). Cambridge University Press.

Hopper, Paul J. & Elizabeth Closs Traugott. 2003. *Grammaticalization*
(Cambridge Textbooks in Linguistics). Cambridge University Press.

Jackendoff, Ray. 1999. Possible stages in the evolution of the language capacity.
Trends in Cognitive Sciences 3(7). 272–279.

Johnson, Mark. 1987. *The body in the mind: The bodily basis of meaning,
imagination, and reason*. University of Chicago Press.

Johnson-Laird, Philip N. 1977. Procedural semantics. *Cognition* 5(3). 189–214.

Kauffman, Stuart A. 1993. *The origins of order: Self-organization and selection in
evolution*. Vol. 209. Oxford University Press.

Kelleher, John D. & Fintan J. Costello. 2009. Applying computational models of
spatial prepositions to visually situated dialog. *Computational Linguistics*
35(2). 271–306. DOI:10.1162/coli.06-78-prep14

Klabunde, Ralf. 1999. Logic – based choice of projective terms. *KI-99: Advances
in Artificial Intelligence*. 697–697.

Kuteva, Tania. 1999. On 'sit'/'stand'/'lie'auxiliation. *Linguistics* 37(2). 191–213.
DOI:10.1515/ling.37.2.191

Kálmán, Rudolf E. 1960. A new approach to linear filtering and prediction
problems. *Transactions of the ASME-Journal of Basic Engineering* 82(1). 35–45.

Lakoff, George & Mark Johnson. 1980. *Metaphors we live by*. Chicago University
Press.

Lass, Roger. 1990. How to do things with junk: Exaptation in language
evolution. *Journal of linguistics*. 79–102.

Lass, Roger. 1997. *Historical linguistics and language change*. Cambridge
University Press.

Lemmens, Maarten. 2002. The semantic network of Dutch posture verbs. In *The
linguistics of sitting, standing and lying*, 103–139. John Benjamins.

Lemmens, Maarten. 2004. Metaphor, image schema and grammaticalisation: A
cognitive lexical-semantic study. *Journée d'Etudes Grammar and figures of
speech* 3(4). 24–46.

Levinson, Stephen C. 1996. Language and space. *Annual Review of Anthropology*
25(1). 353–382.

References

Levinson, Stephen C. 2003. *Space in language and cognition: Explorations in cognitive diversity* (Language, Culture and Cognition 5). Cambridge University Press.

Levinson, Stephen C. & David P. Wilkins. 2006. *Grammars of space.* Cambridge University Press.

Lloyd, Stuart P. 1982. Least squares quantization in PCM. *IEEE Transactions on Information Theory* 28(2). 129–137.

MacLaury, Robert E. 1989. Zapotec body-part locatives: Prototypes and metaphoric extensions. *International Journal of American Linguistics* 55(2). 119–154.

Maddieson, Ian. 1984. *Patterns of sounds.* Cambridge University Press.

Mainwaring, Scott, Barbara Tversky, Motoko Ohgishi & Diane J. Schiano. 2003. Descriptions of simple spatial scenes in English and Japanese. *Spatial Cognition and Computation* 3(1). 3–42.

Miller, George A. & Philip N. Johnson-Laird. 1976. *Language and perception.* Belknap Press.

Moratz, Reinhard & Thora Tenbrink. 2006. Spatial reference in linguistic human-robot interaction: Iterative, empirically supported development of a model of projective relations. *Spatial Cognition & Computation* 6(1). 63–107.

Narayanan, Srini. 1999. Moving right along: A computational model of metaphoric reasoning about events. In *Proceedings of the National Conference on Artificial Intelligence (AAAI'99)*, 121–127. American Association for Artificial Intelligence Menlo Park, CA, USA.

Ostrom, John H. 1974. Archaeopteryx and the origin of flight. *The Quarterly Review of Biology* 49(1). 27–47.

Oudeyer, Pierre-Yves. 2005. The self-organization of speech sounds. *Journal of Theoretical Biology* 233(3). 435–449.

Pauw, Simon & Michael Spranger. 2010. Embodied determiners. In Marija Slavkovik (ed.), *Proceedings of the 15th Student Session of the European Summer School for Logic, Language and Information (ESSLI 2010)*. University of Copenhagen.

Pauw, Simon & Michael Spranger. 2012. Embodied quantifiers. In Daniel Lassiter & Marija Slavkovik (eds.), *New directions in logic, language and computation*, vol. 7415 (Lecture Notes in Computer Science), 52–66. Springer Berlin Heidelberg. DOI:10.1007/978-3-642-31467-4_4

Pickering, Martin J. & Simon Garrod. 2004. Toward a mechanistic psychology of dialogue. *Behavioral and Brain Sciences* 27(2). 169–190.

Pope, Mildred K. 1952. *From Latin to Modern French with especial consideration of Anglo-Norman. Phonology and morphology.* Manchester University Press.

Regier, Terry & Laura A. Carlson. 2001. Grounding spatial language in perception: An empirical and computational investigation. *Journal of Experimental Psychology: General* 130(2). 273–298.

Rizzolatti, Giacomo & Michael A. Arbib. 1998. Language within our grasp. *Trends in neurosciences* 21(5). 188–194.

Roach, Eleanor. 1978. Principles of categorization. In Eleanor Roach & Barbara B. Lloyd (eds.), *Cognition and categorization*, 27–48. Hillsdale, NJ: Lawrence Erlbaum.

Roy, Deb. 2005. Semiotic schemas: A framework for grounding language in action and perception. *Artificial Intelligence* 167(1-2). 170–205.

Schober, Michael F. 1993. Spatial perspective-taking in conversation. *Cognition* 47(1). 1–24.

Schoenemann, P. Thomas. 1999. Syntax as an emergent characteristic of the evolution of semantic complexity. *Minds and Machines* 9(3). 309–346.

Siskind, Jeffrey M. 2001. Grounding the lexical semantics of verbs in visual perception using force dynamics and event logic. *Journal of Artificial Intelligence Research* 15. 31–90.

Smith, Kenny, Simon Kirby & Henry Brighton. 2003. Iterated learning: A framework for the emergence of language. *Artificial Life* 9(4). 371–386.

Sperber, Dan & Deirdre Wilson. 1986. *Relevance: Communication and cognition.* Harvard University Press.

Spranger, Michael. 2008. *World models for grounded language games.* Humboldt-Universität zu Berlin German Diplom Thesis.

Spranger, Michael. 2011. Recruitment, Selection and Alignment of Spatial Language Strategies. In Tom Lenaerts, Mario Giacobini, Hugues Bersini, Paul Bourgine, Marco Dorigo & René Doursat (eds.), *Advances in artificial life, ECAL 2011: Proceedings of the Eleventh European Conference on the Synthesis and Simulation of Living Systems*, 771–778. MIT Press.

Spranger, Michael. 2012a. Potential stages in the cultural evolution of spatial language. In Thomas C. Scott-Phillips, Monica Tamariz, Erica A. Cartmill & James Hurford (eds.), *The evolution of language: Proceedings of the 9th International Conference* (Evolang 9). Singapore: World Scientific.

Spranger, Michael. 2012b. The co-evolution of basic spatial terms and categories. In Luc Steels (ed.), *Experiments in Cultural Language Evolution*, 111–141. John Benjamins.

Spranger, Michael. 2013a. Evolutionary explanations for spatial language – A case study on landmarks. In *Advances in Artificial Life, ECAL 2013*, vol. 12, 1999–1205. MIT Press.

Spranger, Michael. 2013b. Evolving grounded spatial language strategies. English. *KI - Künstliche Intelligenz* 27(2). 97–106. DOI:10.1007/s13218-013-0245-4

Spranger, Michael. 2013c. Grounded lexicon acquisition – Case studies in spatial language. In *Third Joint IEEE International Conference on Development and Learning and on Epigenetic Robotics (ICDL – EPIROB, 2013)*.

Spranger, Michael & Martin Loetzsch. 2009. The semantics of sit, stand, and lie embodied in robots. In N. A. Taatgen & H. van Rijn (eds.), *Proceedings of the 31th Annual Conference of the Cognitive Science Society (Cogsci09)*, 2546–2552. Cognitive Science Society. Austin, TX.

Spranger, Michael & Martin Loetzsch. 2011. Syntactic indeterminacy and semantic ambiguity: A case study for german spatial phrases. In Luc Steels (ed.), *Design patterns in Fluid Construction Grammar*, vol. 11 (Constructional Approaches to Language), 265–298. John Benjamins.

Spranger, Michael, Martin Loetzsch & Simon Pauw. 2010. Open-ended grounded semantics. In Helder Coelho, Rudi Studer & Michael Wooldridge (eds.), *Proceedings of the 19th European Conference on Artificial Intelligence (ECAI 2010)* (Frontiers in Artificial Intelligence and Applications 215), 929–934. IOS Press.

Spranger, Michael, Martin Loetzsch & Luc Steels. 2012. A perceptual system for language game experiments. In Luc Steels & Manfred Hild (eds.), *Language grounding in robots*, 89–110. Springer.

Spranger, Michael & Simon Pauw. 2012. Dealing with Perceptual Deviation – Vague Semantics for Spatial Language and Quantification. In Luc Steels & Manfred Hild (eds.), *Language Grounding in Robots*, 173–192. Springer.

Spranger, Michael, Simon Pauw & Martin Loetzsch. 2010. Open-ended semantics co-evolving with spatial language. In Andrew D. M. Smith, Marieke Schouwstra, Bart de Boer & Kenny Smith (eds.), *The evolution of language* (Evolang 8), 297–304. Singapore: World Scientific.

Spranger, Michael & Luc Steels. 2012. Emergent functional grammar for space. In Luc Steels (ed.), *Experiments in Cultural Language Evolution*, 207–232. John Benjamins.

Spranger, Michael, Simon Pauw, Martin Loetzsch & Luc Steels. 2012. Open-ended procedural semantics. In Luc Steels & Manfred Hild (eds.), *Language Grounding in Robots*, 153–172. Springer.

Steels, Luc. 1997. Constructing and sharing perceptual distinctions. In Maarten van Someren & Gerhard Widmer (eds.), *Proceedings of the ninth european conference on machine learning*, 4–13. Springer.

Steels, Luc. 1998. Synthesising the origins of language and meaning using co-evolution, self-organisation and level formation. In James Hurford, Chris Knight & Michael Studdert-Kennedy (eds.), *Approaches to the evolution of language: Social and cognitive bases*, 384–404. Edinburgh University Press.

Steels, Luc. 2000a. Language as a complex adaptive system. In M. Schoenauer, K. Deb, G. Rudolph, X. Yao, E. Lutton, J.J. Merelo & H-P. Schwefel (eds.), *Proceedings of the 6th International Conference on Parallel Problem Solving from Nature*, vol. 1917 (Lecture Notes in Computer Science), 17–26. Springer.

Steels, Luc. 2000b. The emergence of grammar in communicating autonomous robotic agents. In Werner Horn (ed.), *ECAI 2000: Proceedings of the 14th European Conference on Artificial Intelligence*, 764–769. IOS Publishing.

Steels, Luc. 2001. Language games for autonomous robots. *IEEE Intelligent systems*. 16–22.

Steels, Luc. 2002. Simulating the evolution of a grammar for case. Presented at the 4th International Conference on the Evolution of Language at Harvard University.

Steels, Luc. 2003. Language-reentrance and the 'inner voice'. *Journal of Consciousness Studies* 10(4-5). 173–185.

Steels, Luc. 2005. The emergence and evolution of linguistic structure: From lexical to grammatical communication systems. *Connection Science* 17(3-4). 213–230.

Steels, Luc. 2007. The Recruitment Theory of Language Origins. In Caroline Lyon, Chrystopher L. Nehaniv & Angelo Cangelosi (eds.), *The Emergence of Communication and Language*, 129–151. Springer.

Steels, Luc. 2008. The symbol grounding problem has been solved. So what's next? In Manuel de Vega, Arthur Glenberg & Arthur Graesser (eds.), *Symbols and embodiment: Debates on meaning and cognition*. Oxford University Press.

Steels, Luc. 2009. Cognition and social dynamics play a major role in the formation of grammar. In Derek Bickerton & Eörs Szathmáry (eds.), *Biological foundations and origin of syntax*, vol. 3 (Strungmann Forum Reports), 345–368. MIT Press.

Steels, Luc. 2011a. A design pattern for phrasal constructions. In Luc Steels (ed.), *Design Patterns in Fluid Construction Grammar*. John Benjamins.

Steels, Luc (ed.). 2011b. *Design patterns in Fluid Construction Grammar*. John Benjamins.

Steels, Luc. 2011c. Self-organization and selection in cultural language evolution. In Luc Steels (ed.), *Experiments in Cultural Language Evolution.* John Benjamins.

Steels, Luc (ed.). 2012. *Computational issues in Fluid Construction Grammar* (Lecture Notes in AI). Springer Verlag.

Steels, Luc & Jean-Christophe Baillie. 2003. Shared grounding of event descriptions by autonomous robots. *Robotics and Autonomous Systems* 43(2-3). 163–173.

Steels, Luc & Tony Belpaeme. 2005. Coordinating perceptually grounded categories through language: A case study for colour. *Behavioral and Brain Sciences* 28. 469–529.

Steels, Luc & Joris Bleys. 2005. Planning what to say: Second order semantics for Fluid Construction Grammars. In A. Bugarin Diz & J. Santos Reyes (eds.), *Proceedings of caepia 05.* (Lecture Notes in AI). Springer.

Steels, Luc & Joachim De Beule. 2006. Unify and merge in Fluid Construction Grammar. In Paul Vogt, Yuuya Sugita, Elio Tuci & Chrystopher L. Nehaniv (eds.), *Symbol grounding and beyond: Proceedings of the Third International Workshop on the Emergence and Evolution of Linguistic Communication* (LNAI 4211), 197–223. Springer.

Steels, Luc, Joachim De Beule & Nicolas Neubauer. 2005. Linking in Fluid Construction Grammars. In *Transactions of the Belgian royal society of arts and sciences,* 11–18.

Steels, Luc & Frédéric Kaplan. 1998. Stochasticity as a source of innovation in language games. In Christoph Adami, Richard K. Belew, Hiroaki Kitano & Charles E. Taylor (eds.), *Proceedings of the Sixth International Conference on Artificial Life.* The MIT Press.

Steels, Luc & Frédéric Kaplan. 2002. Bootstrapping grounded word semantics. In Ted Briscoe (ed.), *Linguistic evolution through language acquisition: Formal and computational models,* 53–74. Cambridge University Press.

Steels, Luc & Martin Loetzsch. 2010. Babel: A tool for running experiments on the evolution of language. In *Evolution of communication and language in embodied agents,* 307–313. Springer Verlag. DOI:10.1007/978-3-642-01250-1_20

Steels, Luc & Michael Spranger. 2008. The robot in the mirror. *Connection Science* 20(4). 337–358.

Steels, Luc & Michael Spranger. 2009. How experience of the body shapes language about space. In *IJCAI'09: Proceedings of the 21st international joint conference on Artifical Intelligence,* 14–19. San Francisco: Morgan Kaufmann.

Steels, Luc & Michael Spranger. 2012. Emergent mirror systems for body language. In Luc Steels (ed.), *Experiments in Cultural Language Evolution*, 87–109. John Benjamins.

Steels, Luc, Remi van Trijp & Pieter Wellens. 2007. Multi-level selection in the emergence of language systematicity. In F. Almeida e Costa, L. M. Rocha, E. Costa & I. Harvey (eds.), *Proceedings of the Ninth European Conference on Artificial Life* (LNAI 4648). Springer.

Steels, Luc & Pieter Wellens. 2006. How grammar emerges to dampen combinatorial search in parsing. In Paul Vogt, Yuuya Sugita, Elio Tuci & Chrystopher Nehaniv (eds.), *Symbol grounding and beyond: Proceedings of the Third International Workshop on the Emergence and Evolution of Linguistic Communication* (LNAI 4211), 76–88. Springer.

Talmy, Leonard. 2000. *Toward a cognitive semantics. Vol. 2: Typology and process in concept structuring.* The MIT Press.

Tenbrink, Thora. 2005a. Identifying objects on the basis of spatial contrast: An empirical study. *Spatial Cognition IV. Reasoning, Action, and Interaction.* 124–146.

Tenbrink, Thora. 2005b. *Localising objects and events: Discoursal applicability conditions for spatiotemporal expressions in English and German.* University of Bremen PhD thesis.

Tenbrink, Thora. 2005c. *Semantics and application of spatial dimensional terms in English and German.* SFB/TR 8 (technical report) 004-03/2005. Bremen, Germany: University of Bremen.

Tenbrink, Thora. 2007. *Space, time, and the use of language: An investigation of relationships.* Vol. 36 (Cognitive Linguistics Research). Berlin, DE: Walter de Gruyter.

Tenbrink, Thora. 2011. Reference frames of space and time in language. *Journal of Pragmatics* 43(3). 704–722.

Tinbergen, Nikolaas. 1963. On aims and methods of ethology. *Zeitschrift für Tierpsychologie* 20(4). 410–433.

Tomasello, Michael. 1992. The social bases of language acquisition. *Social Development* 1(1). 67–87.

Tomasello, Michael. 1995. Joint attention as social cognition. In Chris Moore & Philip J. Dunham (eds.), *Joint attention: Its origins and role in development.* Hillsdale, NJ: Lawrence Erlbaum Associates.

Tomasello, Michael, Malinda Carpenter, Joseph Call, Tanya Behne & Henrike Moll. 2005. Understanding and sharing intentions: The origins of cultural cognition. *Behavioral and Brain Sciences* 28(05). 675–691.

Traugott, Elizabeth Closs & Bernd Heine (eds.). 1991. *Approaches to grammaticalization.* Vol. 1 & 2 (Typologogical Studies in Language 19). John Benjamins.

Tversky, Barbara & Bridgette M. Hard. 2009. Embodied and disembodied cognition: Spatial perspective-taking. *Cognition* 110(1). 124–129.

Tversky, Barbara & Paul U. Lee. 1998. How space structures language. In *Spatial cognition,* 157–175. Springer.

Tversky, Barbara, Paul U. Lee & Scott Mainwaring. 1999. Why do speakers mix perspectives? *Spatial Cognition and Computation* 1(4). 399–412.

van Trijp, Remi. 2008. *Analogy and multi-level selection in the formation of a case grammar. a case study in fluid construction grammar.* Antwerp: University of Antwerp PhD thesis.

van Trijp, Remi. 2011. Feature matrices and agreement: a case study for German case. In Luc Steels (ed.), *Design Patterns in Fluid Construction Grammar,* 205–235. John Benjamins.

Vandeloise, Claude. 1991. *Spatial prepositions: A case study from French.* University of Chicago Press.

Vogt, Paul. 2002. Bootstrapping grounded symbols by minimal autonomous robots. *Evolution of Communication* 4(1). 87–116.

Winograd, Terry. 1971. *Procedures as a representation for data in a computer program for understanding natural language.* Massachusetts Institute of Technology PhD thesis.

Worden, Robert. 1998. The evolution of language from social intelligence. In James R. Hurford, Michael Studdert-Kennedy & Chris Knight (eds.), *Approaches to the Evolution of Language: Social and Cognitive Bases,* 148–166. Cambridge University Press.

Wunderlich, Dieter & Michael Herweg. 1991. Lokale und Direktionale. In Arnim von Stechow & Dieter Wunderlich (eds.), *Semantik: Ein internationales Handbuch der zeitgenössischen Forschung.* De Gruyter.

Zhou, Zhonghe. 2004. The origin and early evolution of birds: Discoveries, disputes, and perspectives from fossil evidence. *Naturwissenschaften* 91. 455–471.

Name index

Subject index